Children's Handbook Scotland

....

12th edition

Alison Gillies

Child Poverty Action Group works on behalf of the more than one in four children in the UK growing up in poverty. It does not have to be like this. We use our understanding of what causes poverty and the impact it has on children's lives to campaign for policies that will prevent and solve poverty – for good. We provide training, advice and information to make sure hard-up families get the financial support they need. We also carry out high-profile legal work to establish and protect families' rights. If you are not already supporting us, please consider making a donation, or ask for details of our membership schemes, training courses and publications.

Published by Child Poverty Action Group
30 Micawber Street
London N1 7TB
Tel: 020 7837 7979
staff@cpag.org.uk
www.cpag.org.uk

© Child Poverty Action Group 2019

This book is sold subject to the condition that it shall not, by way of trade or otherwise, be lent, resold, hired out or otherwise circulated without the publisher's prior consent in any form of binding or cover other than that in which it is published and without a similar condition including this condition being imposed on the subsequent purchaser.

A CIP record for this book is available from the British Library

ISBN: 978 1 910715 59 8

Child Poverty Action Group is a charity registered in England and Wales (registration number 294841) and in Scotland (registration number SC039339), and is a company limited by guarantee, registered in England (registration number 1993854). VAT number: 690 808117

Cover design by Colorido Studios
Internal design by Devious Designs
Typeset by DLxml, a division of RefineCatch Limited, Bungay, Suffolk
Printed and bound in the UK by CPI Group (UK) Ltd, Croydon CR0 4YY

The author

Alison Gillies is a welfare rights worker with CPAG in Scotland, working on its Children and Families Project.

Acknowledgements

Grateful thanks are due to Jon Shaw for his time and expertise in checking this *Handbook* and to Judith Paterson for her ongoing support, encouragement and assistance. Many thanks also to the parent advisers at Contact for their expertise and advice.

Many thanks go to everyone at CPAG in Scotland for their invaluable support and practical help.

Thanks to Nicola Johnston for editing and managing the production of the book, Anne Ketley for updating the index and Pauline Phillips for proofreading the text.

CPAG would like to thank the Scottish government for its financial support in the production of this *Handbook*.

Online *Handbook* and further training, information and advice
With the assistance of Scottish government funding, this *Handbook* is available free online at www.onlinepublications.cpag.org.uk. CPAG in Scotland also provides training, advice and information to frontline advisers on benefits and tax credits for families and children. Please contact Alison Gillies on 0141 548 1056 for details of the support we can offer. For specific advice queries, contact our adviser's advice line on 0141 552 0552 on Monday to Thursday between 10am to 4pm and on Fridays between 10am and 12 noon.

We would be very grateful if users of this book could send any comments, corrections or suggestions for inclusion in the next edition to CPAG in Scotland, Unit 9, Ladywell, 94 Duke Street, Glasgow G4 0UW; email staff@cpagscotland.org.uk.

The law covered in this book was correct on 9 August 2019 and includes regulations laid up to this date.

Contents

How to use this *Handbook*	vii
Abbreviations	viii
Means-tested benefit rates 2019/10	ix
Non-means-tested benefit rates 2019/20	xiii
Tax credit rates 2019/20	xv

Chapter 1 Benefits and tax credits	1
1. Introduction	1
2. Attendance allowance	2
3. Best Start grant	3
4. Carer's allowance	5
5. Child benefit	7
6. Council tax reduction	10
7. Disability living allowance	11
8. Employment and support allowance	14
9. Funeral support payment	19
10. Guardian's allowance	20
11. Health benefits	21
12. Housing benefit	23
11. Income support	26
14. Jobseeker's allowance	31
15. Pension credit	34
16. Personal independence payment	36
17. The Scottish Welfare Fund	38
18. Statutory adoption pay	40
19. Tax credits	40
20. Universal credit	46

Chapter 2 Claims, decisions and challenges	52
1. How to claim benefits and tax credits	52
2. Decisions and delays	56
3. Challenging decisions and complaints	58

Chapter 3 Children in hospital	64
1. Child benefit and guardian's allowance	64
2. Means-tested benefits	65
3. Non-means-tested benefits	68
4. Tax credits	68
5. Help visiting your child	69

Chapter 4 Disabled children in care homes	71
1. Benefits and tax credits for children in care homes	71
2. More than one stay in a care home	79
3. When your child comes home	80
Chapter 5 Disabled children at residential school	84
1. Child benefit and guardian's allowance	84
2. Means-tested benefits	84
3. Non-means-tested benefits	89
4. Tax credits	92
5. Help visiting your child	93
Chapter 6 Children who are 'looked after and accommodated'	96
1. Benefits and tax credits for children who are 'looked after and accommodated'	96
2. When your child comes home	102
Chapter 7 Children living with kinship carers	107
1. What is kinship care	107
2. Financial help from the local authority	108
3. Benefits and tax credits if a child is not looked after	110
4. Benefits and tax credits if a child is looked after	119
Chapter 8 Children living with foster carers	129
1. What is foster care	129
2. Benefits and tax credits for foster carers	130
Chapter 9 Adoption	137
1. Adoption allowances	137
2. Benefits and tax credits when a child is placed with you for adoption	139
3. Benefits and tax credits once you have adopted a child	146
Chapter 10 Young people leaving care	153
1. Universal credit	154
2. Income support, income-based jobseeker's allowance and housing benefit	155
3. Other benefits	156
4. Financial support from the local authority for 16/17-year-old care leavers	157
5. Other help from the local authority	159
6. Other help	160
7. Challenging local authority decisions	160
Appendices	
Appendix 1 Useful addresses	167
Appendix 2 Abbreviations used in the notes	169
Index	175

How to use this *Handbook*

This *Handbook* is intended for those who advise and work with children and families in Scotland. It covers situations where a child is living away from home, or away from her/his parents, for a variety of reasons. The *Handbook* covers the rules affecting benefits and tax credits in these circumstances.

Up to date

This *Handbook* is up to date on 9 August 2019. The rates of benefits and tax credits used are those from April 2019.

You can also check the online version of this *Handbook* at www.onlinepublications.cpag.org.uk.

If you are interested in having a link from your organisation's website to the online *Handbook*, please contact us on staff@cpagscotland.org.uk or 0141 552 3303.

Structure of the *Handbook*

Chapter 1 provides information about the main relevant benefits and tax credits. Chapter 2 provides information about claiming, decision making and challenging decisions. The rest of the *Handbook* is divided into chapters about the various situations that may apply to you (eg, children living with kinship carers and children at residential school) and how benefits and tax credits are affected in these circumstances.

Chapters are footnoted with references to the legal sources. Where an abbreviation is used in the footnotes or in the text, this is explained in Appendix 2 and on pviii. If you are challenging a benefit or tax credit decision, you may want to refer to the law.

Abbreviations

AA	attendance allowance
CA	carer's allowance
CTC	child tax credit
CTR	council tax reduction
DLA	disability living allowance
DHP	discretionary housing payment
DWP	Department for Work and Pensions
ESA	employment and support allowance
HB	housing benefit
HMRC	HM Revenue and Customs
ICE	Independent Case Examiner
IS	income support
JSA	jobseeker's allowance
MP	Member of Parliament
MSP	Member of the Scottish Parliament
NI	national insurance
PC	pension credit
PIP	personal independence payment
SAAS	Student Awards Agency for Scotland
SAP	statutory adoption pay
SSPP	statutory shared parental pay
SSS	Social Security Scotland
SPP	statutory paternity pay
SSP	statutory sick pay
UC	universal credit
WTC	working tax credit

Means-tested benefit rates 2019/20

Universal credit
Standard allowance

		£pm
Single	Under 25	251.77
	25 or over	317.82
Couple	Both under 25	395.20
	One or both 25 or over	498.89

Elements

First child (if born before 6 April 2017)		277.08
Second/subsequent/all children born on or after 6 April 2017, subject to two-child limit		231.67
Disabled child addition	Lower rate	126.11
	Higher rate	392.08
Limited capability for work		126.11
Limited capability for work-related activity		336.20
Carer		160.20
Childcare costs	One child	up to 646.35
	Two or more children	up to 1108.04
	Percentage of childcare costs covered	85%

Income support and income-based jobseeker's allowance
Personal allowances £pw
Single	Under 25	57.90
	25 or over	73.10
Lone parent	Under 18	57.90
	18 or over	73.10
Couple	Both under 18 (maximum)	87.50
	One 18 or over (maximum)	114.85
	Both 18 or over	114.85

Premiums
Carer		36.85
Pensioner		140.40
Disability	Single	34.35
	Couple	48.95
Enhanced disability	Single	16.80
	Couple	24.10
Severe disability	One qualifies	65.85
	Two qualify	131.70

Children
(pre-6 April 2004 claims with no child tax credit)

Child under 20 personal allowance	66.90
Family premium	17.45
Disabled child premium	64.19
Enhanced disability premium	26.04

Pension credit
Standard minimum guarantee	Single	167.25
	Couple	255.25
Severe disability addition	One qualifies	65.85
	Two qualify	131.70
Carer addition		36.85
Child addition	Standard amount	53.34
	Standard amount for eldest child born before 6 April 2017	63.84
	Disabled child increase	29.02
	Severely disabled child increase	90.23
Savings credit threshold	Single	144.38
	Couple	229.67

Housing benefit and council tax reduction

Personal allowances

Single	Under 25	57.90
	Under 25 (on main phase ESA)	73.10
	25 or over	73.10
Lone parent	Under 18	57.90
	Under 18 (on main phase ESA)	73.10
	18 or over	73.10
Couple	Both under 18	87.50
	Both under 18 (claimant on main phase ESA)	114.85
	One or both 18 or over	114.85
Dependent children	Under 20	66.90
Pension age	Single	181.00
	Couple	270.60

Premiums

Family (pre-1 May 2016 claims only)	Ordinary rate	17.45
	Some lone parents	22.20
Carer		36.85
Disability	Single	34.35
	Couple	48.95
Disabled child		64.19
Severe disability	One qualifies	65.85
	Two qualify	131.70
Enhanced disability	Single	16.80
	Couple	24.10
	Child	26.04

Components

Work-related activity	29.05
Support	38.55

Income-related employment and support allowance

Personal allowances	Assessment phase £pw	Main phase £pw
Single		
Under 25	57.90	73.10
25 or over	73.10	73.10
Lone parent		
Under 18	57.90	73.10
18 or over	73.10	73.10
Couple		
Both under 18 (maximum)	87.50	114.85
Both 18 or over	114.85	114.85
Premiums		
Carer	36.85	36.85
Severe disability – one qualifies	65.85	65.85
Severe disability – two qualify	131.70	131.70
Enhanced disability		
Single	16.80	16.80
Couple	24.10	24.10
Pensioner		
Couple, no component	140.40	
Couple, work-related activity component	–	111.35
Couple, support component	–	101.85
Components		
Work-related activity	–	29.05
Support	–	38.55

Non-means-tested benefit rates 2019/20

	£pw
Attendance allowance	
Higher rate	87.65
Lower rate	58.70
Carer's allowance	66.15
Child benefit	
Only/eldest child	20.70
Other child(ren)	13.70
Disability living allowance	
Care component	
Highest	87.65
Middle	58.70
Lowest	23.20
Mobility component	
Higher	61.20
Lower	23.20
Employment and support allowance (contributory)	
Assessment phase	
Basic allowance (under 25)	57.90
Basic allowance (25 or over)	73.10
Main phase	
Basic allowance (16 or over)	73.10
Work-related activity component	29.05
Support component	38.55
Guardian's allowance	17.60
Jobseeker's allowance (contribution-based)	
Under 25	57.90
25 or over	73.10

Personal independence payment
Daily living component
Standard rate — 58.70
Enhanced rate — 87.65
Mobility component
Standard rate — 23.20
Enhanced rate — 61.20

Statutory adoption pay (standard rate) — 148.68
Statutory paternity pay (maximum) — 148.68
Statutory shared parental pay (maximum) — 148.68

Tax credit rates 2019/20

Child tax credit	£ per day	£ per year
Family element	1.49	545
Child element	7.60	2,780
Disabled child element	9.17	3,355
Severely disabled child element	3.72	1,360

Working tax credit

	£ per day	£ per year
Basic element	5.36	1,960
Couple element	5.50	2,010
Lone parent element	5.50	2,010
30-hour element	2.22	810
Disabled worker element	8.65	3,165
Severe disability element	3.73	1,365

Childcare element
70% eligible childcare costs to a weekly maximum of:

One child	70% of 175
Two or more children	70% of 300

Income thresholds

Working tax credit only or with child tax credit	6,420
Child tax credit only	16,105

Chapter 1
Benefits and tax credits

This chapter covers:
1. Introduction (below)
2. Attendance allowance (p2)
3. Best Start grant (p3)
4. Carer's allowance (p5)
5. Child benefit (p7)
6. Council tax reduction (p10)
7. Disability living allowance (p11)
8. Employment and support allowance (p14)
9. Funeral support payment (p19)
10. Guardian's allowance (p20)
11. Health benefits (p21)
12. Housing benefit (p23)
13. Income support (p26)
14. Jobseeker's allowance (p31)
15. Pension credit (p34)
16. Personal independence payment (p36)
17. The Scottish Welfare Fund (p38)
18. Statutory adoption pay (p40)
19. Tax credits (p40)
20. Universal credit (p46)

1. Introduction

This chapter gives an outline of the basic conditions of entitlement for the main benefits and tax credits which may be relevant to the situations covered in this *Handbook*. Other chapters look at how benefits and tax credits are affected when a child comes to live with you, goes to live elsewhere or leaves local authority care.

To check your entitlement, first use the chapter covering the circumstances that apply to you. This explains the specific rules that apply to benefits and tax credits in your circumstances. Then use this chapter for an outline of the general conditions of entitlement that apply to everyone. If you need more details, see

Chapter 1: Benefits and tax credits
2. Attendance allowance

CPAG's *Welfare Benefits and Tax Credits Handbook*. Chapter 2 explains how to claim benefits and tax credits, how to challenge a decision if you disagree with it and how to make a complaint.

Future changes
The rules for some benefits are changing in Scotland as certain benefits are devolved to the Scottish parliament. For example, the Best Start grant and carer's allowance supplement have already been introduced and disability benefits (such as personal independence payment and disability living allowance) and carer's allowance will start to be changed from summer 2020.

Benefit cap

There is a 'cap' on the total amount of benefits and tax credits you can receive, although some claimants are exempt.[1] If the total amount of your benefit is capped, the cap is applied by either reducing the amount of your universal credit (UC) or by reducing the amount of your housing benefit (HB). The cap does not apply to you if you have reached pension age (see p35) and there are a number of other situations in which it does not apply – eg, if you or someone in your household gets a disability benefit, or if you or your partner get carer's allowance or guardian's allowance.

If you are getting UC, the cap is set at £1,116.67 (£1,284.17 if in Greater London) a month for single people with no children and £1,666.67 (£1,916.67 if in Greater London) a month for couples and lone parents.

If you are getting HB, the cap is set at £257.69 (£296.35 if in Greater London) a week for single people with no dependent children and £384.62 (£442.31 if in Greater London) a week for couples and lone parents.

2. Attendance allowance

Attendance allowance (AA) is a benefit for people who have reached pension age and who have care needs because of a disability. AA is not means tested and you do not have to have paid any national insurance contributions to get it.

The Department for Work and Pensions is responsible for the administration of AA.

Who can claim attendance allowance

You qualify for AA if you:[2]
- have reached pension age when you first claim. People aged between 16 and pension age may be able to claim personal independence payment (see p36)

and children aged under 16 may be able to claim disability living allowance (DLA) (see p11); *and*
- satisfy certain UK residence and presence conditions and are not a 'person subject to immigration control'. See CPAG's *Welfare Benefits and Tax Credits Handbook* for details; *and*
- satisfy the disability test (see below); *and*
- have satisfied the disability test for the last six months (unless you are terminally ill).

Disability test

You get either a lower or a higher rate of AA. The disability conditions for the lower rate are the same as for the middle rate care component of DLA (see p12). The conditions for the higher rate are the same as for the highest rate care component of DLA (see p12).

Amount of benefit

Weekly rate	£
Lower rate	58.70
Higher rate	87.65

3. Best Start grant

The Best Start grant is made up of three different payments:
- the pregnancy and baby payment of £600 or £300;
- the early learning payment of £250;
- the school-age payment of £250.

You must usually reside in Scotland to get the Best Start grant and satisfy some other residence conditions (see CPAG's *Welfare Benefits and Tax Credits Handbook* for more details).

The Best Start grant is adminstered by Social Security Scotland.

Pregnancy and baby payment

This is a grant of £600 (or £300 if you are responsible for another child aged under 16) to help with the costs of having a new baby. To qualify, unless you are under 18 (or in some situations under 20), you have to be getting a qualifying benefit.[3] You or your partner must be getting one of the following:
- universal credit (UC) (including if your award ended within the last month);
- income support;

- income-based jobseeker's allowance;
- income-related employment and support allowance;
- pension credit (PC);
- housing benefit;
- child tax credit (CTC);
- working tax credit.

You can claim from the 24th week of pregnancy up to six months after the baby is born. You may also qualify if you become responsible for a baby who is under the age of one – eg, as a kinship carer or where a child is placed with you for adoption. In these situations, you have to claim before the child's first birthday and you have to be responsible for the child (see below).[4]

Early learning payment

This is a grant of £250 to help with the costs of having a young child aged between two and three and a half. To qualify, unless you are under 18 (or in some situations under 20), you have to be getting one of the qualifying benefits and be responsible for the child (see below). You must claim between the child's second birthday and the date six months after her/his third birthday.[5]

School-age payment

This is a grant of £250 to help with the costs of a child reaching school age. To qualify, unless you are under 18 (or in some situations under 20), you have to be getting a qualifying benefit and be responsible for the child (see below).

If your child's date of birth falls between 1 March 2014 and 28 February 2015 (inclusive), you have to claim between 3 June 2019 and 29 February 2020.

If your child's date of birth falls between 1 March 2015 and 29 February 2016 (inclusive), you have to claim between 1 June 2020 and 28 February 2021.[6]

Responsible for the child

You count as responsible for a child for the Best Start grant if any of the following applies on the day you claim.[7]
- The child is your dependant. S/he counts as your dependant if:
  - you are getting child benefit for her/him;
  - you are getting CTC and s/he is included in your award;
  - you are getting UC and s/he is included in your award; or
  - you are getting a child amount for her/him in your PC.
- You are under 20, the parent of the child, you normally live with her/him and you are a dependant in someone else's child benefit, CTC, UC or PC.
- You have adopted the child under Scottish law, or under the law of another jurisdiction recognised under Scottish law.

- The child has been placed with you for adoption by an approved adoption agency.
- You are the appointed guardian of the child.
- You are an approved kinship for the child and the child lives with you either under the terms of a kinship care order or under an agreement with a local authority where the child is a looked after child.
- You have been granted a parental order following a surrogate pregnancy.

4. Carer's allowance

Carer's allowance (CA) is a benefit for people who spend at least 35 hours a week looking after a disabled adult or disabled child. You do not have to have paid any national insurance contributions to get CA.

The Department for Work and Pensions is responsible for the administration of CA.

CA will eventually transfer to the Scottish government. Before then, you get a carer's allowance supplement if you get CA and you live in Scotland (see p6).

Who can claim carer's allowance

You qualify for CA if you:[8]
- are aged at least 16; *and*
- are caring for a person receiving either the highest or the middle rate care component of disability living allowance (DLA), either rate of the daily living component of personal independence payment (PIP), either rate of attendance allowance (AA), armed forces independence payment or constant attendance allowance with an industrial injury benefit or war pension; *and*
- are providing care that is regular and substantial (at least 35 hours a week); *and*
- are not gainfully employed. This means your earnings must be no more than £123 a week; *and*
- are not a full-time student; *and*
- are not a 'person subject to immigration control' and you satisfy the residence conditions. See CPAG's *Welfare Benefits and Tax Credits Handbook* for details.

The disabled person's benefit

Your entitlement to CA depends on the person for whom you care continuing to get her/his disability benefit. If her/his benefit stops, your benefit should also stop. To avoid being overpaid, make sure you tell the Carer's Allowance Unit (see Appendix 1) if the disabled person's AA, PIP or DLA stops being paid, or if you are no longer providing care for 35 hours or more a week.

If you are caring for a disabled adult, it is not always financially prudent to claim CA. Although it may mean more money for you, it could result in the person for whom you care losing some income support (IS), income-based jobseeker's allowance (JSA), income-related employment and support allowance (ESA), pension credit (PC), housing benefit (HB) or council tax reduction (CTR). S/he may be getting a severe disability premium/addition included in these benefits. S/he cannot continue to get this premium if you get CA for her/him. See CPAG's *Welfare Benefits and Tax Credits Handbook* for details.

Breaks from caring

You can have a short, temporary break from caring and still remain entitled to CA. You can have a break of up to four weeks in any period of 26 weeks, or a break of 12 weeks if either you or the person for whom you care is receiving treatment in hospital for at least eight of the 12 weeks, providing the person you care for is still getting her/his disability benefit.

Overlapping benefits

Although CA is not means tested, you cannot receive it at the same time as contributory ESA, incapacity benefit, maternity allowance, severe disablement allowance, widow's pension, widowed parent's allowance, retirement pension or contribution-based JSA. If you are eligible for more than one of these benefits, you generally get whichever is worth the most.

Carer element, carer premium and carer addition

In universal credit, a carer element is included if you satisfy the rules for CA or would satisfy them except that your earnings are too high.[9] If you are entitled to CA (even if you are not paid it because of the overlapping benefit rules), a carer premium or carer addition is included in your IS, income-based JSA, income-related ESA, PC, HB and CTR.

Amount of benefit

Weekly rate	£66.15

Carer's allowance supplement

The carer's allowance supplement is an extra payment for people who get CA and live in Scotland. If you get CA on the 'qualifying date', you are entitled to a payment of £226.20 which is for a six-month period. The qualifying dates for 2019 are 15 April 2019 and 14 October 2019. You must actually be receiving CA (either full or part payment) on the qualifying date: an 'underlying' entitlement is not enough. The carer's allowance supplement is disregarded for all means-tested benefits and tax credits. There is no need to make a claim for carer's allowance supplement: it should be paid automatically.

Carer's allowance supplement is administered by Social Security Scotland.

Young carer grant

A young carer grant is planned to be introduced in Scotland in autumn 2019. At the time of writing, the rules were not finalised. It is expected that the grant will be £300 a year and be aimed at young carers aged 16–18 who care for a disabled person for an average of 16 hours or more a week and who are not entitled to CA.[10]

The young carer grant will be administered by Social Security Scotland.

5. Child benefit

Child benefit is paid to people who are responsible for a child or children. Child benefit is paid for each child for whom you are responsible, with a higher amount paid for the eldest child. You do not have to be the child's parent to get child benefit for her/him. Child benefit is not means tested and so is not affected by any income or savings you have. In certain situations, child benefit is not payable for a child, even though you are caring for her/him. See the chapter relevant to your circumstances for more details. You do not have to have paid any national insurance contributions to get child benefit.

If you or your partner has an annual income of over £50,000, any child benefit you or your partner receive may be withdrawn through additional income tax. This is called the high income child benefit charge. You can elect not to be paid child benefit if this applies to you.[11]

HM Revenue and Customs (HMRC) is responsible for the administration of child benefit.

Who can claim child benefit

You qualify for child benefit if:[12]
- the child counts as a 'child' or 'qualifying young person' (see p8). **Note:** in the rest of this chapter the term 'child' is used for both a child and qualifying young person; *and*
- you are responsible for the child (see p9); *and*
- you have priority over other claimants (see p9); *and*
- you and the child satisfy certain presence and residence conditions; *and*
- you are not a 'person subject to immigration control'.

For details about the residence and presence conditions, and who is subject to immigration control, see CPAG's *Welfare Benefits and Tax Credits Handbook*.

There is no lower age limit, so if you have a baby and are under 16 you can claim child benefit.

Who counts as a child
Anyone aged under 16 counts as a **'child'** for child benefit purposes.[13]

Who counts as a qualifying young person
A **'qualifying young person'** is someone who:[14]
- has left relevant education or training and is aged 16, up to and including 31 August after her/his 16th birthday; *or*
- is aged 16 or 17; *and*
  - has left relevant education or training; *and*
  - registered for work, education or training with Skills Development Scotland within three months of leaving; *and*
  - is not in full-time work (24 hours or more a week); *and*
  - is within her/his 'extension period' (see below); *or*
- is aged 16 or over but under 20 and in relevant education (see below) or on an approved training course (see below). A 19-year-old is only included if s/he started, enrolled on or was accepted on the course or training before her/his 19th birthday; *or*
- is aged 16 or over but under 20, is not in full-time work (24 hours or more a week) and has left relevant education or approved training but has not passed her/his 'terminal date' (see p9).

If your child counts as a qualifying young person under more than one heading, s/he will be a qualifying young person until the last date that applies.

Relevant education
'Relevant education' means a full-time (more than 12 hours a week during term time) non-advanced course. This includes:
- school qualifications such as National Qualifications from Access level to Advanced Higher level;
- SVQ levels 1 to 3;
- National Certificates.

Approved training
'Approved training' means Employability Fund activity. This must not be provided under a contract of employment.

Extension period
The **'extension period'** runs for 20 weeks starting from the Monday after the child leaves education or training. You must apply in writing for child benefit to be paid during the extension period within three months of the child leaving school.

Terminal date

Your child's **'terminal date'** is the first of the following dates that falls after the day her/his relevant education or approved training ends:
- the last day of February; *or*
- 31 May; *or*
- 31 August; *or*
- 30 November.

Responsible for a child

You are responsible for a child in any week in which:
- you have the child living with you. **'Living with you'** means the child lives in the same house or residence and has a settled course of daily living with you;[15] *or*
- you are contributing to the cost of supporting the child. To satisfy this condition, you must be contributing at least the amount of child benefit.

There are special rules about when child benefit can be paid if a child is absent from home. Whether or not child benefit continues to be paid depends on the circumstances. See the relevant chapter of this *Handbook* for more information on what happens to child benefit when a child is away from home. There are also special rules that mean some people cannot get child benefit for a child, even though the child is living with them. See the relevant chapter of this *Handbook* for how you may be affected.

You cannot get child benefit for a child who claims certain benefits in her/his own right or, in most cases, who is married or cohabiting with a partner, or in prison or other custody. See CPAG's *Welfare Benefits and Tax Credits Handbook* for more information.

Priority between claimants

Only one person can get child benefit for a particular child. If more than one person has claimed child benefit for a child, claimants take priority in the following order:[16]
- the person with whom the child lives;
- the wife, if a husband and wife are living together;
- a parent, including a step-parent or adoptive parent;
- the mother (including stepmother), if the parents are unmarried and living together;
- in any other case, the person agreed by the claimants;
- if there is no agreement, the person selected by the decision maker at HMRC. There is no right of appeal against this decision, although you can request a revision and see p60 for information on how to complain.

Chapter 1: Benefits and tax credits
6. Council tax reduction

If a new claim takes priority over an existing claim, child benefit continues to be paid to the existing claimant for three weeks after the new claim, unless the existing claimant gives up her/his entitlement at an earlier date.

Amount of benefit

Weekly rate	£
Eldest child	20.70
Other children (each)	13.70

6. Council tax reduction

Council tax reduction (CTR) is a means-tested scheme to help low-income households with council tax payments. You can get help through CTR whether or not you are in work, provided you satisfy the conditions of entitlement.

Your local authority is responsible for the administration of CTR.

Who can claim council tax reduction

You qualify for CTR if:
- you or your partner are liable for council tax for the home in which you live; *and*
- you are 'habitually resident' in the UK, Ireland, Channel Islands or Isle of Man, have a 'right to reside' in the UK, and are not a 'person subject to immigration control'. These terms are explained in CPAG's *Welfare Benefits and Tax Credits Handbook*; *and*
- you and your partner have savings of £16,000 or less, unless you are on guarantee credit of pension credit (PC), in which case your capital is not taken into account; *and*
- your income is sufficiently low.

Amount of reduction

The amount of CTR you get depends on your income compared with the amount the law says you need to live on. This section gives a brief outline of how CTR is calculated, so you can see how a change in your circumstances or in your income may affect your entitlement. CTR is calculated in a very similar way to housing benefit (HB) (see p24).

Step one: calculate maximum council tax reduction

This is your net weekly council tax liability, after any discounts, reductions and non-dependant deductions have been made.

Step two: if you get some means-tested benefits
If you get income support (IS), income-based jobseeker's allowance (JSA), income-related employment and support allowance (ESA) or PC (guarantee credit), you get your maximum CTR (Step one). In this case, you do not need to continue with the remainder of these steps.

Step three: if you do not get these means-tested benefits
If you do not get IS, income-based JSA, income-related ESA or PC (guarantee credit), you must compare your income with your 'applicable amount'. If you are not on universal credit (UC), follow the same process as for HB (see p25).

The calculation of your CTR is different if you get UC. If you get UC, it is important to apply to your local authority for CTR as soon as you can.

The local authority must either use the DWP's figures for your UC maximum amount as your 'applicable amount' for CTR, and the DWP's assessment of your income and capital (both converted to weekly figures), or an estimated average weekly income and estimated UC payment if your income, or that of your partner, frequently changes. In either case, for each child or young person in your family, your applicable amount is increased by £16.73. See the relevant chapter of this *Handbook* for information on how your UC applicable amount is affected in specific circumstances.

Step four: work out your weekly income
Some kinds of income are ignored.

See the relevant chapters of this *Handbook* for more information on how specific income (eg, fostering allowances and payments from the local authority) is treated.

Step five: calculate your council tax reduction
If your income is less than or the same as your applicable amount, CTR is the amount worked out at Step one – ie, your maximum CTR.

If your income is more than your applicable amount, work out 20 per cent of the difference. Your CTR is the amount you worked out at Step one minus 20 per cent of the difference between your weekly income and your applicable amount.

7. Disability living allowance

Disability living allowance (DLA) is a benefit for people with mobility problems and/or care needs as a result of a disability. For claimants aged between 16 and pension age, DLA is being replaced by personal independence payment (PIP) (see p36). New claims for DLA can now normally only be made by claimants aged under 16.

Chapter 1: Benefits and tax credits
7. Disability living allowance

DLA has two components:
- a care component, paid at either the lowest, middle or highest rate;
- a mobility component, paid at either the lower or the higher rate.

You can get either the care component or the mobility component, or both. DLA is not means tested and you do not have to have paid any national insurance contributions to get it.

The Department for Work and Pensions is responsible for the administration of DLA.

Who can claim disability living allowance

You qualify for DLA if:[17]
- you are under age 16 when you first claim. Those aged between 16 and pension age may be able to claim PIP and those who have reached pension age may be able to claim attendance allowance; *and*
- you satisfy certain UK residence and presence conditions, and are not a 'person subject to immigration control'. See CPAG's *Welfare Benefits and Tax Credits Handbook* for details; *and*
- you satisfy the disability test for the care component (see below) and/or the mobility component (see p13); *and*
- you have satisfied the disability test for the last three months and are likely to continue to do so for the next six months (unless you are terminally ill).

Disability test: care component

To get the care component, you must have a physical or mental disability which means you need the following kind of care from another person. What is important is the help you need rather than the help you actually get.

You get either the lowest, middle or highest rate.

You get the **lowest rate** if you need attention in connection with your bodily functions (see p13) for a significant portion of the day. This attention might be given all at once or spread out. It should normally add up to about an hour or more, or be made up of several brief periods.

You get the **middle rate** if you need care either during the day or during the night, but not both. You get the middle rate if you meet one (or both) of the day care conditions *or* one (or both) of the night care conditions.

You get the **highest rate** if you need care both during the day and the night. You get the highest rate if you meet one (or both) of the day care conditions *and* one (or both) of the night care conditions. Alternatively, you should get the highest rate if you are terminally ill. This means that you have a progressive disease and can reasonably be expected to die as a result within six months.

There is no lower age limit for the care component. If you are under 16, you must show that your need for attention or supervision is substantially in excess of the normal needs of other children of the same age without a disability or similar to those of a younger child without a disability.

Day care conditions
- You need frequent attention throughout the day in connection with your bodily functions (see below). This means you may qualify if you need help several times (not just once or twice), spread throughout the day. If you need help just in the mornings and evenings, for instance, you might get the lowest rate.
- You need continual supervision throughout the day in order to avoid substantial danger to yourself or others. The supervision needs to be frequent or regular, but need not be literally continuous.

Night care conditions
- You need prolonged or repeated attention at night in connection with your bodily functions (see below). You should qualify if you need help once in the night for 20 minutes or more. You should also qualify if you need help twice in the night (or more often), however long it takes.
- In order to avoid substantial danger to yourself or others, you need another person to be awake at night for a prolonged period (20 minutes or more) or at frequent intervals (three times or more) to watch over you.

Attention with bodily functions
This is help from someone to do personal things you cannot do entirely by yourself. Bodily functions are things like breathing, hearing, seeing, eating, drinking, walking, sitting, sleeping, getting in or out of bed, dressing, undressing, communicating and using the toilet. Any help in connection with an impaired bodily function counts if it involves personal contact (physical or verbal in your presence) and it is reasonably required.

Disability test: mobility component
You can get either the lower or higher rate mobility component.

The **lower rate** is for people who can walk but who need guidance or supervision. You qualify if you are able to walk, but because of your mental or physical disability you cannot walk outdoors without guidance or supervision from someone else most of the time.

You can still qualify if you are able to manage on familiar routes. If you cannot manage without guidance or supervision on unfamiliar routes, or you cannot manage anywhere, you should qualify.

The **higher rate** is for people who cannot walk or have great difficulty walking because of a physical disability. You qualify if:
- you are unable to walk; *or*
- you have no legs or feet; *or*

Chapter 1: Benefits and tax credits
8. Employment and support allowance

- you are virtually unable to walk. This takes account of the distance you can walk before you feel severe discomfort. There is no set distance at which you pass or fail the test. Some people have passed who can walk 100 metres; others have failed who can walk only 50 metres. The speed at which you walk and how you walk also count; *or*
- the exertion required to walk would lead to a danger to your life or could cause a serious deterioration in your health; *or*
- you are deaf and blind; *or*
- you are severely visually impaired.

Someone who is severely mentally impaired may also qualify if s/he gets the highest rate care component and meets other conditions. This can help a child with severe learning disabilities and disruptive behaviour to get the higher rate mobility component even if s/he is physically able to walk.

You have to be at least age three to get the higher rate mobility component and at least age five to get the lower rate mobility component. For the lower rate, you must need substantially more guidance or supervision than a child of your age without a disability would normally need.

Disability living allowance for over-16s

Some people aged 16 or over are currently getting DLA. All existing DLA claimants, except those who were already 65 on 8 April 2013, will be invited to claim PIP. Their existing DLA awards will end. See CPAG's *Welfare Benefits and Tax Credits Handbook* for details.

Amount of benefit

Weekly rate	£
Care component	
Lowest rate	23.20
Middle rate	58.70
Highest rate	87.65
Mobility component	
Lower rate	23.20
Higher rate	61.20

8. Employment and support allowance

Employment and support allowance (ESA) is a benefit for people who have limited capability for work because of illness or disability. There are two types: income-related ESA (see p15) and contributory ESA (see p18).

'Limited capability for work' is assessed by the Department for Work and Pensions (DWP), usually at a medical examination.

The DWP is responsible for the administration of ESA.

Income-related employment and support allowance

Income-related ESA is means tested and is for people with a low income who have 'limited capability for work'.

Income-related ESA is being replaced by universal credit (UC) and you cannot normally make a new claim for income-related ESA. Eventually, claimants who are on income-related ESA will be transferred to UC.

Who can claim income-related employment and support allowance

If you are not in the UC system, you qualify for income-related ESA if:[18]

- you have 'limited capability for work'; *and*
- you are aged at least 16 and under pension age; *and*
- you are not getting income support (IS), jobseeker's allowance (JSA), pension credit (PC) or statutory sick pay (SSP); *and*
- your partner is not getting IS, income-based JSA, PC or income-related ESA; *and*
- you are not working or, if you are, it is 'permitted work'; *and*
- your partner is not working 24 hours or more a week (there are some exceptions to this); *and*
- you are not in education (this is the general rule, but part-time students and some full-time students can claim); *and*
- you are in Great Britain, you are not a 'person subject to immigration control' and you satisfy the habitual residence test, including having the 'right to reside'; *and*
- you have no more than £16,000 capital; *and*
- your income is less than the set amount the law says you need to live on (known as your 'applicable amount' – see p16).

For details of these qualifying conditions, including how your imited capability for work is assessed, see CPAG's *Welfare Benefits and Tax Credits Handbook*.

Amount of benefit

The amount of income-related ESA you get depends on your circumstances and the circumstances of your partner, if you have one. The amount also depends on your income and capital. It is calculated by going through the following steps.

Step one: work out your capital

If your capital is over £16,000, you cannot get income-related ESA.[19] Some kinds of capital are ignored.

Chapter 1: Benefits and tax credits
8. Employment and support allowance

Step two: work out your applicable amount

This is an amount for basic weekly needs. It is made up of personal allowances (see below), premiums (see p17), housing costs (see p17) and either a work-related activity component or a support component (see p17).

Work out your applicable amount by adding together your personal allowance, premiums, eligible housing costs and, once you have been getting ESA for 13 weeks, either the work-related activity component or the support component. **Note:** from 3 April 2017, the work-related activity component was abolished for most new claims.

The first 13 weeks is called the 'assessment phase' and from week 14 it is called the 'main phase'. Income-related ESA does not include amounts for children.

Personal allowance

Your personal allowance is paid at either the single, lone parent or couple rate depending on your situation. The amount depends on your age and whether you are in the assessment phase or the main phase.

Weekly rate	Assessment phase (weeks 1–13) £	Main phase (week 14 onwards) £
Single		
Under 25	57.90	73.10
25 or over	73.10	73.10
Lone parent		
Under 18	57.90	73.10
18 or over	73.10	73.10
Couple		
Both under 18 (higher rate)	87.50	114.85
Both under 18	57.90	73.10
(if not eligible for higher rate)		
One under 18, one 18 or over (higher rate)	114.85	114.85
One under 18, one 18–24	57.90	73.10
(if not eligible for higher rate)		
One under 18, one 25 or over	73.10	73.10
(if not eligible for higher rate)		
Both 18 or over	114.85	114.85

If you are both under 18, you get the higher rate if:
- one of you is responsible for a child; *or*
- both you and your partner would be eligible to claim income-related ESA if you were single; *or*
- your partner would qualify for IS if s/he were single; *or*

Chapter 1: Benefits and tax credits
8. Employment and support allowance

- your partner would qualify for income-based JSA or severe hardship payments of JSA.

If one of you is under 18 and the other is 18 or over, you get the higher rate if the younger person would:
- qualify for IS or income-related ESA if s/he were single; *or*
- qualify for income-based JSA or severe hardship payments of JSA.

Premiums

Whether or not you qualify for premiums depends on your circumstances. You qualify for:
- **pensioner premium** of £140.40 if your partner has reached pension age (see p35). In the main phase, these amounts are reduced by the amount of the work-related activity component or support component for which you qualify;
- **carer premium** of £36.85 in the same way as you would for IS (see p29);
- **enhanced disability premium** if you or your partner get the highest rate disability living allowance care component, the enhanced rate of personal independence payment daily living component or you get the ESA support component. It is not included if either partner is over pension age. It is £16.80 if you are single and £24.10 for a couple;
- **severe disability premium** of £65.85 in the same way as you would for IS (see p30).

Housing costs

If you own your own home, income-related ESA can help with certain service charges. Normally, help only starts once you have been getting ESA for 39 weeks.

Components

In the main phase, which usually starts 14 weeks after you claim, you are placed in either the 'work-related activity' group or the 'support' group depending on your ability to undertake work-focused interviews and other work-related activity. If you are in the support group, you get a support component of £38.55 a week. For claims that started before 3 April 2017, or are linked to a claim which existed before that date, if you are in the work-related activity group you get a work-related activity component of £29.05 a week. New claims made from 3 April 2017 do not include the work-related activity component. For more detail about these rules, see CPAG's *Welfare Benefits and Tax Credits Handbook*.

Step three: work out your weekly income

Some kinds of income are ignored. For details, see CPAG's *Welfare Benefits and Tax Credits Handbook*.

See the relevant chapters of this *Handbook* for more information on how specific income (eg, fostering allowances and payments from the local authority) is treated.

Step four: deduct weekly income from applicable amount

If your income is *less* than your applicable amount, income-related ESA equals the difference between the two.

If your income is *the same as or more than* your applicable amount, you cannot get income-related ESA.

Contributory employment and support allowance

Contributory ESA is not means tested and is for people who have paid sufficient national insurance (NI) contributions.

Who can claim contributory employment and support allowance

You qualify for contributory ESA if:[20]
- you have limited capability for work. See CPAG's *Welfare Benefits and Tax Credits Handbook* for more details of how this is assessed; *and*
- you are aged at least 16 and under pension age; *and*
- you are in Great Britain (there are some exceptions allowed); *and*
- you are not getting IS, JSA or SSP; *and*
- you satisfy the NI contribution conditions (see below).

National insurance contributions

You must meet two contribution conditions.
- You must have paid at least 26 weeks' class 1 or class 2 NI contributions on earnings at the lower earnings limit in one of the two complete tax years (6 April to 5 April) before the start of the benefit year (running from the first Sunday in January) in which you claim.
- You must have paid or been credited with class 1 or class 2 NI contributions on earnings of 50 times the lower earnings limit in each of the last two complete tax years before the start of the benefit year in which you claim.

In certain situations, for example if you are a carer, the contribution conditions are relaxed. For more information on contribution conditions, see CPAG's *Welfare Benefits and Tax Credits Handbook*.

Amount of benefit

Contributory ESA only includes an amount for you. There are no additions for partners and children. Contributory ESA is made up of a basic allowance and, after an assessment phase, the support component or, for some claimants only, the work-related activity component. The work-related activity component was abolished for most new claims made from 3 April 2017. During the 13-week assessment phase at the start of your claim, the basic allowance is paid at a lower rate if you are under 25. After the assessment phase, the basic allowance is paid at the same rate regardless of your age (the main phase).

Unless you are in the support group, your contributory ESA is only paid for one year.

See CPAG's *Welfare Benefits and Tax Credits Handbook* for more information.

Weekly rate	£
Assessment phase	
Under 25	57.90
25 or over	73.10
Main phase	
Basic allowance	73.10
Work-related activity component	29.05
Support component	38.55

9. Funeral support payment

A funeral support payment is made to help with burial or cremation costs. It is expected to be available from last summer 2019.

Social Security Scotland is responsible for the administration of funeral support payments.

Who can claim a funeral support payment

To qualify for a funeral support payment, you must get:[21]
- universal credit (including if your award ended in the last month);
- income support;
- income-based jobseeker's allowance;
- income-related employment and support allowance;
- child tax credit;
- working tax credit including the disabled worker or severe disability element;
- pension credit; *or*
- housing benefit.

You must have accepted responsbility for the funeral costs and it must be reasonable for you to have accepted responsbility.[22] Usually, it will be reasonable for the person with the closest relationship to the person who has died to accept responsibility, but other factors, such as estrangement, may also be relevant. You must normally reside in Scotland and the person who has died must have normally resided in the UK. Usually, the funeral must take place in the UK, but a funeral in a European Economic Area state may sometimes qualify.

You must claim within six months of the funeral.

10. Guardian's allowance

Guardian's allowance is a benefit paid to people looking after a child who is effectively an orphan. It is not means tested and so is not affected by any income or savings you have. However, if a local authority is paying you to look after a child you are fostering this might affect guardian's allowance (see Chapter 8). You do not have to have paid any national insurance contributions to get guardian's allowance.

HM Revenue and Customs is responsible for the administration of guardian's allowance.

Who can claim guardian's allowance

You can claim guardian's allowance for a child if:[23]
- you are entitled to child benefit for the child. **Note:** you still count as being entitled to child benefit if you have chosen not to claim to avoid the high income child benefit charge; *and*
- the child is an 'eligible child' (see below); *and*
- the child is living with you, or you (or your spouse/civil partner) are contributing to the cost of supporting the child at a rate of at least £17.60 a week (in addition to any payment you make which means you are entitled to child benefit for the child); *and*
- the residence conditions are satisfied (see CPAG's *Welfare Benefits and Tax Credits Handbook* for more information).

Who is an eligible child

A child is an **'eligible child'** if:
- both her/his parents have died; *or*
- one of her/his parents has died and, when s/he died, you did not know where the other parent was and all reasonable efforts to trace her/him have been unsuccessful; *or*
- one of her/his parents has died and the other is in prison (with at least two years of her/his sentence still to serve at the date of the death) or detained in hospital (under particular legislation).

Parents and adoptive parents

The general rule is that parents cannot claim guardian's allowance for their own child. Adoptive parents count as parents and, therefore, cannot get guardian's allowance for an adopted child. The exception to this is if an adoptive parent is entitled to guardian's allowance for the child immediately before the adoption.[24]

Amount of benefit

Weekly rate
Each eligible child   £17.60

11. Health benefits

You may be able to get some help with the cost of:
- glasses and contact lenses;
- dental treatment;
- travel to hospital.

You may be exempt from these charges or be able to claim a reduction on low income grounds.[25] Pregnant women or parents or carers of young children may also be able to get Best Start food payment cards.

There is no charge for NHS eye and dental checks, prescriptions, wigs or fabric supports in Scotland.

Who is exempt from charges

You can be exempt either because you are getting a 'qualifying benefit' or because you are in one of the exempt groups.

Qualifying benefits

You get NHS dental treatment, vouchers for glasses, and certain fares to hospital if you get:
- universal credit (UC) and have no earnings, or you earn £435 or less a month (if your UC does not include a a child, limited capability for work or limited capability for work-related activity element) or £935 or less a month (if your UC includes one or more of these elements); *or*
- income support (IS); *or*
- income-based jobseeker's allowance (JSA); *or*
- income-related employment and support allowance (ESA); *or*
- child tax credit (CTC), with or without working tax credit (WTC), and your income for tax credit purposes is £15,276 or less; *or*
- WTC with a disability or severe disability element and your income for tax credit purposes is £15,276 or less; *or*
- guarantee credit of pension credit (PC).

Exempt groups

You are eligible for **free NHS dental treatment** if:
- you are under 18; *or*

- you are under 19 in full-time education; *or*
- you are pregnant or have given birth in the last year; *or*
- you are under the Community Dental Service (for people who have difficulty getting treatment for reasons such as a disability); *or*
- you are an asylum seeker getting asylum support; *or*
- you get a war pension and need treatment for your war disablement; *or*
- you are a care leaver getting support from the local authority under section 29 of the Children (Scotland) Act 1995.

You are eligible for **vouchers for glasses or contact lenses** if:
- you are under 16; *or*
- you are under 19 in full-time education; *or*
- you have a prescription for complex lenses; *or*
- you are a Hospital Eye Service patient; *or*
- you are an asylum seeker getting asylum support; *or*
- you get a war pension and need treatment for your war disablement; *or*
- you are a care leaver getting support from the local authority under section 29 of the Children (Scotland) Act 1995.

You are eligible for **help with fares to hospital** if:
- the hospital is 30 or more miles away, or it involves a journey of five miles or more by sea, and you live in the Highlands or Islands – ie:
    - the Highland region, Western Isles, Orkney Islands, Shetland Islands;
    - Arran, Great Cumbrae, Little Cumbrae;
    - the area formerly covered by Argyll and Bute District Council;
    - parts of Moray (Aberlour, Cabrach, Dallas, Dyke, Edinkillie, Forres, Inveravon, Kinloss, Kirkmichael, Knockando, Mortlach, Rafford, Rothes); *or*
- you are an asylum seeker getting asylum support; *or*
- you get a war pension and need treatment for your war disablement; *or*
- you are a care leaver getting support from the local authority under section 29 of the Children (Scotland) Act 1995.

Low income scheme

If you are not on a qualifying benefit or in an exempt group and your capital is £16,000 or less, you may still be able to get help with the cost of dental treatment, glasses/contact lenses and fares to hospital under the low income scheme. Whether or not you get any help depends on how much income you have compared with a set level (based on IS but with some differences).

Best Start foods

You can get a payment card to buy certain foods under the Best Start foods scheme if you are pregnant or have a child under three and you get a qualifying benefit (if you are under 18 you do not have to getting a qualifying benefit).[26]

The qualifying benefits are:[27]
- UC with earnings under £610 a month;
- IS;
- income-based JSA;
- income-related ESA;
- PC;
- housing benefit with income under £311 a week;
- CTC (with no WTC) with income under £16,190 a year;
- WTC (with or without CTC) with income under £7,320 a year.

12. Housing benefit

Housing benefit (HB) is a means-tested benefit that helps low-income households with rent payments. You can get HB whether or not you are in work, provided you satisfy the conditions of entitlement.

Your local authority is responsible for the administration of HB.

For most people under pension age, HB is being replaced by universal credit (UC) and you cannot normally make a new claim for HB. Eventually, most claimants who are on HB will be transferred to UC.

Who can claim housing benefit

If you are not in the UC system, you qualify for HB if:[28]
- you or your partner are liable to pay rent on the dwelling you occupy as your home; *and*
- you are not in a category that is excluded from HB (see below); *and*
- you satisfy the 'habitual residence test', including having a 'right to reside', and are not a 'person subject to immigration control'. These terms are explained in CPAG's *Welfare Benefits and Tax Credits Handbook*; *and*
- you and your partner have savings of £16,000 or less, unless you are on guarantee credit of pension credit (PC), in which case your capital is not taken into account; *and*
- your income is sufficiently low.

Who cannot claim housing benefit

Some groups of people are excluded from HB – eg, most (but not all) full-time students, most people who live in care homes, and people whose agreement to pay rent is not on a commercial basis or whose liability to pay rent has been created to take advantage of the HB scheme. For more information, see CPAG's *Welfare Benefits and Tax Credits Handbook*. Most 16/17-year-old care leavers are excluded (see Chapter 10).

Chapter 1: Benefits and tax credits
12. Housing benefit

Amount of benefit

The amount of HB you get depends on your income compared with the amount the law says you need to live on. Also, there are limits set on how much rent HB will cover. This section just gives an outline of how HB is calculated, so you can see how a change in your circumstances or in your income might affect your entitlement.

Step one: calculate the maximum housing benefit

This is the maximum amount the local authority can pay. HB does not cover some charges, such as those for fuel and meals. Your maximum HB may not be as much as your actual rent. Most private tenants have their maximum HB determined by a 'local housing allowance'. This is a flat rate based on the area in which you live and on the size of your household.

Working-age tenants in the social rented sector (ie, local authority or housing association tenants) have their maximum HB reduced if they are deemed to be under-occupying their home – ie, if they have one or more spare bedrooms. This is commonly known as the 'bedroom tax'. **Note:** this does not apply to you if you are over pension age and there are some other exceptions – eg, if you have a disabled child and s/he cannot share a room due to her/his disability. See CPAG's *Welfare Benefits and Tax Credits Handbook* for more details of this reduction. See the relevant chapter of this *Handbook* for how it affects your particular situation. If you are affected by the bedroom tax, you should claim a discretionary housing payment (see p26).

Step two: deduct amounts for non-dependants from maximum housing benefit

A **'non-dependant'** is someone aged 18 or over, usually a friend or adult relative, who lives with you but not on a commercial basis. A non-dependant deduction is made to reflect an assumed contribution from her/him to the household, whether or not s/he pays anything. Sometimes no non-dependant deduction is made – eg, if the non-dependant is under 25 and gets certain benefits, or is someone who normally lives elsewhere. If you or your partner gets attendance allowance, the daily living component of personal independence payment or the care component of disability living allowance, or are certified as severely sight-impaired or blind by a consultant ophthalmologist, no non-dependant deduction is made.

Non-dependant deductions are made at a fixed rate, depending on the income and circumstances of the non-dependant. See CPAG's *Welfare Benefits and Tax Credits Handbook* for details.

Step three: if you get means-tested benefits

If you get income support (IS), income-based jobseeker's allowance (JSA), income-related employment and support allowance (ESA), PC (guarantee credit) or UC, your HB is your maximum HB minus any amount for non-dependants. You do not need to continue with the remainder of these steps.

Step four: if you do not get means-tested benefits
If you do not get IS, income-based JSA, income-related ESA, PC (guarantee credit) or UC, you must compare your income with your 'applicable amount'. Your applicable amount is made up of:
- personal allowances; *and*
- premiums; *and*
- components.

The applicable amount includes allowances, premiums and components for yourself and for your partner, if you have one. It also includes allowances and premiums for dependent children. The amounts for HB are the same as for IS (see p28), except:
- personal allowances:
  - the child allowance is included in HB. This may be subject to the 'two-child limit' (see CPAG's *Welfare Benefits and Tax Credits Handbook* for details);
  - single people under 25 and lone parents under 18 who are entitled to main-phase ESA get £73.10;
  - young couples get £114.85, unless both are under 18 and the claimant is not entitled to main-phase ESA, in which case they get £87.50;
  - single people who have reached pension age have a personal allowance of £181.00;
  - couples where one or both have reached pension age get £270.60.
- premiums:
  - family premium (£17.45, or £22.20 for some lone parents), disabled child premium (£64.19) and enhanced disability premium for a child (£26.04) are included in HB. The family premium is only included if you were getting it before 1 May 2016, you are still getting HB and have not made a new claim for HB since then;
  - you do not get a disability premium if you have been assessed as having limited capability for work for ESA and you (ie, not your partner, if you have one) are the HB claimant;
- components:
  - instead of a disability premium, include a work-related activity component of £29.05 if you have claimed ESA and been assessed as having limited capability for work, or a support component of £38.55 if you also have limited capability for work-related activity (see p14 for more about ESA). You will only get the work-related activity component if it is included in your ESA (see p17).

Step five: work out your weekly income

Some kinds of income are ignored. For details, see CPAG's *Welfare Benefits and Tax Credits Handbook*.

See the relevant chapters of this *Handbook* for more information on how specific income (eg, fostering allowances and payments from the local authority) is treated.

Step six: calculate your housing benefit

If your income is less than or the same as your applicable amount, HB is the amount worked out at Step two – ie, your maximum rent less any non-dependant deductions.

If your income is more than your applicable amount, work out 65 per cent of the difference. Your HB is the amount you worked out at Step two minus 65 per cent of the difference between your weekly income and your applicable amount.

Discretionary housing payments

Discretionary housing payments (DHPs) are extra payments that can be paid by the local authority in addition to your UC or HB.

A local authority can pay you a DHP if:[29]
- you are entitled to HB or UC which includes a housing costs element for rent; *and*
- you appear to need additional financial help to meet your housing costs.

The local authority has discretion whether or not to pay you, how much to pay you and over what period. Certain expenses cannot be met by DHPs – eg, a need for financial assistance that arises because of a reduction in HB to recover an overpayment, or a need that arises as a consequence of ineligible service charges under the HB scheme.

DHPs can be particularly important if your HB is reduced because of the bedroom tax or the benefit cap.

13. Income support

Income support (IS) provides basic financial support for some people under pension age (see p35) who are not expected to 'sign on' as available for work – eg, lone parents with a child under a certain age and people caring for a disabled person. IS is a means-tested benefit, so any income and savings you have may affect how much IS you get or whether you are entitled. You do not have to have paid any national insurance contributions to get IS.

The Department for Work and Pensions is responsible for the administration of IS.

IS is being replaced by universal credit (UC) and you cannot usually make a new claim for IS. Eventually, claimants who are on IS will be transferred to UC.

Who can claim income support

If you are not in the UC system, you qualify for IS if:[30]
- you are at least 16 and under pension age (see p35); *and*
- you fit into one of the groups of people who can claim IS (see below); *and*
- you are not working for 16 hours or more a week; *and*
- your partner, if you have one, is not working for 24 hours or more a week (there are some exceptions to this); *and*
- you are not studying full time (there are some exceptions to this rule); *and*
- you are not entitled to jobseeker's allowance (JSA); *and*
- you are not entitled to employment and support allowance (ESA) and your partner, if you have one, is not entitled to income-related ESA; *and*
- your partner, if you have one, is not entitled to income-based JSA or PC; *and*
- you are present in Great Britain, satisfy the 'habitual residence test', including having the 'right to reside', and are not a 'person subject to immigration control'. (You can sometimes be paid IS for the first four or eight weeks you are outside Britain.) These terms are explained in CPAG's *Welfare Benefits and Tax Credits Handbook*; *and*
- you have no more than £16,000 capital; *and*
- your income is less than the set amount the law says you need to live on (known as your 'applicable amount' – see p28).

Groups of people who can claim income support

You can claim IS if:[31]
- you are a carer and you get carer's allowance (CA) (see p5), or you are looking after someone who is getting attendance allowance (AA) (see p2), either rate of the daily living component of personal independence payment (PIP) (see p36), or the middle or highest rate care component of disability living allowance (DLA) (see p11), or you are looking after someone who has claimed these benefits in the last 26 weeks and is waiting for a decision;
- you are a lone parent with a child aged under five;
- you are on statutory sick pay (SSP);
- you are looking after your partner or child because s/he is temporarily ill;
- you are looking after a child whose parent is temporarily ill or away;
- you are fostering a child aged under 16 through the local authority (or an agency on behalf of the local authority) and you do not have a partner;
- you are a kinship carer of a looked-after child aged under 16 and you do not have a partner;
- you are not a member of a couple and a child aged under 16 has been placed with you for adoption;

- you are expecting a child in less than 11 weeks, you had a baby in the last 15 weeks, or you are incapable of work because of your pregnancy.

Some young people in full-time, non-advanced education can also claim IS – eg, young people who are orphaned or estranged from their parents.

There are some additional groups of people who can claim IS. For more details, see CPAG's *Welfare Benefits and Tax Credits Handbook*.

If you are a member of a couple, one of you must claim IS for both of you. Your joint income and capital is taken into account.

Amount of benefit

The amount of IS you get depends on your circumstances and on the circumstances of your partner, if you have one. The amount also depends on your income and capital. Go through the following steps to work out the amount of IS to which you are entitled.

Step one: work out your capital

If your capital is over £16,000, you cannot get IS.[32] Some kinds of capital are ignored. For details, see CPAG's *Welfare Benefits and Tax Credits Handbook*.

Step two: work out your applicable amount

This is an amount for basic weekly needs. It is made up of personal allowances (see below), premiums (see p29) and housing costs (see p30). On 6 April 2004, personal allowances and premiums for children were abolished for all new IS claims and for anyone claiming child tax credit (CTC). Amounts for children are paid through CTC and child benefit instead. If you were getting IS with amounts for children included before 6 April 2004, your IS continues to include these until you claim CTC.

If a child becomes part of your family for the first time or returns to the family, you cannot get IS personal allowances and premiums for that child unless you already get these for another child in the family. See p30 for details of child personal allowances and premiums.

Personal allowance

Your personal allowance is made up of a personal allowance at either the single, lone parent or couple rate, depending on your situation.[33]

Circumstances	£ per week	Conditions
Single		
Under 25	57.90	No special conditions.
25 or over	73.10	No special conditions.

Lone parent		
Under 18	57.90	No special conditions.
18 or over	73.10	No special conditions.
Couple		
Both aged 16/17 (lower rate)	57.90	For couples who cannot get a higher rate (see below).
Both aged 16/17 (higher rate)	87.50	You get the higher rate if: – you or your partner are responsible for a child; *or* – you and your partner would be eligible to claim IS or income-related ESA if you were single; *or* – your partner is eligible for income-based JSA or entitled to severe hardship payments of JSA.
One aged 16/17 (certain cases)	114.85	Your partner is under 18 and is eligible for IS or income-related ESA, or would be if s/he were single, or s/he is eligible for income-based JSA or entitled to severe hardship payments of JSA.
One aged 16/17, one 18–24	57.90	If the rate above does not apply.
One aged 16/17, one 25 or over	73.10	If the rate above does not apply.
Both aged 18 or over	114.85	No special conditions.

Premiums

Whether or not you qualify for premiums depends on your circumstances. You can qualify for either:
- disability premium of £34.35 (£48.95 for a couple); *or*
- pensioner premium of £140.40 for couples.

In addition, you may qualify for:[34]
- carer premium of £36.85; *and/or*
- enhanced disability premium of £16.80 (£24.10 for a couple); *and/or*
- severe disability premium of £65.85.

You get a **carer premium** if you or your partner are entitled to CA (see p5). If you are entitled to CA but not paid it because it overlaps with another benefit (eg, ESA), you still qualify for a carer premium. You get two carer premiums if both you and your partner qualify.

You get a **disability premium** if you or your partner get:[35]
- DLA;
- AA;

Chapter 1: Benefits and tax credits
13. Income support

- PIP;
- long-term incapacity benefit;
- severe disability allowance;
- working tax credit with a disabled worker or severe disability element;
- war pensioner's mobility supplement;
- armed forces independence payment;
- constant attendance allowance;
- exceptionally severe disablement allowance.

You also qualify if:
- you are certified as severely sight impaired or blind or have stopped being certified within the last 28 weeks; *or*
- you have been entitled to SSP for a continuous period of 196 days and you are terminally ill (breaks in entitlement of up to eight weeks are ignored); *or*
- you have claimed IS on the grounds of incapacity for at least 364 days.

If you are the IS claimant and you have a partner, you get disability premium if s/he gets any of the qualifying benefits or is blind.

You get an **enhanced disability premium** if you get the highest rate DLA care component or the enhanced rate of PIP daily living component. It is paid at the rate of £16.80 if you qualify and are single or a lone parent, or £24.10 if you have a partner and one or both of you qualifies.[36]

People who have reached pension age claim PC rather than IS. However, you get a **pensioner premium** if you are claiming IS and you have a partner who has reached pension age (see p35).[37]

The **severe disability premium** is for severely disabled people who live alone, or can be treated as living alone. You qualify for this premium if you get the middle or highest rate care component of DLA, the daily living component of PIP or either rate of AA and no one gets CA for looking after you. You will not get it if you live with another person aged 18 or over (eg, a friend or parent), unless s/he is separately liable for rent, you only share a bathroom or hallway, or in some other circumstances.[38] See CPAG's *Welfare Benefits and Tax Credits Handbook* for details.

If you have a partner, you do not qualify unless s/he also qualifies in her/his own right or is certified as severely sight impaired or blind. If you both qualify, you get two premiums.

Housing costs

If you own your own home, IS can help with certain service charges.[39] The rules about who can get help with housing costs and when help starts are explained in CPAG's *Welfare Benefits and Tax Credits Handbook*.

Claiming for children

Since 6 April 2004, personal allowances and premiums for children have no longer been included in new IS claims or for anyone claiming CTC. Amounts for children are paid through CTC and child benefit instead. If you were getting IS with amounts for children included before 6 April 2004 you may still be getting them.

The personal allowance for each dependent child is £66.90. This may be subject to the 'two-child limit' (see CPAG's *Welfare Benefits and Tax Credits Handbook* for more details). Also included are whichever of the following premiums applies:
- family premium of £17.45;
- disabled child premium of £64.19 for each qualifying child;
- enhanced disability premium (child) of £26.04.

You get a **family premium** if you have a dependent child (under 16, or under 20 and a qualifying young person – see p8). You get one premium per family, not per child.[40]

You get a **disabled child premium** for each dependent child who gets DLA, PIP or is certified as severely sight impaired or blind or has stopped being certified in the last 28 weeks.[41]

You get an **enhanced disability premium** for each child who gets the highest rate care component of DLA or enhanced rate daily living component of PIP.[42]

Step three: work out your weekly income
Some kinds of income are ignored. For details, see CPAG's *Welfare Benefits and Tax Credits Handbook*.

See the relevant chapters of this *Handbook* for more information on how specific income (eg, fostering allowances and payments from the local authority) is treated.

Step four: deduct weekly income from applicable amount
If your income is *less* than your applicable amount, IS equals the difference between the two.

If your income is *the same as or more than* your applicable amount, you cannot get IS.

14. Jobseeker's allowance

Jobseeker's allowance (JSA) provides basic financial support for people of working age who are not working full time and who are expected to 'sign on' as available for work. There are two types of JSA: income-based JSA (see p32) and contribution-based JSA (see p33).

The Department for Work and Pensions (DWP) is responsible for the administration of JSA.

Chapter 1: Benefits and tax credits
14. Jobseeker's allowance

Income-based jobseeker's allowance

Income-based JSA is means tested and is for people with a low income. You do not have to have paid any national insurance (NI) contributions to get income-based JSA. Income-based JSA is being replaced by universal credit (UC) and you cannot normally make a new claim for income-based JSA. Eventually, claimants who are on income-based JSA will be transferred to UC. See p46 and CPAG's *Welfare Benefits and Tax Credits Handbook* for more details.

Who can claim income-based jobseeker's allowance

If you are not in the UC system, you qualify for income-based JSA if:[43]

- you are aged 18 or over (some people can get income-based JSA if they are aged 16 or 17 but there are extra rules) and you are under pension age; *and*
- you are available for work. You must be willing and able to take up work immediately (although some people are allowed notice). You must be prepared to work at least 40 hours a week. Disabled people and people caring for a child or for a disabled person can restrict themselves to fewer than 40 hours; *and*
- you are actively seeking work; *and*
- you enter into a jobseeker's agreement. The DWP calls this a 'claimant commitment'. This sets out, for instance, the hours you have agreed to work, the type of work you are looking for and any restrictions on travel and pay; *and*
- any work you do is for less than 16 hours a week; *and*
- your partner, if you have one, is not working for 24 hours or more a week (there are some exceptions to this); *and*
- you or your partner (if you have one) are not getting income support (IS), income-related employment and support allowance (ESA) or pension credit; *and*
- you are not a qualifying young person – eg, aged 16 to 19 in full-time non-advanced education; *and*
- you do not have limited capability for work (although you can continue to get JSA for limited periods while sick); *and*
- you are present in Great Britain, satisfy the 'habitual residence test', including having the 'right to reside', and are not a 'person subject to immigration control'. These terms are explained in CPAG's *Welfare Benefits and Tax Credits Handbook*; *and*
- your income is below the amount set for your basic living needs (known as your 'applicable amount'); *and*
- you have no more than £16,000 capital.

If you are a member of a couple, one of you must claim income-based JSA for both of you, and your joint income and capital is taken into account. Many couples have to make a **joint claim** for income-based JSA. This means you both have to satisfy the conditions of entitlement – eg, you both have to 'sign on' as available for and actively seeking work. You have to make a joint claim unless:

- you have a dependent child; *or*
- you are both under 18.

Amount of benefit

The amount of income-based JSA you get depends on your circumstances and the circumstances of your partner (if you have one). The amount also depends on your income and capital. Some kinds of income are ignored. For details, see CPAG's *Welfare Benefits and Tax Credits Handbook*.

Income-based JSA is worked out in the same way as IS (see p28). The amount you get is made up of:
- personal allowances (see p28); *and*
- premiums (see p29); *and*
- housing costs (see p30).

The total of these is called your 'applicable amount'. If you have no other income, you are paid your full applicable amount. Otherwise, any income you do have is topped up with income-based JSA to the level of your applicable amount. If your weekly income is above your applicable amount, you are not entitled to income-based JSA. See p28 for how to work out your applicable amount. The rules are almost the same as those for IS, except that:
- the higher rates of personal allowance are payable to couples under 18 in slightly different circumstances;
- joint-claim couples can get a disability premium (at the couple rate) if one has had limited capability for work for 364 days (196 days if terminally ill). You need to claim ESA to establish limited capability for work even if you will not get it.

See the relevant chapters of this *Handbook* for more information on how specific income (eg, fostering allowances and payments from the local authority) is treated.

Contribution-based jobseeker's allowance

Contribution-based JSA is not means tested. You must have paid NI contributions to get contribution-based JSA. It can only be paid for up to 26 weeks.

Who can claim contribution-based jobseeker's allowance

You qualify for contribution-based JSA if:[44]
- you are under pension age; *and*
- you are available for work. You must be willing and able to take up work immediately (although some people are allowed notice). You must be prepared to work at least 40 hours a week. Disabled people and people caring for a child or for a disabled person can restrict themselves to fewer than 40 hours; *and*
- you are actively seeking work; *and*

Chapter 1: Benefits and tax credits
15. Pension credit

- you enter into a jobseeker's agreement. The DWP calls this a 'claimant commitment'. This sets out, for instance, the hours you have agreed to work, the type of work you are looking for and any restrictions on travel and pay; *and*
- if you are doing any work, it is for less than 16 hours a week; *and*
- you are not in relevant education; *and*
- you do not have limited capability for work (you can continue to get JSA for limited periods while sick); *and*
- you are not getting IS; *and*
- you are present in Great Britain; *and*
- you have paid sufficient NI contributions (see below).

National insurance contributions

You must have paid at least 26 weeks' class 1 contributions on earning at the lower earnings limit in one of the two complete tax years (6 April to 5 April) before the start of the benefit year (which runs from the first Sunday in January) in which you claim. You must also have paid or been credited with class 1 contributions on earnings of 50 times the lower earnings limit in both of these years.

For more information on contribution conditions, see CPAG's *Welfare Benefits and Tax Credits Handbook*.

Amount of benefit

Contribution-based JSA is paid at different weekly rates, depending on your age.

Weekly rate	£
Under 25	57.90
25 or over	73.10

You may get less than this if you have part-time earnings, or an occupational or personal pension. Other income does not affect the amount you get. Contribution-based JSA is only paid for up to 26 weeks. Unlike income-based JSA, you only get amounts for yourself, not for a partner.

15. Pension credit

Pension credit (PC) is a benefit paid to people who have reached pension age (see p35) whose income is below a certain level. You do not have to have paid any national insurance contributions to get PC.

PC consists of two different elements:
- **guarantee credit**, designed to bring your income up to a minimum level; *and*
- **savings credit**, which is paid to some people who have been able to make provision for retirement over and above the basic state retirement pension.

Chapter 1: Benefits and tax credits
15. Pension credit

You can qualify for either or both credits. The savings credit is being phased out.[45]

The Pension Service (part of the Department for Work and Pensions) is responsible for the administration of PC.

Who can claim pension credit

You qualify for PC if:[46]
- you have reached pension age. If you have a partner and you are claiming after 14 May 2019, your partner must also have reached pension age (there are some exceptions to this rule: see CPAG's *Welfare Benefits and Tax Credits Handbook*) (see below); *and*
- you are in Great Britain (with some exceptions for periods of temporary absence) and you satisfy the 'habitual residence test', including having the 'right to reside', and are not a 'person subject to immigration control'. These terms are explained in CPAG's *Welfare Benefits and Tax Credits Handbook*; *and*
- your income is below a set level.

If you are a member of a couple, one of you must claim PC for both. Your joint income is taken into account.

Pension age

The **'qualifying age'** for PC is the minimum age that you can receive your state retirement pension. For claimants born on or after 6 April 1950, this is increasing until it reaches 66 by 2020 and will eventually go up to 68. For more information, see CPAG's *Welfare Benefits and Tax Credits Handbook*.

Amount of benefit

PC is means tested and the amount you get depends on your income and whether you have any disabilities, caring responsibilities and eligible housing costs. From 1 February 2019, PC claimants who become responsible for a child or qualifying young person may get an additional amount (instead of getting child tax credit – CTC).

Guarantee credit

There are three steps for calculating your entitlement to guarantee credit.[47]

Step one: calculate your appropriate minimum guarantee

This is the minimum weekly income the government decides you need to live on. It is made up of fixed amounts depending on your personal circumstances:[48]
- the standard minimum guarantee of £167.25 if you are single, or £255.25 if you have a partner;
- a severe disability addition of £65.85 if you satisfy the conditions that apply for the income support (IS) severe disability premium (see p29);

- a carer addition of £36.85 if you satisfy the conditions that apply for the IS carer premium (see p29);
- eligible housing costs if you are a homeowner – ie, certain service charges. The rules about who can get help with housing costs, when help starts and how much you get are explained in CPAG's *Welfare Benefits and Tax Credits Handbook;*
- an additional amount for dependent child(ren). This may apply if you become responsible for a child or qualifying young person after 1 February 2019 and you are not getting CTC for her/him. The amount for the eldest or only child if s/he was born before 6 April 2017 is £63.84. The amount for any other children is £53.34. An additional £90.23 is added if the child is severely sight impaired or blind or is entitled to the highest rate of the care component of DLA or the enhanced daily living component of PIP. Alternatively, an additional £29.02 is added if the child gets any other rate of DLA or PIP.[49]

Step two: work out your weekly income

This is the amount you have from any pension and other sources each week. Not all your income counts. For details, see CPAG's *Welfare Benefits and Tax Credits Handbook.*

See the relevant chapters of this *Handbook* for how specific income (eg, fostering allowances and payments from the local authority) is treated.

Step three: deduct income from appropriate minimum guarantee

The resulting amount is your guarantee credit. If your income is more than your appropriate minimum guarantee, you are not entitled to guarantee credit.

Savings credit

The maximum weekly savings credit you can get is £13.72 if you are single, and £15.35 if you have a partner. For details of how it is calculated, see CPAG's *Welfare Benefits and Tax Credits Handbook.*

16. Personal independence payment

Personal independence payment (PIP) is a benefit for people with mobility problems and/or care needs as a result of a disability who are aged between 16 and pension age. It replaces disability living allowance (DLA) for claimants in this age range. If you are aged 16 or over and are already on DLA, you will be invited to claim PIP, unless you were already aged 65 or over on 8 April 2013.

PIP has two components:
- **a daily living component,** paid at either the standard rate or the enhanced rate;

- a mobility component, paid at either the standard or the enhanced rate.

You can get either the daily living component or the mobility component, or both. PIP is not means tested and you do not have to have paid any national insurance contributions to get it.

The Department for Work and Pensions is responsible for the administration of PIP.

Who can claim personal independence payment

You can qualify for PIP if:[50]
- you are aged 16 or over and, in most cases, under pension age. Your pension age will be after you turn 65 if you were born on or after 6 December 1953 (ie, if you reached 65 on or after 6 December 2018) and it is due to rise to 66 by September 2020;
- you satisfy certain UK residence and presence conditions and are not a 'person subject to immigration control'. See CPAG's *Welfare Benefits and Tax Credits Handbook* for details;
- you satisfy the disability conditions (see below) for the daily living component, the mobility component or both;
- you satisfy the 'required period condition', which means that you have met the disability conditions for at least three months and are expected to continue to meet them for a further nine months. This condition does not apply if you are terminally ill.

Disability conditions

In addition to satisfying the basic conditions of entitlement, you qualify for a component of PIP if your ability to undertake either 'daily living activities' or 'mobility activities' is limited by your mental or physical condition (for the standard rate), or it is severely limited by your mental or physical condition (for the enhanced rate).[51] Your ability is assessed by a points-based test which considers how your mental or physical condition affects your ability to undertake specific activities.

The relevant **'daily living activities'** are:
- preparing food;
- taking nutrition;
- managing therapy or monitoring a health condition;
- washing and bathing;
- managing toilet needs or incontinence;
- dressing and undressing;
- communicating verbally;
- reading and understanding signs, symbols and words;
- engaging with other people face to face;
- making budgeting decisions.

The relevant **'mobility activities'** are:
- planning and following journeys;
- moving around.

Under each of the activities, there is a list of statements (called 'descriptors') which describe different difficulties or types of help needed with the activity. Each descriptor has a points score, and you are awarded one descriptor for each activity. Your entitlement to a component is assessed by:[52]
- adding together the descriptors that you satisfy for each activity relevant to that component; *and*
- comparing your total score with a 'threshold' for entitlement to the standard or enhanced rates of the component. The threshold is eight points for the standard rate and 12 points for the enhanced rate.

You are only assessed as being able to undertake an activity at a level described by the descriptor if you can complete it 'reliably'. This means that you are only awarded a particular descriptor (rather than a higher scoring one) if you can undertake the activity:[53]
- safely – ie, in a way that is unlikely to cause harm to you or anyone else;
- to an acceptable standard;
- repeatedly – ie, as often as it is required;
- within a reasonable time period – ie, not more than twice the maximum time normally taken by someone with no health problems or disability to complete the activity.

Amount of benefit

Weekly rate	£
Daily living	
Enhanced	87.65
Standard	58.70
Mobility	
Enhanced	61.20
Standard	23.20

17. The Scottish Welfare Fund

The Scottish Welfare Fund makes two types of payments:
- crisis grants; *and*
- community care grants.

Local authorities are responsible for administering the Scottish Welfare Fund on behalf of the Scottish government.

Scottish Welfare Fund grants can be cash, vouchers or goods.

Crisis grants

Crisis grants are intended to help with expenses in an emergency or a disaster if you have no other money to meet your immediate needs. For example, you may get a crisis grant if:
- you have lost money that you need to live on, your regular income has not been paid and you are in hardship;
- there has been a disaster like a fire or flood that has caused damage.

Community care grants

A community care grant is intended to help you and your family stay independent in the community by helping you pay for items such as furniture, clothing or removal expenses. There is no ceiling on the amount you can apply for. To qualify, you must be on a low income. You are automatically treated as having a low income if you get:
- universal credit; *or*
- income support; *or*
- income-based jobseeker's allowance; *or*
- income-related employment and support allowance; *or*
- pension credit.

Even if you are not on one of these benefits, your local authority can still decide that you are on a low income.

A community care grant can be paid:
- to help you, a member of your family or a person for whom you care establish yourself (or her/himself) in the community following a stay in institutional or residential accommodation;
- to help you, a member of your family or a person for whom you care remain in the community rather than enter institutional or residential accommodation;
- to help you set up home in the community as part of a planned resettlement programme, following a period during which you have been homeless or without a settled way of life;
- to ease exceptional pressures on you or your family;
- to allow you, or your partner, to care for a prisoner or young offender on temporary release.

18. **Statutory adoption pay**

You can get statutory adoption pay (SAP) for 39 weeks if you are adopting a child and are earning at least £118 a week from employment. If a couple (including a same-sex couple) is adopting a child, one can claim SAP and the other may be able to claim statutory paternity pay (SPP) for two weeks. They may also be able to claim statutory shared parental pay (SSPP).

SAP, SPP and SSPP are paid by your employer.

Who can claim statutory adoption pay

You can get SAP if:[54]
- you are adopting a child; *and*
- you have worked for the same employer for 26 weeks ending with the week in which you are told you have been matched with a child for adoption; *and*
- your average gross earnings are at least £118 a week; *and*
- you give your employer the correct notice.

Amount of benefit

Weekly rate	First six weeks:
	90% of average weekly earnings
	Remaining 33 weeks:
	£148.68 (or 90% of earnings if less)

If your partner is adopting a child or if you are jointly adopting a child with your partner, you may be able to get SPP. SPP is either £148.68 or 90 per cent of earnings, whichever is the lower. It is only payable for two weeks. You cannot get both SAP and SPP (see p139). You may also be able to get SSPP if your partner is adopting a child or you are jointly adopting a child with your partner. SSPP allows one partner to give up her/his SAP early and the remaining pay to be 'shared' with her/his partner. See p142 for more details.

19. **Tax credits**

Tax credits comprise child tax credit (CTC) and working tax credit (WTC). You can be entitled to either CTC or WTC, or both.

CTC can be paid whether you are in or out of work if you have a dependent child. Your entitlement and how much you get depends on how much income you have. WTC can be paid if you are working for at least 16 hours (or in some cases 24 or 30 hours) a week and have a low income.

If you are single, you make a single claim for tax credits. If you have a partner, you make a couple claim.

HM Revenue and Customs (HMRC) is responsible for the administration of tax credits.

Tax credits are being replaced by universal credit (UC) and you cannot normally make a new claim for tax credits. Eventually, claimants who are on tax credits will be transferred to UC.

Child tax credit

CTC is a payment made to people who have children. It can be paid whether you are working or not working. You get a higher amount if you have a child with a disability. The amount of CTC depends on your income in the tax year.

Who can claim child tax credit

If you are not in the UC system, you qualify for CTC if:[55]
- you are aged 16 or over; *and*
- you are responsible for a child or 'qualifying young person' (see below); *and*
- you are 'present and ordinarily resident' in the UK, not a 'person subject to immigration control' and have a 'right to reside'. These terms are explained in CPAG's *Welfare Benefits and Tax Credits Handbook*; *and*
- your income is not too high (see p42).

Who counts as a child

A child counts for CTC purposes up to her/his 16th birthday.[56]

Who counts as a qualifying young person

A **'qualifying young person'** is someone who:[57]
- is aged 16, until 31 August after her/his 16th birthday; *or*
- is aged 16 or 17; *and*
  - has left education or training; *and*
  - has, within three months of leaving education or training, notified HMRC that s/he has registered for work, education or training with Skills Development Scotland; *and*
  - is within 20 weeks of the date s/he left education or training; *or*
- is aged over 16 but under 20 and on a full-time course of non-advanced education (see p8) or on an approved training course (see p8). A 19-year-old is only included if s/he started, enrolled or was accepted onto the course or training before her/his 19th birthday.

Responsible for a child

You are treated as responsible for a child if:[58]
- s/he normally lives with you; *or*

Chapter 1: Benefits and tax credits
19. Tax credits

- you have the main responsibility for her/him (this second test only applies where you and someone else make competing claims for CTC for the same child).

Only one person (or one couple in a joint claim) can get tax credits for a particular child.[59] You should get tax credits if the child 'normally lives with you'.[60] HMRC says this means that the child 'regularly, usually, typically' lives with you.[61]

If a child normally lives in more than one household (eg, s/he shares her/his time between two different households), there may be more than one potential claimant for tax credits. You can decide between you who should make the claim. If you cannot agree, HMRC decides whose claim should take priority by establishing who has 'main responsibility' for the child.[62] HMRC is likely to take account of:[63]
- whether there is a court order setting out where the child is to live, or who is to care for her/him. However, the terms of a court order should not outweigh the facts of the case;[64]
- how many days a week the child lives in the different households;
- who pays for the child's food and clothes;
- where the child's belongings are kept;
- who is the main contact for nursery, school or childcare provider;
- who does the child's laundry;
- who looks after the child when s/he is ill and takes her/him to the doctor.

If you disagree with HMRC's decision (eg, it decides that you cannot get CTC because another person has the main responsibility for a child), you can ask for a review and then appeal against it (see Chapter 2).

There are special rules about when CTC can be paid if a child is absent from home. Whether CTC continues to be paid depends on the circumstances. See the relevant chapter of this *Handbook* for information on what happens to CTC when a child is away from home. There are also special rules which mean that some people cannot get CTC for a child even though s/he is living with them. See the relevant chapter of this *Handbook* for how you might be affected.

Amount of child tax credit
The maximum CTC you can get is made up of:
- **child element** of £2,780 a year for each child. This may be subject to a 'two-child limit' (see p43); *plus*
- **family element** of £545 a year. One family element is payable if you are responsible for a child born before 6 April 2017. If you are not responsible for a child born before 6 April 2017 your CTC does not include the family element; *plus*

- **disabled child element** of £3,355 a year for each child who gets disability living allowance (DLA), personal independence payment (PIP) or is certified as severely sight impaired or blind or was in the last 28 weeks; *plus*
- **severely disabled child element** of £1,360 a year for each child who gets the highest rate care component of DLA or the enhanced rate of the daily living component of PIP.

These are the amounts for the tax year April 2019 to April 2020. You will get less than the maximum if your income is more than a set threshold.

A 'two-child limit' was introduced on 6 April 2017. In general, this means that a child element is not payable for a child born on or after 6 April 2017 if you already have two or more children included in your CTC award, unless s/he is covered by the exceptions. The exceptions include some adoption and kinship care situations – see the relevant chapter of this *Handbook* for more information.

Example
Meg has two children, Bella (aged two) and Meena (aged four). Meena has asthma and gets the lowest rate care component of DLA. Meg's maximum CTC for the tax year April 2019 to April 2020 is:

Two child elements	£2,780
	£2,780
Family element	£545
Disabled child element	£3,355
Total maximum CTC	**£9,460**

Whether she gets maximum CTC or a reduced amount depends on her income.

The income threshold is £16,105 unless you are working and eligible for WTC (see p44), in which case it is £6,420. If your income is below this, you get maximum CTC. If your income is above this threshold, you get a reduced amount.

If you are entitled to CTC and are also getting income support (IS), income-based jobseeker's allowance (JSA), income-related employment and support allowance (ESA) or pension credit (PC), you get maximum CTC.[65]

For details of how income is treated and how your CTC award is calculated, see CPAG's *Welfare Benefits and Tax Credits Handbook*.

See the relevant chapters of this *Handbook* for more information on how specific income (eg, fostering allowances and payments from the local authority) is treated.

Working tax credit

WTC helps supplement low wages. It can only be paid to those who are working (employed or self-employed) for at least 16 hours a week or, in some cases, 24 or

Chapter 1: Benefits and tax credits
19. Tax credits

30 hours a week. You get a higher amount if you work 30 hours or more or have a disability. If you get CTC, you can also get childcare costs paid with WTC. The amount of WTC you get depends on your income in the tax year.

Who can claim working tax credit

If you are not in the UC system, you qualify for WTC if:[66]
- you are aged at least 16; and
- you (or your partner) are in full-time paid work (see below); and
- your income is low enough; and
- you are present and ordinarily resident in the UK and you are not a 'person subject to immigration control'. These terms are explained in CPAG's *Welfare Benefits and Tax Credits Handbook*.

Full-time paid work

You count as being in full-time paid work if:[67]
- you are a single claimant, have a dependent child (see p41) and you work for at least 16 hours a week; or
- you are a couple, have a dependent child and your combined working hours are at least 24 a week. If you both work, one must do at least 16 hours. If only one of you works, you must do at least 24 hours. **Note:** if the non-working partner is incapacitated, a hospital in-patient, in prison or entitled to carer's allowance, you can qualify if you work at least 16 hours a week. See CPAG's *Welfare Benefits and Tax Credits Handbook* for more details; or
- you have a disability that puts you at a disadvantage in getting a job and you work for at least 16 hours a week. For more details, see CPAG's *Welfare Benefits and Tax Credits Handbook*; or
- you are aged at least 60 and you work at least 16 hours a week; or
- you are aged at least 25 and you work at least 30 hours a week.

Sometimes you count as being in full-time work even when you are not – eg, while you are getting statutory adoption pay or maternity pay, or, in certain cases, for up to 28 weeks of sickness.

Work can be as an employed or self-employed earner. Fostering and, in certain cases, kinship care can count as self-employed work. See Chapters 7 and 8 for more details.

Amount of working tax credit

The WTC you can get is made up of a **basic element** of £1,960 a year, plus whichever of the following elements apply:
- **lone parent or couple element** of £2,010 a year;
- **30-hour element** of £810 a year if you work at least 30 hours a week. If you have a child, you can add your hours to those of your partner to make up the 30 hours, providing one of you works at least 16 hours a week;

- **disabled worker element** of £3,165 a year if you qualify for WTC as a disabled worker;
- **severe disability element** of £1,365 a year if you or your partner get the highest rate of the DLA care component or the enhanced rate of the PIP daily living component;
- **childcare element.** You may get up to 70 per cent of childcare costs up to a limit of £175 for one child or £300 a week for two or more children for whom you get CTC – ie, a maximum of £122.50 or £210. Childcare must be of a certain type, including a registered childminder, nursery or playscheme, an out-of-hours club or sitter service. You do not get help with childcare at home provided by a relative. Generally, to get the childcare element, you, and you partner if you have one, must be working 16 hours or more a week. If you claim as a couple, you can still be entitled if one of you is working 16 hours ore more a week and the other is incapacitated, entitled to CA, in hospital or in prison.

These are the amounts for the tax year April 2019 to April 2020. You get less than the maximum if your income is more than a set threshold.

The income threshold is £6,420. If your income is below this, you get maximum WTC. If your income is above this threshold, you get a reduced amount.

For details of how income is treated and how your WTC award is calculated, see CPAG's *Welfare Benefits and Tax Credits Handbook*.

See the relevant chapters of this *Handbook* for more information on how specific income (eg, fostering allowances and payments from the local authority) is treated.

Changes of circumstances and tax credits

If your circumstances change, tell HMRC immediately to avoid being overpaid or underpaid. For example, you should inform it if:
- you stop, or start, being part of a couple;
- you stop being responsible for a child – eg, a child stops living with you;
- you start being responsible for a child – eg, a child comes to live with you or you have a baby;
- a child for whom you claim stops counting as a child or qualifying young person – eg, s/he leaves education;
- your hours of work fall below 16, 24 or 30;
- your hours of work increase;
- your childcare costs change by more than £10 a week for four weeks in a row;
- you, your partner or a dependent child is awarded DLA or PIP, or an award of DLA or PIP stops;
- you stop being entitled to IS, income-based JSA, income-related ESA or PC;
- you have an unexpected change in your income.

20. Universal credit

Universal credit (UC) is a means-tested benefit which is being gradually introduced across the UK.
UC replaces the following benefits and tax credits:
- income support (IS);
- income-based jobseekers' allowance (JSA);
- income-related employment and support allowance (ESA);
- child tax credit;
- working tax credit;
- housing benefit (HB), for most claimants.

For most people, if you have to make a new benefit claim and you would previously have claimed one of the benefits being replaced by UC (often called 'legacy benefits'), you will have to claim UC instead. If you are already on a legacy benefit and you have a change of circumstances which means you have to make a new claim, you will probably have to claim UC. The exception is people who are affected by the 'severe disability premium gateway' rules (see below). Eventually, people who are on legacy benefits will be transferred to UC.

The Department for Work and Pensions is responsible for the administration of UC.

Who can claim universal credit

You can claim UC if:[68]
- you are aged 18 or over (although certain 16- and 17-years-olds can claim); *and*
- you are not receiving education (although there are exceptions to this); *and*
- you satisfy certain residence and presence conditions, and are not a 'person subject to immigration control'. See CPAG's *Welfare Benefit and Tax Credits Handbook* for details; *and*
- you have accepted a 'claimant commitment' (see p49); *and*
- your savings and other capital are £16,000 or less; *and*
- your income is low enough.

Severe disability premium gateway

If you are entitled to the severe disability premium (see p30) in IS, income-based JSA, income-related ESA or HB, you are prevented from claiming UC and are able to stay on, or reclaim, the legacy benefit. This also applies if you have been entitled to the severe disability premium within the last month and have continued to satisfy the entitlement conditions for it.

Amount of benefit

The amount of UC you get depends on your circumstances and the circumstances of your partner, if you have one. It also depends on whether you have dependent children. The steps set out below show how UC is calculated.

Step one: capital

If your capital is over £16,000 you cannot get UC. Some kinds of capital are ignored. For details, see CPAG's *Welfare Benefits and Tax Credits Handbook*.

Step two: work out your maximum amount

This is an amount for basic needs. It is worked out on a monthly basis and includes a 'standard allowance', plus additional amounts ('elements') if you have dependent children, certain housing costs or some other additional expenses.

Standard allowance

Your standard allowance is paid at either a single or couple rate.

Circumstances	£ per month
Single	
Under 25	251.77
25 or over	317.82
Couple	
Both under 25	395.20
One or both over 25	498.89

Additional elements

You get one **'child element'** for each dependent child who normally lives with you (subject to a 'two-child limit' – see below).[69] You get £277.08 a month for your only or oldest child if that child was born before 6 April 2017, and £231.67 a month each for any other child. You get an additional amount for a child who gets disability living allowance (DLA), personal independence payment (PIP) or has a visual impairment.[70] This is paid at £126.11 a month or £392.08 a month if your child gets DLA highest rate care component, PIP enhanced daily living component or is severely sight impaired or blind.

A 'two-child limit' was introduced on 6 April 2017.[71] In general, this means that a child element is not payable for a child born on or after 6 April 2017 if you already have two or more children included in your UC award, unless s/he is covered by an exception – eg, in some adoption and kinship care situations. See the relevant chapter of this *Handbook* for more information on the exceptions to the two-child limit.

There are special rules about when the child element is paid where a child is absent from home. Whether it continues to be paid depends on the circumstances.

Chapter 1: Benefits and tax credits
20. Universal credit

See the relevant chapter of this *Handbook* for information on what happens to the child element when a child is away from home. There are also special rules which mean that some people cannot get the child element for a child even though the child is living with her/him. See the relevant chapter of this *Handbook* to see how you might be affected.

You may get an amount for rent or certain service charges if you own your home. This is called the **'housing costs element'**. The amounts are limited and may, for example, not cover all your rent. See CPAG's *Welfare Benefits and Tax Credit Handbook* for more information.

For claims that started before 3 April 2017, or are linked to a claim which existed before that date, if you have limited capability for work you get the **'limited capabilty for work element'** of £126.11 a month. New claims made from 3 April 2017 do not include the limited capability for work element. For more detail about these rules see CPAG's *Welfare Benefits and Tax Credits Handbook*. Alternatively, if you have limited capability for work-related activity, you get a **'limited capability for work-related activity element'** of £336.20 a month. The tests used in ESA are used to decide whether you should get either of these elements.

You get a **'carer element'** of £160.20 a month if you satisfy the rules for carer's allowance (CA) or would satisfy them except that your earnings are too high.[72] You must be caring for someone who is in receipt of certain disability benefits. Your caring responsibilities must be for at leat 35 hours a week. You do not have to have claimed CA to get the carer element. You cannot get an element for being a carer and an element for your own illness. If you are entitled to both, you only get the one which is higher.

You get a **'childcare element'** if you are working and have childcare costs in respect of a dependent child.[73] You can get help with up to 85 per cent of these costs, up to a maximum limit. You must be in paid work and the childcare costs must be necessary to allow you to work. If you have a partner, you must both be in paid work unless your partner is ill, disabled or a carer.

Step three: work out your earnings and how much can be ignored

Some of your earnings may be ignored for UC: this is called the 'work allowance'. You only get a work allowance if you have a dependent child or children or if you have limited capability for work. There are two levels of work allowance depending on whether you are getting help in your UC with housing costs. If you do not have a housing costs element in your UC, your work allowance is £503 a month. If you have a housing costs element in your UC, your work allowance is £287 a month.

If your earnings are less than your work allowance, they are ignored. If they are more than your work allowance, 63 per cent of the excess counts as income. If you do not have a work allowance, 63 per cent of your earnings counts as income.

Step four: work out your other income and how much can be ignored

If you have other income apart from earnings (eg, other benefits), unless it is ignored, it reduces the UC maximum amount pound for pound. See CPAG's *Welfare Benefits and Tax Credits Handbook* for more details of what income is ignored. See the relevant chapter of this *Handbook* for more information on how specific income (eg, fostering allowances and payments from the local authority) is treated.

Step five: calculate your total income

Add together the income that is to be taken into account under steps three and four.

Step six: calculate your universal credit entitlement

Deduct your total income (Step five) from your maximum UC (Step two). This is your UC entitlement.

Claimant commitment

You cannot get UC unless you sign a 'claimant commitment'. This sets out what you must do to receive your UC. You are placed in one of four groups based on whether you are subject to:
- no work-related requirements – eg, if you are caring for a severely disabled person or you are the main carer of a child aged under one;
- the work-focused interview requirement only – eg, if you are the main carer of a child aged one;
- the work preparation and work-focused interview requirements – eg, if you have limited capability for work;
- all work-related requirements, including work availability and work search requirements for most people.

See CPAG's *Welfare Benefits and Tax Credits Handbook* for more details of the claimant commitment, work-related requirements and sanctions if you do not meet your work-related requirements. See the relevant chapters of this *Handbook* for more information about the work-related requirements for specific groups of people.

Chapter 1: Benefits and tax credits
Notes

Notes

1. **Introduction**
   1 s96 WRA 2012

2. **Attendance allowance**
   2 s64 SSCBA 1992; reg 2 SS(AA) Regs

3. **Best Start grant**
   3 Regs 11 and 12 and Sch 2 para 1(e) EYA(BSG)(S) Regs
   4 Sch 2 EYA(BSG)(S) Regs
   5 Sch 3 EYA(BSG)(S) Regs
   6 Sch 4 EYA(BSG)(S) Regs
   7 Regs 9 and 10 EYA(BSG)(S) Regs

4. **Carer's allowance**
   8 s70 SSCBA 1992; regs 3 and 9 SS(ICA) Regs
   9 Regs 29 and 30 UC Regs
   10 The Carer's Assistance (Young Carer Grants) (Scotland) Regulations 2019 (draft)

5. **Child benefit**
   11 See www.gov.uk/child-benefit-tax-charge/stop-child-benefit
   12 ss141-44 SSCBA 1992; s115 IAA 1999; reg 23 CB Regs
   13 s142(1) SSCBA 1992
   14 Regs 3-5 and 7 CB Regs
   15 R(F) 2/81
   16 Sch 10 SSCBA 1992

7. **Disability living allowance**
   17 ss71, 72 and 73 SSCBA 1992

8. **Employment and support allowance**
   18 s1 and Sch 1 para 6 WRA 2007
   19 Reg 110 ESA Regs
   20 s1 and Sch 1 paras 1-5 WRA 2007

9. **Funeral support payment**
   21 Reg 10 FEA(S) Regs
   22 Reg 7 FEA(S) Regs

10. **Guardian's allowance**
    23 ss77 and 122(5) SSCBA 1992; reg 7 GA(Gen) Regs
    24 s77(11) SSCBA 1992

11. **Health benefits**
    25 NHS(TERC)(S) Regs
    26 WF(BSF)(S) Regs
    27 Reg 10 WF(BSF)(S)Regs

12. **Housing benefit**
    28 s130 SSCBA 1992; s115 IAA 1999; reg 10 HB Regs; reg 10 HB(SPC) Regs
    29 s69 CSPSSA 2000; reg 2(1) DFA Regs

11. **Income support**
    30 s124 SSCBA 1992
    31 Reg 4ZA and Sch 1B IS Regs
    32 s134 SSCBA 1992; reg 45 IS Regs
    33 Sch 2 para 1 IS Regs
    34 Sch 2 para 6 IS Regs
    35 Sch 2 paras 11 and 12 IS Regs
    36 Sch 2 paras 13A and 15(8) IS Regs
    37 Sch 2 paras 9, 9A and 10 IS Regs
    38 Sch 2 para 13 IS Regs
    39 Sch 3 IS Regs
    40 Sch 2 para 3 IS Regs
    41 Sch 2 para 14 IS Regs
    42 Sch 2 para 13A IS Regs

14. **Jobseeker's allowance**
    43 ss1, 3 and 13 JSA 1995
    44 ss1 and 2 JSA 1995

15. **Pension credit**
    45 Sch 12 para 89 PA 2014
    46 ss1-4 SPCA 2002; Part 2 SPC Regs
    47 s2(2) SPCA 2002
    48 s2(3) SPCA 2002; Schs 1 and 2 SPC Regs
    49 Sch IIA para 9 and 10 SPC Regs

16. **Personal independence payment**
    50 ss77(2) and (3) and 83 WRA 2012; Part 6 SS(PIP) Regs
    51 ss78 and 79 WRA 2012
    52 Regs 5 and 6 SS(PIP) Regs
    53 Reg 4(2A) and (4) SS(PIP) Regs

18. **Statutory adoption pay**
    54 s171ZL(2)-(4) SSCBA 1992; reg 3(2) SPPSAP(G) Regs

19. **Tax credits**
    55 ss3(3) and (7), 8 and 42 TCA 2002; regs 3-5 CTC Regs; reg 3 TC(R) Regs; reg 3 TC(Imm) Regs
    56 Reg 2 CTC Regs
    57 Regs 2, 4 and 5(2)-(4) CTC Regs
    58 Reg 3(1) rr1 and 2 CTC Regs
    59 Reg 3(1) r2.2 CTC Regs
    60 Reg 3(1) rr1 and 2 CTC Regs
    61 para 02202 TCTM
    62 Reg 3(1) r3.1 CTC Regs
    63 para 02204 TCTM
    64 *GJ v HMRC (TC)* [2013] UKUT 561 (AAC)
    65 ss7(2) and 13 TCA 2002; reg 4 TC(ITDR) Regs
    66 ss3(3) and (7), 10 and 42 TCA 2002; regs 4-8 WTC(EMR) Regs; reg 3 TC(R) Regs; reg 3 TC(Imm) Regs
    67 Reg 4 WTC(EMR) Regs

20. **Universal credit**
    68 ss3, 4 and 5 WRA 2012; reg 9 UC Regs
    69 Reg 24 UC Regs
    70 Reg 24(2) UC Regs
    71 Reg 24A UC Regs
    72 Regs 29 and 30 UC Regs
    73 Regs 31-33 UC Regs

Chapter 2

Claims, decisions and challenges

This chapter covers:
1. How to claim benefits and tax credits (below)
2. Decisions and delays (p56)
3. Challenging decisions and complaints (p58)

1. How to claim benefits and tax credits

Child benefit, guardian's allowance and tax credits are administered by HM Revenue and Customs (HMRC). Statutory adoption pay, statutory paternity pay and statutory shared parental pay are administered by your employer, but any dispute is dealt with by HMRC. Best Start grants, Best Start foods and funeral support payments are administered by Social Security Scotland (SSS). Housing benefit (HB), council tax reduction (CTR) and the Scottish Welfare Fund are administered by your local authority and health benefits by the NHS. All the other benefits referred to in this *Handbook* are administered by the Department for Work and Pensions (DWP).

The table explains how to claim benefits and tax credits.

Benefit/tax credit	How to claim
Attendance allowance	Claim on Form AA1, available from the attendance allowance (AA) helpline (tel: 0800 731 0122; textphone: 0800 731 0317), or download a claim form from www.gov.uk. It is usually better to phone the helpline as that secures your date of claim.
Best Start grant and Best Start foods	Claim online at www.mygov.scot/best-start/, download the claim form or telephone 0800 182 2222.

Chapter 2: Claims, decisions and challenges
1. How to claim benefits and tax credits

Carer's allowance	Claim on Form DS700 (or Form DS700(SP) if you get a retirement pension), available from the Carer's Allowance Unit (tel: 0800 731 0297; textphone: 0800 731 0317), or claim online or download a claim form from www.gov.uk.
Child benefit	Claim on Form CH2, available from the Child Benefit Office (tel: 0300 200 3100; textphone: 0300 200 3103), or download a claim form from www.gov.uk.
Council tax reduction	Contact your local authority to check how to make a claim.
Disability living allowance (under 16)	Claim on Form DLA1A Child, available from the disability living allowance (DLA) helpline (tel: 0800 121 4600; textphone: 0800 121 4523), or download a claim form from www.gov.uk.
Employment and support allowance	If you come under the universal credit (UC) system, claim on Form NSESAF1 (available at www.gov.uk) or by telephone (tel: 0800 328 5644; textphone: 0800 328 1344). If you do not come under the UC system, claim by telephone (tel: 0800 169 0350; textphone 0800 023 4888). You can download a claim form (ESA1) from www.gov.uk.
Funeral support payment	Check www.mygov.scot for how to claim.
Guardian's allowance	Claim on Form BG1, available from the Guardian's Allowance Unit at the Child Benefit Office (tel: 0300 200 3101; textphone: 0300 200 3103), or download from www.gov.uk.
Health benefits – eg, dental care	To claim on the grounds of low income, complete Form HC1, available from Jobcentre Plus offices and NHS hospitals, download a claim form from www.nhsbsa.nhs.uk or telephone 0131 275 6386.
Housing benefit	Some local authorities allow claims by telephone, online or by email. Otherwise, claim by using the form that your local authority has issued and return it to the office designated for that purpose by the local authority.
Income support	You are usually expected to start your claim by telephone (tel: 0800 169 0350; textphone: 0800 023 4888), or you can download a claim form from www.gov.uk.

Chapter 2: Claims, decisions and challenges
1. How to claim benefits and tax credits

Jobseeker's allowance	Claim at www.gov.uk or by telephone (tel: 0800 055 6688; textphone 0800 023 4888).
Pension credit	Claim by telephone (tel: 0800 991 234; textphone: 0800 169 0133).
Personal independence payment	Claim by telephone (tel: 0800 917 2222; textphone: 0800 917 7777).
Scottish Welfare Fund	Contact your local authority to check how to make a claim.
Statutory adoption pay	No claim form required, but you must give your employer the required notice and information.
Statutory paternity pay	No claim form required, but you must give your employer the required notice and information.
Statutory shared parental pay	No claim form required, but you must give your employer the required notice and information.
Tax credits	Claim both child tax credit and working tax credit by calling the Tax Credit helpline (tel: 0345 300 3900; textphone 0345 300 3909).
Universal credit	Claim at www.gov.uk. If you need support to claim, telephone 0800 328 5644 (textphone 0800 328 1344).

Information to support your claim

You are expected to provide information and evidence to support your claim for all benefits and tax credits. The type of information needed should be explained when you make your claim. You are usually given one month to provide any missing information without its affecting your date of claim. You (and your partner if you are making a joint claim) must usually have a national insurance number when you make a claim, or show you have applied for one.

Backdating

Sometimes it is possible to get your benefit paid from a date before you made your claim, if you met the entitlement conditions during that time. This is called 'backdating'. There are different backdating rules for different benefits. The table below gives a brief outline of the main rules. See CPAG's *Welfare Benefits and Tax Credits Handbook* for more information.

Chapter 2: Claims, decisions and challenges
1. How to claim benefits and tax credits

Benefit/tax credit	Backdating
Attendance allowance	No backdating.
Carer's allowance	Up to three months. No special reasons required. If you claim within three months of the person you care for being awarded DLA care component (middle or highest rate), PIP daily living component or AA, carer's allowance can be backdated to the date DLA, PIP or AA was awarded.
Child benefit	Up to three months. No special reasons required. Backdating may not be possible, however, if someone else was getting child benefit for the child during the three-month period.
Disability living allowance	No backdating.
Employment and support allowance	Up to three months. No special reasons required.
Guardian's allowance	Up to three months. No special reasons required.
Health benefits – eg, free dental treatment	If you pay for an item that you could have got free or at a reduced cost, you can apply for a refund. You should do so within three months of paying for the item, although this time limit can be extended if you show good cause.
Housing benefit/council tax reduction	If under pension age, up to one month for HB and six months for CTR if you can show continuous good cause. If you have reached pension age and neither you nor your partner are on income support (IS), income-based jobseeker's allowance (JSA), income-related employment and support allowance or UC, up to three months and no special reasons required.
Income support	In prescribed circumstances, up to one month, and in other prescribed circumstances, up to three months. Backdating for more than three months is possible if a qualifying benefit, such as PIP or DLA, has been awarded and an earlier claim for IS was refused.

Chapter 2: Claims, decisions and challenges
2. Decisions and delays

Jobseeker's allowance	In prescribed circumstances, up to one month, and in other prescribed circumstances, up to three months. Backdating for more than three months is possible if a qualifying benefit, such as DLA, has been awarded, and an earlier claim for JSA was refused.
Pension credit	Up to three months. No special reasons required.
Personal independence payment	No backdating.
Statutory adoption and paternity pay	Usually, you must give your employer 28 days' notice. If you are not able to do so, and your employer accepts you gave notice as soon as reasonably practicable, statutory adoption/paternity pay can be paid from the date you have chosen to start your adoption/paternity leave.
Statutory shared parental pay	Usually, you must give your employer eight weeks' notice before the start of the period for which you want to claim.
Tax credits	Up to one month. No special reasons required.
Universal credit	In prescribed circumstances, up to one month.

2. Decisions and delays

Decisions about benefits and tax credits are made by decision makers from the relevant authority – eg, the Department for Work and Pensions. You are entitled to written notification of all decisions. Decisions should be made within a reasonable timescale. If there are long delays, you should make a complaint (see p59) and check whether you could get a short-term advance, interim payment or payment on account.

Interim payments and short-term advances

If your claim or payment of child benefit or guardian's allowance is delayed, you can ask for an interim payment. If your claim for another benefit is delayed, you can ask for a short-term advance. The rules do *not* apply to tax credits, attendance allowance, disability living allowance, personal independence payment, statutory adoption pay, statutory paternity pay or statutory shared parental pay. See p57 for the rules about payments on account of housing benefit (HB).

An interim payment of child benefit or guardian's allowance can be made if it seems you are, or may be, entitled to benefit and:

- there is a delay in you making a claim, including being able to satisfy the national insurance number requirement straight away; or
- you have claimed it but not in the correct way (eg, you have filled in the wrong form, or filled in the right form incorrectly or incompletely) and you cannot put in a correct claim immediately; or
- you have claimed correctly, but it is not possible for the claim, or for a revision or supersession request which relates to it, to be dealt with immediately; or
- you have been awarded benefit, but it is not possible to pay you immediately other than by means of an interim payment.

A short-term advance (for universal credit, a 'universal credit advance') can be made where there is a delay in dealing with your claim or paying your benefit and, because of the delay, you are in financial need. Financial need means that because you have not received your benefit, there is serious risk of harm to the health or safety of you or of your family.

You cannot appeal to the First-tier Tribunal if you are refused an interim payment or short-term advance. It may be possible to apply for judicial review (see p63). You could contact your MP to see if s/he can help get the decision to refuse you an interim payment or short-term advance reconsidered.

An interim payment or short-term advance can be deducted from any later payment of benefit. If it is more than your actual entitlement, the overpayment can be recovered.

Payments on account of housing benefit

If you are a private or housing association tenant and the local authority has not been able to assess your HB within 14 days, you should receive an interim payment (known as a 'payment on account') while your claim is being sorted out.[1]

Some local authorities treat interim payments as though they are discretionary. However, the local authority *must* pay you an amount which it considers reasonable, given what it knows about your circumstances.[2]

Interim payments can only be refused if it is clear you will not be entitled to HB, or the reason for the delay is that you have been asked for information or evidence to support your claim and you have failed, without good cause, to provide it.[3]

If the delay has been caused by a third party (eg, the rent officer, your bank or employer), this does not affect your right to an interim payment. If your local authority has not made a payment on account, you should complain (see p61).

If the local authority makes a payment on account, it should notify you of the amount and that it can recover any overpayment that occurs if your actual HB entitlement is less than the interim amount.

If your payment on account is less than your entitlement, your future HB can be adjusted to take account of the underpayment.[4]

Chapter 2: Claims, decisions and challenges
3. Challenging decisions and complaints

Crisis grants

If you are experiencing financial hardship, you could claim a crisis grant from the Scottish Welfare Fund to help you with your living expenses (see p38).

3. Challenging decisions and complaints

Appeals

Most decisions about benefit or tax credit entitlement can be challenged by appealing to an independent tribunal. In most cases, you first have to ask for the decision to be looked at again (see below). Decisions about Scottish Welfare Fund payments can be challenged initially by requesting an internal review and then by applying to the Scottish Public Service Ombudsman for a further review. Decisions about council tax reduction (CTR) can be challenged initially by asking for an internal review (within two months of the decision), and then by applying to the Council Tax Reduction Review Panel (within 42 days of the review decision) for a further review. Decisions about benefits administered by Social Security Scotland (SSS) can be challenged by asking for a 'redetermination' (within 31 days of the decision being notified to you), and then by appealing to a First-tier Tribunal (within 31 days of the redetermination being notified to you).

Decisions about all other benefits and tax credits apart from housing benefit (HB) can only be appealed against once you have asked for a revision or review (often called a 'mandatory reconsideration'). If you want to challenge a HB decision, you can appeal without first having to ask for a mandatory reconsideration. The normal time limit for asking for a mandatory reconsideration is one month from the date of the decision being challenged, or 30 days for tax credits. This time limit can be extended by up to one year if you have special reasons for applying late and it is reasonable to grant your application. If a late application is refused, you may be able to appeal to the First-tier Tribunal provided it is within the absolute time limit of 13 months.[5]

If you are still unhappy with a decision following a mandatory reconsideration, you can appeal to a First-tier Tribunal.

You must appeal about a decision on a benefit within one month of the date of the mandatory reconsideration decision, or within 30 days if it is an appeal about tax credits. This time limit can be extended by one year from the date the ordinary time limit expired. If your appeal is late, you must give reasons why. A late appeal can be accepted by the First-tier Tribunal if it is fair and just to do so.[6]

How to appeal

You must usually appeal in writing, preferably using the appropriate appeal form. For HB and CTR, use the form provided by your local authority. For tax credits, child benefit and guardian's allowance, use form SSCS5. For benefits administered

Chapter 2: Claims, decisions and challenges
3. Challenging decisions and complaints

by SSS, appeal using the form you have been sent with the redetermination notice or telephone 0800 182 2222. For other benefits, use form SSCS1.

For more information on appeals and on other ways of changing benefit and tax credit decisions (revisions and supersessions), see CPAG's *Welfare Benefits and Tax Credits Handbook*.

Complaints

If you experience delays in getting your benefit or tax credit claim decided, or if you are unhappy with the service you receive in some other way, you could use the Department for Work and Pensions (DWP), HM Revenue and Customs (HMRC), SSS or local authority complaints procedure.

Department for Work and Pensions complaints

Complaining about the Department for Work and Pensions

The DWP has a complaints procedure that applies to all its agencies. The individual agencies include: the Pension Service, Jobcentre Plus and the Disability and Carers Service.

The DWP's preferred method of dealing with complaints is by telephone, although for jobseeker's allowance and universal credit there is an online complaints service at https:/makeacomplaint.dwp.gov.uk/. The DWP should normally resolve or deal with a complaint within 15 working days at each stage of the procedure. To complain, contact the office which dealt with your claim. If you are still dissatisfied, you can ask for your complaint to be dealt with by a more senior DWP officer. The officer should contact you about your complaint and keep you updated about its progress. If you are still dissatisfied, you can make a further complaint which is dealt with by a senior DWP manager. If you are not satisfied following this, complain to the Independent Case Examiner. You may also have grounds to make a complaint to the Ombudsman (see p61).

Complaining to the Independent Case Examiner

The Independent Case Examiner (ICE) deals with complaints about DWP agencies and its contracted providers. A complaint can only be made to the ICE if you have already completed the complaints procedure of the agency concerned. Complaints can be made by telephone (0800 414 8529; textphone: 18001 0800 414 8529), in writing to PO Box 209, Bootle L20 7WA or by email to ice@dwp.gov.uk. You need to give all the relevant information. A complaint should be made within six months after the final response from the agency you are complaining about.

The ICE first considers whether or not it can accept the complaint. If it can, it will attempt to settle it by suggesting ways in which you and the agency can come to an agreement. If this fails, the ICE prepares a formal report, setting out how the complaint arose and how it believes it should be settled. The ICE considers whether there has been maladministration. It cannot deal with matters of law or cases that are subject to judicial review action or under appeal.

HM Revenue and Customs complaints

Complaining to HM Revenue and Customs

You can complain about how HMRC has dealt with your tax credit, child benefit or guardian's allowance claim or with your national insurance credits or contributions, online using a Government Gateway account, by telephone or in writing (see www.gov.uk/complain-about-hmrc). If you are not happy with the initial response, ask HMRC to review your complaint. The review should be carried out by a different customer service adviser, who will give you HMRC's final reply to your complaint.

If you are not happy with HMRC's final reply, you can ask the Adjudicator to look into it and recommend appropriate action.

Complaining to the Adjudicator

The Adjudicator's Office can investigate complaints about the way in which HMRC deals with tax credits, child benefit and guardian's allowance. Complaints can be made about delays, staff behaviour, misleading advice or any other form of maladministration. The Adjudicator cannot, however, investigate disputes about matters of law. The Adjudicator can only investigate a complaint if you have first exhausted the HMRC internal complaints procedure. A complaint should be made in writing using the form available from www.adjudicatorsoffice.gov.uk. A complaint should be made within six months of the final correspondence with HMRC.

The Adjudicator can recommend that compensation be paid, and HMRC should follow her/his recommendations in all but exceptional circumstances. If you are unhappy with the Adjudicator's response to your complaint, you can ask your MP to put your complaint to the Ombudsman (see below). As well as looking at your complaint about HMRC, the Ombudsman may also look into the way in which the Adjudicator has investigated your complaint.

Using your MP

If you are not satisfied with the reply you receive after you have made a complaint about the DWP or HMRC, the next step is to take up the matter with your MP.

Most MPs have surgeries in their areas where they meet constituents to discuss problems. You can get the details of your MP and how to contact her/him from www.parliament.uk/mps-lords-and-offices/mps or from the House of Commons Enquiry Service (tel: 0800 112 4272). You can either go to the surgery, email or write to your MP.

Your MP will probably want to write to the benefit authority for an explanation of what has happened. If you are not satisfied with the reply, the next stage is to complain to the Ombudsman (see p61).

Social Security Scotland complaints

If you are not happy about the way you have been treated by SSS, you can complain by telephone (tel: 0800 182 2222) or in writing (Social Security Scotland, General Enquiries, PO Box 10301, Dundee DD1 9FW). SSS states it will try to resolve your complaint within a week, unless it is more complex, then it will try to resolve it within four weeks. If you are still unhappy after your complaint has been considered by SSS, you can complain to the Scottish Public Services Ombudsman (see p62).

Local authority complaints

Local authorities are required to have a complaints procedure and you should ask for details of how this works. If there is no formal procedure, begin by writing to the supervisor of the person dealing with your claim, making it clear why you are dissatisfied. If you do not receive a satisfactory reply, take up the matter with someone more senior in the department and ultimately the principal officer. Send a copy of the letter to your local councillor and to the councillor who chairs the council committee responsible for HB/CTR, or the Scottish Welfare Fund, as local authority officers are always accountable to the councillors. If this does not produce results, or if the delay is causing you severe hardship, consider a complaint to the Scottish Public Services Ombudsman (see p62) or judicial review (see p63).

Complaining to the Ombudsman

The Ombudsman investigates complaints from members of the public who believe they have experienced an injustice because of maladministration by a government department. Maladministration means poor administration and can include avoidable delays, failure to advise about appeal rights, refusal to answer reasonable questions or respond to correspondence, discourteousness, racism or sexism. The Parliamentary and Health Service Ombudsman deals with complaints about central government and the Scottish Public Services Ombudsman deals with complaints about local government and SSS.

The Ombudsman cannot usually investigate a complaint unless you have first exhausted the internal complaints procedure. However, if the authority is not acting upon your complaint, or there are unreasonable delays, this delay may also form part of your complaint. The normal time limit for lodging a complaint with the Ombudsman is 12 months from the date you were notified of the matter you are complaining about, although it possible for a complaint which is made after 12 months to be looked at if there are good reasons for the delay.

The Parliamentary and Health Service Ombudsman

The Parliamentary and Health Service Ombudsman deals with complaints about central government departments such as the DWP and HMRC, as well as any agencies carrying out functions on their behalf. In order to make a complaint,

Chapter 2: Claims, decisions and challenges
3. Challenging decisions and complaints

you must contact your MP, who will then refer the complaint to the Ombudsman. You can find out who your MP is and how to contact her/him at www.parliament.uk/mps-lords-and-offices/mps or from the House of Commons Enquiry Service (tel: 0800 112 4272). The Ombudsman can only investigate complaints of maladministration and not disputes about entitlement, which should be dealt with by the First-tier Tribunal. The Ombudsman has extensive powers to look at documents held by the benefit authority on your claim. You may be interviewed to check any facts. The Ombudsman can recommend financial compensation if you have been unfairly treated or experienced a loss as a result of the maladministration.

The Scottish Public Services Ombudsman

If you have tried to resolve your complaint with the local authority or with SSS but you are still not satisfied with the outcome, you can apply to the Scottish Public Services Ombudsman. The Ombudsman can investigate any cases of maladministration by local authorities or by SSS.

You can apply to the Ombudsman by writing to the office (see Appendix 1), downloading a complaint form or completing it online at www.spso.org.uk/complain/form. The Ombudsman has extensive powers to look at documents on your claim. You may be interviewed to check any facts. The Ombudsman can recommend financial compensation if you have been unfairly treated or experienced a loss as a result of the maladministration.

Compensation payments

You should expect prompt, courteous and efficient service from staff dealing with your claim. If you are dissatisfied with the way your claim has been administered, you can seek compensation. The organisations administering social security benefits and tax credits sometimes pay compensation if you can show that you have lost out through their error or delay.

The DWP uses a guide, *Financial Redress for Maladministration*,[7] to help it decide when and how much compensation (known as an 'extra-statutory' or ex gratia payment) should be paid. HMRC's *Complaints and Remedy Guidance*[8] sets out when it makes 'financial redress'.

Judicial review

If there is no right of appeal against a decision of a public body (such as the DWP, HMRC, SSS or local authority) or, in certain circumstances, if the body is refusing to make a decision or to exercise its discretion properly, you may be able to threaten and pursue judicial review proceedings. You cannot normally take judicial review action if you have another independent means of appeal (such as to the First-tier Tribunal). You need to consult a solicitor or law centre about judicial review. You should apply for judicial review within three months of the decision you want to challenge. This time period can be extended.[9]

Notes

2. **Decisions and delays**
   1 Reg 93(1) HB Regs; reg 74(1) HB(SPC) Regs
   2 paras A6/6.158 and 6.159 GM
   3 Reg 93(1) HB Regs; reg 74(1) HB(SPC) Regs; *R v Haringey LBC ex parte Azad Ayub* [1992] 25 HLR 566 (QBD)
   4 Reg 93(3) HB Regs; reg 74(3) HB(SPC) Regs

3. **Challenging decisions and complaints**
   5 *R (CJ) v SSWP* (ESA) [2017] UKUT 324 (AAC) reported as [2018] AACR 5
   6 rr2 and 5(3)(a) TP(FT) Rules
   7 www.gov.uk/government/publications/compensation-for-poor-service-a-guide-for-dwp-staff
   8 www.gov.uk/hmrc-internal-manuals/complaints-and-remedy-guidance
   9 s27A Court of Session Act 1988

Chapter 3

Children in hospital

This chapter covers:
1. Child benefit and guardian's allowance (below)
2. Means-tested benefits (p65)
3. Non-means-tested benefits (p68)
4. Tax credits (p68)
5. Help visiting your child (p69)

Hospital inpatient
Your child counts as a hospital inpatient if s/he is being maintained free of charge while having medical or other treatment as an inpatient in an NHS hospital or similar institution.[1]
If your child is being treated as a private patient, s/he does not count as an inpatient for benefit purposes.
'Medical or other treatment' is treatment by a doctor, dentist or professionally qualified or trained nurse, or by someone under the supervision of such a person.[2]

1. Child benefit and guardian's allowance

If your child is in hospital, your child benefit – and guardian's allowance if you get it – continues unaffected for 12 weeks.[3] When counting the 12 weeks, two or more periods in hospital (and/or residential accommodation) separated by 28 days or less count as the same period.[4] After 12 weeks, your child benefit (and guardian's allowance) continues, provided you spend money on your child's behalf – eg, on clothing, pocket money, snacks, books and comics.[5] The amount of money you must spend is not stipulated. If you do not spend any money on your child's behalf, your child benefit stops after 20 weeks in hospital.[6]

2. Means-tested benefits

Universal credit

Your child continues to be included in your universal credit (UC) claim if the child's stay in hospital is temporary. However, s/he is no longer included in your claim if the hospital stay is expected to last for more than six months, or has lasted for more than six months.[7] While the child is still included in your UC claim, you continue get the child element and any disabled child element.[8] Your work allowance (see p48) is calculated taking into account that you have a dependent child.[9] However, if you receive the carer element, this stops if you no longer have 'regular and substantial' caring responsibilities for your child (see p47).[10] If you are in rented accommodation, the housing costs element is calculated as if the child is living with you for the first six months your child is in hospital.[11] If you receive help with childcare costs in your UC, this may change if you are no longer paying for childcare because your child is in hospital.

Note: if the only reason you are exempt from the benefit cap (p2) is because a child for whom you are responsible is entitled to disability living allowance (DLA) (or personal independence payment – PIP), this exemption will end if the child is no longer part of your UC claim.[12]

Income support and income-based jobseeker's allowance

During the first 12 weeks of a temporary absence, your child is still treated as part of your household for income support (IS) or income-based jobseeker's allowance (JSA).[13] After 12 weeks' absence s/he is still treated as part of your household, provided you are still in regular contact with her/him.[14] Regular contact is not defined. Department for Work and Pensions (DWP) guidance says that regular contact includes visits, letters and telephone calls that take place regularly or frequently, and that weekly or monthly visits are considered regular contact.[15] The DWP normally continues to treat the child as part of your household for the first year of absence, provided child benefit remains in payment for her/him.[16] After 52 weeks in hospital, a child is normally no longer treated as being part of your household, but there are exceptions (see p66).[17]

How your benefit is actually affected depends on whether or not you still get amounts in your IS/income-based JSA for your child (see below).

If you do not get amounts for your child

Most people who are on IS/income-based JSA do not get amounts in IS/income-based JSA for their child(ren), and instead get child tax credit (CTC) (see p41). In this situation, the amount of benefit you get should be unaffected by your child's stay in hospital, unless you stop being entitled to carer's allowance (CA) for the child or the child no longer counts as part of your household (see above). If you stop being entitled to CA for the child, entitlement to the carer premium stops

Chapter 3: Children in hospital
2. Means-tested benefits

eight weeks after this date (see p68).[18] If claiming CA was the only basis for your IS claim, eight weeks after CA stops, you can no longer claim IS on this basis.[19] If the child no longer counts as part of your household, your benefit may be affected. For example, if you no longer count as responsible for a child aged under five, you cannot claim IS as a lone parent. If you have no other basis for your IS award, you can no longer claim IS.

If you still get amounts for your child

You will only be getting amounts for your child in your IS/income-based JSA if you have been claiming for a child since before 6 April 2004 and you have not claimed CTC (see p30). While your child is still considered part of your household, you continue to get a child personal allowance and family premium. If you are getting the disabled child premium and/or the enhanced disability premium, this will also continue.

If you have been getting CA and you stop being entitled, the **carer premium** stops eight weeks after your CA stops (see p68).[20] If you are getting IS only because you were getting CA, eight weeks after CA stops, you can no longer claim IS on this basis.

If your child is in hospital for more than 52 weeks

If the hospital stay is expected to last for more than 52 weeks, or if it has lasted for more than 52 weeks, the child is usually no longer treated as part of your household for IS/income-based JSA purposes.[21] This means that if you have still been getting amounts for your child in your IS/income-based JSA, these will stop. The exception to this rule is if:[22]

- there are exceptional circumstances – eg, s/he is in hospital and you have no control over the length of her/his absence; *and*
- the absence is unlikely to be to be substantially more than 52 weeks.

If this applies, the child can still be treated as part of your household for more than 52 weeks. However, the enhanced disability premium and the disabled child premium will stop after 52 weeks.[23]

Income-related employment and support allowance

There are no amounts in employment and support allowance (ESA) for dependent children and, therefore, your ESA is not normally affected if your child goes into hospital. The exception is if you are entitled to CA and this stops. The **carer premium** (part of your income-related ESA applicable amount) stops eight weeks after your entitlement to CA stops (see p68).[24]

Pension credit

If you are entitled to CA and it stops, the **carer addition** (part of your pension credit (PC)) stops eight weeks after your entitlement to CA stops (see p68).[25] Some

PC claimants who are responsible for a child or qualifying young person get an additional amount for her/him in their PC (instead of getting CTC). If you get a PC additional amount for a child and s/he goes into hospital, the additional amount continues during a temporary period in hospital which is unlikely to last for more than 52 weeks, or unlikely to last for substantially more than 52 weeks.[26]

Housing benefit and council tax reduction

If you are on IS, income-based JSA, income-related ESA or the guarantee credit of PC, you get maximum housing benefit (HB)/council tax reduction (CTR). This means your HB/CTR does not normally change as a result of your child's being in hospital, provided you remain on one of these benefits.

If you are not on one of these benefits, provided your child's absence is temporary and expected to last for no more than 52 weeks, s/he continues to be treated as part of your household for HB/CTR for up to 52 weeks (sometimes for longer – see below).[27] This usually means that your applicable amount (see p25) continues to include any relevant amounts and premiums for the child, although it may be different if you get UC and CTR.

If you have been getting CA and you stop being entitled, the **carer premium** stops eight weeks after your CA stops (see p68).[28]

If your child is in hospital for more than 52 weeks

Your child continues to be treated as part of your household for HB (and therefore you continue to get the child personal allowance, family premium, and enhanced disability and disabled child premium if appropriate) if s/he is in hospital for more than 52 weeks, provided:[29]
- there are exceptional circumstances – eg, s/he is in hospital and you have no control over the length of her/his absence. This is an example given in the law; *and*
- the absence is unlikely to be to be substantially more than 52 weeks.

Your child is treated as part of your household for CTR if her/his absence is temporary.[30] There is no '52-week' rule for CTR. This gives local authorities more flexibility with CTR than with HB.

Note: if the only reason you are exempt from the benefit cap (see p2) is because a child for whom you are responsible is entitled to DLA (or PIP), this exemption will end if the child no longer counts as part of your household.[31]

3. Non-means-tested benefits

Disability living allowance and personal independence payment

Provided your child is under 18 on the day s/he enters hospital as an inpatient, disability living allowance (DLA) (both components) or personal independence payment (PIP) (both components) continue to be paid regardless of how long s/he remains in hospital. DLA (or PIP if 16 or over) can be awarded and paid after a child aged under 18 has gone into hospital.[32] If a child reaches 16 while s/he is still in hospital and s/he is already on DLA, s/he will not have to claim PIP while still in hospital and will be able to continue to get DLA.[33]

Carer's allowance

Providing your child is getting the appropriate rate of DLA care component middle or highest rate (or PIP daily living component), you can continue to get carer's allowance (CA) while your child is in hospital, as long as you continue to meet the normal conditions of entitlement – eg, you continue to care for your child for 35 hours or more a week.

Time off from caring

You can still be entitled to CA during temporary breaks from caring. You can have a break from caring of up to four weeks in any period of 26 weeks, or a break of up to 12 weeks if either you or the person for whom you care is receiving treatment in a hospital for at least eight of the 12 weeks.[34]

Carer element, carer premium and carer addition

The carer element in your universal credit (UC) stops if you no longer have 'regular and substantal' caring responsibilities for your child (see p47).[35] If your entitlement to CA stops, the carer premium or carer addition (see p6) in your income support, income-based jobseeker's allowance, income-related employment and support allowance, pension credit or housing benefit stops eight weeks later. This rule applies to council tax reduction unless you also get UC.[36]

4. Tax credits

Child tax credit (CTC) remains payable for a child, provided s/he normally lives with you.[37] Guidance from HM Revenue and Customs (HMRC) says this means that the child 'regularly, usually, typically' lives with you, and that this allows for temporary or occasional absences.[38]

You remain entitled to CTC if your child is in hospital on a temporary basis, because your child should still be treated as normally living with you. S/he also continues to count as a dependent child for working tax credit (WTC) purposes.

The amount of tax credits

If your child is in hospital, you remain entitled to the disabled child and severely disabled child elements (see p42) in your CTC, even if your child's disability living allowance or personal independence payment has stopped. This is not likely to have happened if your child is under 18, but may have happened if s/he was 18 or over when s/he entered hospital.[39]

If you are getting help with childcare costs in your WTC (the childcare element), this may change if your child is in hospital for a prolonged period. If your childcare costs stop or go down by £10 or more over a period of four weeks, you must let HMRC know about this change.

Make sure you report changes to HMRC to avoid underpayments or overpayments.

5. Help visiting your child

If you are on a low income you may be able to get help with the cost of visiting your child in hospital from the Scottish Welfare Fund (see p38).

If you are eligible, it may be possible to get a community care grant or crisis grant to help with travel expenses to visit your child in hospital.[40] The amount awarded normally covers the cost of standard public transport. If public transport is not available or suitable, the cost of petrol or a taxi may be given. Payment may be by a travel voucher.

If you are on universal credit, income support, income-based jobseeker's allowance, income-related employment and support allowance or pension credit, it should be accepted that you are on a low income, but you do not need to be on one of these benefits to get help from the Scottish Welfare Fund.

Chapter 3: Children in hospital
Notes

1 Reg 2(4) SS(HIP) Regs
2 *SSWP v Slavin* [2011] EWCA Civ 1515

1. Child benefit and guardian's allowance
3 s143(3)(b) and (4) SSCBA 1992; reg 10(1) CB Regs
4 s143(3) SSCBA 1992; reg 10(2) CB Regs
5 s143(4) SSCBA 1992
6 s143(2) SSCBA 1992, 12 weeks' 'hospital' absence plus eight weeks' normal absence

2. Means-tested benefits
7 Reg 4(7) UC Regs
8 Reg 24(2) UC Regs
9 Reg 22 UC Regs
10 Regs 29 and 30 UC Regs
11 Reg 4(7)(a) and Sch 4 para 11 UC Regs
12 Regs 79 and 83 UC Regs
13 **IS** Reg 16(1) and (5)(b) IS Regs
   JSA Reg 78(1) and (5)(c) JSA Regs
14 **IS** Reg 16(5)(b) IS Regs
   JSA Reg 78(5)(c) JSA Regs
15 para 22074 DMG
16 para 22075 DMG
17 **IS** Reg 16(2) IS Regs
   JSA Reg 78(2) JSA Regs
18 **IS** Sch 2 para 14ZA(2) IS Regs
   JSA Sch 1 para 17(3) JSA Regs
19 Sch 1B para 5 IS Regs
20 **IS** Sch 2 para 14ZA(3) IS Regs
   JSA Sch 1 para 17(3) JSA Regs
21 **IS** Reg 16(2) IS Regs
   JSA Reg 78(2) JSA Regs
22 **IS** Reg 16(2)(b) IS Regs
   JSA Reg 78(2)(b) JSA Regs
23 **IS** Reg 2(1) and Sch 2 paras 13A(2)(a)(ii) and 14(2)(b) IS Regs
   JSA Reg 1 and Sch 1 paras 15A(2)(ii) and 16(2)(b) JSA Regs
24 Sch 4 para 8(2) ESA Regs
25 Sch 1 para 4(3) SPC Regs
26 Sch 2A para 6 SPC Regs
27 **HB** Reg 21(1) and (2) HB Regs; reg 21(1) and (2) HB(SPC) Regs
   CTR Reg 11(1) CTR(S) Regs; reg 11(1) CTR(SPC)(S) Regs
28 **HB** Sch 3 para 17(2) HB Regs; Sch 3 para 9(2) HB(SPC) Regs
   CTR Sch 1 para 14(2) CTR(S) Regs; Sch 1 para 10(2) CTR(SPC)(S) Regs
29 Reg 21 HB Regs; reg 21 HB(SPC) Regs
30 Reg 11(1) CTR(S) Regs; reg 11(1) CTR(SPC)(S) Regs
31 Regs 75A and 75F HB Regs

3. Non-means-tested benefits
32 **DLA** Regs 8 and 12A SS(DLA) Regs
   PIP Reg 29 SS(PIP) Regs
33 Regs 2, 3(4A) and (5A) and 19 PIP(TP) Regs
34 Reg 4(2) SS(ICA) Regs
35 Regs 29 and 30 UC Regs
36 **IS** Sch 2 para 14ZA(3) IS Regs
   JSA Sch 1 para 17(3) JSA Regs
   ESA Sch 4 para 8(4) ESA Regs
   PC Sch 1 Part II para 4(3) SPC Regs
   HB Sch 3 para 17(2) HB Regs; Sch 3 para 9(2) HB(SPC) Regs
   CTR Sch 1 para 14(2) CTR(S) Regs; Sch 1 para 10(2) CTR(SPC)(S) Regs

4. Tax credits
37 Reg 3 CTC Regs
38 para 02202 TCTM
39 Reg 8(2)-(4) CTC Regs

5. Help visiting your child
40 SWFG para 6.5

Chapter 4
Disabled children in care homes

This chapter covers:
1. Benefits and tax credits for children in care homes (below)
2. More than one stay in a care home (p79)
3. When your child comes home (p80)

If your child is in a care home for a reason other than disability, see Chapter 6.

1. Benefits and tax credits for children in care homes

Child benefit and guardian's allowance

If your child is in a care home, your child benefit – and guardian's allowance if you get it – continues unaffected for 12 consecutive weeks.[1] When counting the 12 weeks, two or more periods in a care home which are separated by 28 days or less count as the same period.[2] See p79 for more details of how this rule works. After 12 weeks, your child benefit (and guardian's allowance) continues, provided you spend money on your child's behalf – eg, on clothing, pocket money, snacks, books, comics and toys or on fares to visit her/him.[3] The amount of money you must spend is not stipulated. If you do not spend any money on your child's behalf, your child benefit stops after 20 weeks in a care home.[4]

Means-tested benefits

Universal credit

If your child counts as looked after

If your child is in a care home and counts as 'looked after' by the local authority, s/he is no longer included in your universal credit (UC) claim, unless it is a 'planned short break' (respite).[5]

This means that any child element you receive stops.[6] If you are in rented accommodation, the housing costs element is calculated as if the child is still

Chapter 4: Disabled children in care homes
1. Benefits and tax credits for children in care homes

living with you for the first six months of absence from home.[7] If your UC includes the carer element, this stops when you no longer have 'regular and substantial' caring responsibilities for your child (see p47), including if your child's disability living allowance (DLA) care component or personal independence payment (PIP) daily living component has stopped being paid.[8] If the child element has stopped and you have no other dependent children, you will not get a work allowance (see p48) unless you or your partner have limited capability for work.[9] If you receive help with childcare costs for the child in your UC, this will stop.[10] The work-related requirements which apply to you may also change (see page 49).

Note: if the only reason you are exempt from the benefits cap (see p2) is because a child for whom you are responsible is entitled to DLA (or PIP), this exemption ends if the child no longer counts as part of your household.[11]

If your child does not count as looked after

If your child does not count as 'looked after' by the local authority, s/he should still be included in your UC claim if her/his absence from home is temporary. However, s/he is no longer included in the claim if the stay away from home is expected to last for more than six months, or has lasted for more than six months.[12] There is no rule 'linking' two or more periods of absence and, therefore, arguably, even a brief stay at home followed by a return to a care home could start a new temporary period of absence. While the child is still included in your UC claim, you continue to get the child element and any disabled child element, even if DLA care component or PIP daily living component has stopped being paid (see p77).[13] Your work allowance (see p48) is calculated taking into account that you have a dependent child.[14] If your UC includes the carer element, this stops when you no longer have 'regular and substantial' caring responsibilities for your child (see p47), including if your child's DLA care component or PIP daily living component has stopped being paid.[15] If you receive help with childcare costs in your UC, this may change if you are no longer paying for childcare because your child is in a care home.

Note: if the only reason you are exempt from the benefit cap (see p2) is because a child for whom you are responsible is entitled to DLA (or PIP), this exemption ends if the child no longer counts as part of your household (either because s/he counts as 'looked after' (see above), or because s/he has been away for more than six months).[16]

Income support and income-based jobseeker's allowance

During the first 12 weeks of a temporary absence, your child is still treated as part of your household for income support (IS) and income-based jobseeker's allowance (JSA).[17] After 12 weeks' absence, s/he is still treated as part of your household provided you are still in 'regular contact' with her/him.[18] 'Regular contact' is not defined. Department for Work and Pensions (DWP) guidance says

Chapter 4: Disabled children in care homes
1. Benefits and tax credits for children in care homes

that regular contact includes visits, letters and telephone calls that take place regularly or frequently, and that weekly or monthly visits are considered regular contact.[19] The DWP usually continues to treat the child as part of your household for the first year of absence, provided child benefit remains in payment for her/him.[20] After 52 weeks in a care home, a child is usually no longer treated as being part of your household, but there are exceptions (see below).

How your IS/income-based JSA is affected depends on whether or not you still get amounts in your benefit for your child (see below).

If you do not get amounts for your child

Most claimants do not get amounts in their IS/income-based JSA for their child(ren) and instead get child tax credit (CTC) (see p30). In this situation, the amount of benefit you get should be unaffected by your child being in a care home, unless you stop being entitled to carer's allowance (CA) for her/him or s/he no longer counts as part of your household (see below). If you stop being entitled to CA for the child, entitlement to the carer premium stops eight weeks after this date (see p77).[21] If claiming CA was the only basis of your IS claim, from eight weeks after your CA ends you are no longer able to claim IS on that basis.[22] If the child no longer counts as part of your household, your benefit may be affected. For example, if you no longer count as caring for a child aged under five, you cannot claim IS as a lone parent.

If you still get amounts for your child

Your IS/income-based JSA may still include amounts for your child (child allowances and premiums). This will only be the case if you have been claiming IS/income-based JSA including amounts for a child since before 6 April 2004 and have not claimed CTC. See p30 for more details.

In most cases, providing your child's stay in a care home is temporary, s/he continues to be treated as part of your household for IS/income-based JSA, and you continue to get a child personal allowance and family premium in your applicable amount for up to 52 weeks (sometimes for longer – see p74).

However, the amount of IS/income-based JSA may change during the 52-week period because of the impact on premiums (part of your 'applicable amount' – see p28).

- The **carer premium** stops eight weeks after your CA stops (see p77).[23]
- The **disabled child premium** stops when your child's DLA care component or PIP daily living component stops (see p77), unless there is another basis for getting it – ie, your child is still getting DLA mobility component, PIP mobility component or is severely sight impaired or blind.[24]
- The **enhanced disability premium** stops when your child's DLA care component or PIP daily living component stops (see p77).[25]

Chapter 4: Disabled children in care homes
1. Benefits and tax credits for children in care homes

When a child stops being treated as part of your household

If the stay in a care home is expected to last for more than 52 weeks, or if it has lasted for more than 52 weeks, the child is no longer treated as part of your household for IS/income-based JSA purposes.[26] This means that if you have still been getting amounts for your child in your IS/income-based JSA, these will stop. The exception to this rule is if:[27]

- there are exceptional circumstances; *and*
- the absence is unlikely to be substantially more than 52 weeks.

Note: when a place in a care home has been arranged by the local authority and the child is away from home for more than 24 hours, technically the child is 'looked after' by the local authority.[28] Applied strictly, the rules mean that the child should not be treated as part of your household for IS/income-based JSA after s/he has been in a care home for 24 hours.[29] In practice, however, it seems that the DWP applies the rules described above.

Income-related employment and support allowance

There are no amounts in employment and support allowance (ESA) for dependent children and, therefore, your ESA is not normally affected if your child goes into a care home. The exception is if you are entitled to CA and this stops (see p77). The **carer premium** (part of your income-related ESA applicable amount) stops eight weeks after your entitlement to CA stops.[30]

Pension credit

If you are entitled to CA and this stops, the **carer addition** (part of your pension credit (PC)) stops eight weeks after your entitlement to CA stops (see p77).[31] Some PC claimants who are responsible for a child or qualifying young person get an additional amount for the child(ren) in their PC (instead of getting CTC). If you get a PC additional amount for a child and s/he goes into a care home, and the child does not count as 'looked after' by the local authority, the additional amount continues during a temporary period in a care home which is unlikely to last for more than 52 weeks or, in exceptional circumstances, unlikely to last for substantially more than 52 weeks.[32] The extra amount that you may get if your child has a disability (see p35) continues during a temporary absence even if your child's DLA or PIP has stopped being paid (see p77).[33] If your child is in a care home and counts as looked after by the local authority, you no longer get the PC additional amount, unless it is a 'planned short break' (respite).[34]

Housing benefit and council tax reduction

Housing benefit (HB) and council tax reduction (CTR) may be affected in several ways if your child is in a care home. How they are affected can depend on whether s/he counts as 'looked after' by the local authority.[35] Ask the social work

Chapter 4: Disabled children in care homes
1. Benefits and tax credits for children in care homes

department of your local council if you are not sure whether your child counts as 'looked after'.

If your child counts as looked after

A child who is in a care home for more than 24 hours, arranged by the local authority, is technically a 'looked-after' child.[36] If s/he is in the care home for less than a week, or if s/he comes home for at least part of every week, your HB and CTR are not affected, provided the local authority considers it reasonable to assess benefit as though the child were at home.[37] A longer stay, however, may affect your benefit. Your entitlement to the personal allowance and any premiums for the child (including **family premium** if s/he is your only dependent child) may stop as soon as s/he goes into the care home.[38] Your **carer premium** stops eight weeks after your CA stops.

If you are on IS, income-based JSA, income-related ESA or the guarantee credit of PC, changes to the personal allowance and premiums in your applicable amount do not affect the amount of HB/CTR you get, as you are 'passported' to maximum HB/CTR. However, your HB may still be reduced because of the number of bedrooms you are deemed to require (the 'size criteria'). This means that if your HB is calculated using the local housing allowance rules (see p24), it may be affected if the child no longer counts as occupying the home and as a result you need fewer bedrooms.[39] If you are under pension age and living in the social rented sector and your child no longer counts as occupying the home, you may be deemed to need fewer bedrooms and be subject to the 'under-occupation penalty' (bedroom tax).[40] It may be possible to argue that, even though the child is not part of your 'household' for HB, s/he should still count as an 'occupier' and s/he should still be included in the size criteria – eg, if s/he is not likely to be away indefinitely.[41] Seek advice if you are in this situation.

If your HB is reduced, you can ask for a discretionary housing payment (see p26) to make up some or all of the difference. Because these are discretionary, it is important to say why you need financial assistance. As well as explaining how the reduction of benefit will affect you financially, you could explain that your child is in the 'looked-after' system only because this is a consequence of her/him having to go into a care home as a result of disability, and that the rules were never intended to reduce benefit for disabled children in these circumstances.

Note: if the only reason you are exempt from the benefit cap (see p2) is because the child for whom you are responsible is entitled to DLA (or PIP), this exemption ends if the child no longer counts as part of your household.[42]

If your child does not count as looked after

If your child does not count as a 'looked-after' child (eg, the care is not arranged through the local authority or the local authority does not treat her/him as such for HB/CTR purposes), provided her/his absence is temporary, s/he continues to

Chapter 4: Disabled children in care homes
1. Benefits and tax credits for children in care homes

be treated as part of your household for HB/CTR for up to 52 weeks (sometimes for longer).[43]

However, the amount of HB/CTR may change during the 52-week period because of the impact on premiums (part of your 'applicable amount' – see p25).
- The **carer premium** stops eight weeks after your CA stops.[44]
- The **disabled child premium** stops when the child's DLA care component or PIP daily living component stops, unless there is another basis for getting it – ie, your child is still getting DLA mobility component, PIP mobility component or is severely sight impaired or blind.[45]
- The **enhanced disability premium** (child) stops when the child's DLA care component or PIP daily living component stops.[46]

If the absence is likely to last for more than 52 weeks, or if it has lasted for more than 52 weeks, the child is usually no longer treated as part of your household for HB. This means that the amounts in your HB applicable amount for the child will stop. The exception to this rule is if:[47]
- there are exceptional circumstances and you have no control over the length of her/his absence; *and*
- the absence is unlikely to be to be substantially more than 52 weeks.

If you are on IS, income-based JSA, income-related ESA or the guarantee credit of PC, changes to the personal allowance and premiums in your applicable amount will not affect the amount of HB/CTR you get, as you are 'passported' to maximum HB/CTR. However, your HB may still be reduced because of the impact on the number of bedrooms you are deemed to require (the 'size criteria'). This means that if your HB is calculated using the local housing allowance rules (see p24), it may be affected if the child no longer counts as occupying the home and as a result you need fewer bedrooms.[48] If you are under pension age and living in the social rented sector and your child no longer counts as occupying the home, you may be deemed to need fewer bedrooms and be subject to the 'under-occupation penalty' (bedroom tax).[49] It may be possible to argue that, even though the child is not part of your 'household' for HB/CTR, s/he should still count as an 'occupier' and s/he should still be included in the size criteria – eg, if s/he is not likely to be away indefinitely.[50] Seek further advice if you are in this situation and look at claiming a discretionary housing payment (see p26).

For CTR, a child is treated as part of your household if her/his absence is temporary.[51] There is no '52-week rule' for CTR. This gives local authorities more flexibility with CTR than with HB.

Note: if the only reason you are exempt from the benefit cap (see p2) is because a child for whom you are responsible is entitled to DLA (or PIP), this exemption ends if the child no longer counts as part of your household – eg, because s/he has been absent for more than 52 weeks.[52]

Chapter 4: Disabled children in care homes
1. Benefits and tax credits for children in care homes

Non-means-tested benefits

Disability living allowance and personal independence payment

If your child is in a care home and the local authority is paying some or all of the costs, the care component of DLA or daily living component of PIP for the child stops after four weeks.[53] The mobility component of DLA or PIP is not affected and continues to be paid. If, instead, the local authority places the child with a family (eg, for a period of respite), both the care and mobility components of DLA or PIP continue to be paid.[54]

Linking rules

When counting the four weeks, two or more periods in a care home which are separated by 28 days or less count as the same period.[55] See p79 for more details of how the linking rules work and for details of how days in a care home are counted.

Carer's allowance

If you are getting CA for caring for your child, there are two main reasons why your entitlement may be affected if s/he goes into a care home.
- You cannot get CA unless the person for whom you care is getting DLA care component at the middle or highest rate or PIP daily living component. If your child has been in a care home for more than four weeks, the care component/daily living component stops. This means your CA stops.
- In order to qualify for CA, you must be caring for the disabled person for at least 35 hours a week. If your child is in a care home, you are unlikely to satisfy this rule. However, you can have some time off from caring and still be entitled to CA.

Time off from caring

You can still be entitled to CA during temporary breaks from caring. You can have a break from caring of up to four weeks in any 26-week period (or a break of up to 12 weeks if either you or the person for whom you care is having treatment in a hospital for at least eight of the 12 weeks[56]). However, if the person you care for has stopped getting DLA care component/PIP daily living component, you cannot continue to get CA.

Arranging care breaks

A 'week off' caring is a week in which you spend less than 35 hours caring for the disabled person. A 'week' for CA runs from Sunday to Saturday.[57] This means that, if you can arrange a care home for your child from midweek to midweek (eg, for respite), you may still be caring for her/him for at least 35 hours in the week s/he goes into the care home and in the week s/he comes home. These weeks do not count as 'weeks off' caring.

Time spent preparing for your child's time at home, and cleaning and washing after s/he has gone, can count as time spent caring for her/him. For example, any

Chapter 4: Disabled children in care homes
1. Benefits and tax credits for children in care homes

shopping or cooking that relate solely to the visit and any cleaning up afterwards can count as caring.[58]

Carer element, carer premium and carer addition

If you are on UC, the carer element stops when you no longer have 'regular and substantial' caring responsibilities for your child (see p48), including if your child's DLA care component or PIP daily living component has stopped being paid.[59]

If your entitlement to CA stops, the carer premium or carer addition in your IS, income-based JSA, income-related ESA, PC or HB stops eight weeks after your entitlement to CA stops. This rule also applies to CTR, unless you are also getting UC.[60]

If you were entitled to IS only because you were getting CA, eight weeks after CA stops you can no longer claim IS on that basis.

See Chapter 1 for more information about carer element, carer premium and carer addition.

Tax credits

If the care home placement has been arranged solely because of your child's disability or health, you continue to be responsible for the child for tax credit purposes if you were responsible for her/him before s/he went into the care home.[61] This means that you should receive CTC indefinitely for your child even though s/he is in a care home (because of her/his disability). Your child also continues to count as a dependent child for working tax credit purposes. However, the amount of tax credits you get might change (see below).

Amount of tax credits

If your child's DLA care component or PIP daily living component has stopped (see p77), this affects the disabled child and severely disabled child elements as follows.[62]

- The disabled child element stops being included in your CTC calculation from the date the DLA care component or PIP daily living component stops, unless there is another basis for getting it – ie, your child is still getting DLA or PIP mobility component, or is severely sight impaired or blind.
- The severely disabled child element stops being included in your CTC calculation from the date the DLA care component or PIP daily living component stops.

Make sure you report changes to HMRC to avoid underpayments and overpayments.

Help visiting your child

If you are on a low income you may be able to get help from the Scottish Welfare Fund (see p38) for the cost of visiting your child in a care home.[63]

If you are eligible, it may be possible to get a community care grant or crisis grant to help with travel expenses to visit your child in a care home. The amount awarded will normally cover the cost of standard public transport. If public transport is not available or suitable, the cost of petrol or a taxi may be given. A travel voucher may be issued.

If you are on UC, IS, income-based JSA, income-related ESA or PC, it should be accepted that you are on a low income, but you do not need to be on one of these benefits to get help from the Scottish Welfare Fund.

2. More than one stay in a care home

Linking rules

For child benefit, disability living allowance (DLA) and personal independence payment (PIP), if your child has two or more periods in a care home separated by 28 days or less, it counts as the same period.[64]

For DLA and PIP, your child does not count as being in a care home on the day s/he goes in or on the day s/he comes home.[65]

Example
Beth's daughter, Julie, is aged six and is disabled. She gets the DLA higher rate mobility component and middle rate care component. Julie goes into a care home on 1 March and comes home again on 15 March.
For DLA purposes, this counts as 13 days in a care home.
Julie then goes back into the care home on 5 April and comes home on 5 July.
For DLA purposes, the two periods are separated by 22 days. The two periods in the care home count as the same period because they are separated by 28 days or less.
Julie's DLA care component stops on 21 April because on that date she counts as having been in a care home for four weeks.

If your child has regular stays in a care home (eg, for respite), you may be able to arrange them so that the separate periods do not link together and affect her/his DLA or PIP entitlement. For example, if your child has regular respite care every fourth week, eventually the DLA care component/PIP daily living component will stop each time s/he goes for respite, if each period in the home is linked by a period of 28 days or less. To ensure this does not happen, you could try to arrange her/his respite so that more than 28 days separate each period s/he is in the care home.

Chapter 4: Disabled children in care homes
3. When your child comes home

3. When your child comes home

When your child comes home from a care home, any benefits/tax credits that were affected should start to be paid as normal again. This section covers the benefits/tax credits that are most likely to have been affected.

Child benefit

Child benefit is only likely to have stopped if your child was in the care home for a prolonged period and you did not continue to spend money on her/his behalf (see p71). If this has happened, you have to reclaim child benefit once your child returns home. See Chapter 2 for details of how to do this.

Means-tested benefits

Universal credit

If you have stopped getting the child element in your universal credit (UC), either because your child counts as 'looked after' by the local authority or because s/he has been away from home for more than six months, tell the Department for Work and Pensions (DWP) as soon as your child comes home so the child element is included again and your work allowance and childcare element can be adjusted, if relevant. If the carer element has stopped, tell the DWP as soon as you have 'regular and sustantial' caring responsibilities for your child again (see p47).

Income support and income-based jobseeker's allowance

If you are still getting amounts in your income support (IS) or income-based jobseeker's allowance (JSA) for your child, but the amount of IS/income-based JSA has changed because the disabled child premium and/or the enhanced disability premium stopped, tell the DWP when your child comes home and disability living allowance (DLA)/personal independence payment (PIP) payments start again.

If you were getting amounts in your IS/income-based JSA for your child and these have stopped altogether, you cannot get these amounts back when your child comes home unless you have continued to get amounts for another child in your IS/income-based JSA.

If you were getting a carer premium and this has stopped because carer's allowance (CA) has stopped, tell the DWP when your CA starts again. If you lost entitlement to benefit (eg, IS) because you lost the carer premium or for some other reason, you will usually have to claim UC instead.

Housing benefit and council tax reduction

If your housing benefit (HB) or council tax reduction (CTR) amount has changed because the carer premium stopped (eight weeks after CA stopped), tell the local authority when your CA starts again. If your HB/CTR amount has changed because the disability and/or enhanced disability premium stopped (when the DLA care component/PIP daily living component stopped), tell the local authority when your child's DLA care component/PIP daily living component starts again.

If your child has stopped being treated as part of your household, tell the local authority as soon as s/he comes home and ask it to include the appropriate amounts in your HB/CTR applicable amount and to apply the correct 'size criteria'.

If you have lost entitlement to HB because of reduced amounts in your applicable amount or for some other reason and you are under pension age, you will usually have to claim UC instead.

Non-means-tested benefits

Disability living allowance and personal independence payment

If payment of DLA care component or PIP daily living component has stopped because your child was in a care home, it should be reinstated when s/he comes home. You do not have to reclaim DLA/PIP, but you must tell the Disability Service Centre (see Appendix 1) that your child has come home.

Carer's allowance

If your CA has stopped, either because your child's DLA care component/PIP daily living component has stopped being paid, or because you have had a break from caring, you have to reclaim CA once you are entitled again (see Chapter 2).

Carer element, carer premium and carer addition

Once you are entitled to CA again, your carer element, carer premium or carer addition in any means-tested benefit should also be reinstated. Make sure you tell the DWP and/or local authority when you become entitled to CA again.

Tax credits

If your child tax credit has been affected because you lost the disabled child and/or severely disabled child element, tell HMRC as soon as your child comes home and her/his DLA care component/PIP daily living component is reinstated.

Chapter 4: Disabled children in care homes
Notes

1. Benefits and tax credits for children in care homes
1   s143(3) SSCBA 1992; regs 9 and 10(1) CB Regs
2   Reg 10(2) CB Regs
3   s143(4) SSCBA 1992
4   s143(2) SSCBA 1992, 12 weeks' 'care home' absence plus eight weeks' 'normal' absence
5   Regs 4 and 4A(1)(a) UC Regs
6   Reg 24 UC Regs
7   Sch 4 Part 3 para 11(2)(a) UC Regs
8   Regs 29 and 30 UC Regs
9   Reg 22 UC Regs
10 Reg 33 UC Regs
11 Regs 79 and 83 UC Regs
12 Reg 4(7) UC Regs
13 Reg 24(2) UC Regs
14 Reg 22 UC Regs
15 Regs 29 and 30 UC Regs
16 Regs 79 and 83 UC Regs
17 **IS** Reg 16(1) and (5)(b) IS Regs
    JSA Reg 78(1) and 5(c) JSA Regs
18 **IS** Reg 16(5)(b) IS Regs
    JSA Reg 78(5)(c) JSA Regs
19 para 22074 DMG
20 para 22075 DMG
21 **IS** Sch 2 para 14ZA(3) IS Regs
    JSA Sch 1 para 17(3) JSA Regs
22 Sch 1B para 5 IS Regs
23 **IS** Sch 2 para 14ZA(3) IS Regs
    JSA Sch 1 para 17(3) JSA Regs
24 **IS** Sch 2 para 14 IS Regs, pre-amendment by SI 2003/455
    JSA Sch 1 para 16 JSA Regs, pre-amendment by SI 2003/455
25 **IS** Sch 2 para 13A IS Regs, pre-amendment by SI 2003/455
    JSA Sch 1 para 15A JSA Regs, pre-amendment by SI 2003/455
26 **IS** Reg 16(2) IS Regs
    JSA Reg 78(2) JSA Regs
27 **IS** Reg 16(2) IS Regs
    JSA Reg 78(2) JSA Regs
28 s17(6) and 25(8) C(S)A 1995
29 **IS** Reg 16(5)(c) IS Regs
    JSA Reg 78(4)(f) JSA Regs
30 Sch 4 para 8(2) ESA Regs
31 Sch 1 para 4(3) SPC Regs
32 Sch IIA para 6 SPC Regs
33 Sch IIA para 9 SPC Regs
34 Sch IIA para 4 SPC Regs
35 As defined in s17(6) C(S)A 1995
36 ss17(6) and 25(8) C(S)A 1995; Scottish government guidance, *Children Looked After by Local Authorities: the legal framework*, p69
37 **HB** Reg 21(5) HB Regs; reg 21(5) HB(SPC) Regs
    CTR Reg 11(4) CTR(S) Regs; reg 11(4) CTR(SPC)(S) Regs
38 **HB** Reg 21(4)(a) HB Regs; reg 21(4)(a) HB(SPC) Regs
    CTR Reg 11(3)(a) CTR(S) Regs; reg 11(3)(a) CTR(SPC)(S) Regs
39 Regs 13D and 21(1) and (2) HB Regs; regs 13D and 21(1) and (2) HB(SPC) Regs
40 **HB** Reg B13 HB Regs
    CTR Sch 1 para 14(4) CTR(S) Regs; Sch 1 para 10(2) CTR(SPC)(S) Regs
41 Regs B13 and 13D HB Regs define 'occupier' as a person whom the local authority is satisfied occupies the claimant's dwelling as her/his home
42 Regs 75A and 75F HB Regs
43 **HB** Reg 21(1) and (2) HB Regs; reg 21(1) and (2) HB(SPC) Regs
    CTR Reg 11(1) CTR(S) Regs; reg 11(1) CTR(SPC)(S) Regs
44 **HB** Sch 3 para 17(2) HB Regs; Sch 3 para 9(2) HB(SPC) Regs
    CTR Sch1 para 14(2) CTR(S) Regs; Sch 1 para 10(2) CTR(SPC)(S) Regs
45 **HB** Sch 3 para 16 HB Regs; Sch 3 para 8 HB(SPC) Regs
    CTR Sch 1 para 13 CTR(S) Regs; Sch 1 para 9 CTR(SPC)(S) Regs
46 **HB** Sch 3 para 15 HB Regs; Sch 3 para 7 HB (SPC) Regs
    CTR Sch 1 para 12 CTR(S) Regs; Sch 1 para 8 CTR(SPC)(S) Regs
47 Reg 21(2)(b) HB Regs; reg 21(2)(b) HB(SPC) Regs
48 Reg 13D HB Regs; reg 13D HB(SPC) Regs
49 Reg B13 HB Regs

Chapter 4: Disabled children in care homes
Notes

50 Regs B13(5) and 13D(12) HB Regs define 'occupier' as a person whom the relevant authority is satisfied occupies the claimant's dwelling as her/his home
51 Reg 11(1) CTR(S) Regs; reg 11(1) CTR(SPC)(S) Regs
52 Regs 75A and 75F HB Regs
53 Regs 9 and 10 SS(DLA) Regs; regs 28 and 30 SS(PIP) Regs
54 Reg 9(4) and (5) SS(DLA) Regs; reg 28(3) and (4) SS(PIP) Regs
55 Reg 10(5) SS(DLA) Regs; reg 32(4) SS(PIP) Regs
56 Reg 4(2) SS(ICA) Regs
57 s122 SSCBA 1992
58 CG/006/1990; para 60041 DMG
59 Regs 29 and 30 UC Regs
60 **IS** Sch 2 para 14ZA IS Regs
 JSA Sch 1 para 17(3) JSA Regs
 ESA Sch 4 para 8(4) ESA Regs
 PC Sch 1 para 4 SPC Regs
 HB Sch 3 para 17(2) HB Regs; Sch 3 para 9(2) HB(SPC) Regs
 CTR Sch 1 para 14(4) CTR(S) Regs; Sch 1 para 10(2) CTR(SPC)(S) Regs
61 Reg 3 r4.2 CTC Regs
62 Reg 8 CTC Regs
63 SWFG para 6.5

2. More than one stay in a care home
64 Reg 10(2) CB Regs; reg 10(5)(a) SS(DLA) Regs; reg 32(4) SS(PIP) Regs
65 Reg 9(7) SS(DLA) Regs; reg 32(2) SS(PIP) Regs

Chapter 5

Disabled children at residential school

This chapter covers:
1. Child benefit and guardian's allowance (below)
2. Means-tested benefits (below)
3. Non-means-tested benefits (p89)
4. Tax credits (p92)
5. Help visiting your child (p93)

This chapter explains what happens to benefits and tax credits if your child lives away from home in a residential school because s/he has a disability and the cost is met by public funds. It explains whether or not benefits and tax credits are paid while your child is away from home and what happens when s/he comes home for a temporary period – eg, at the weekends or holidays.

In this chapter, the term 'away at school' is used for when your child is staying at a residential school because of her/his disability.

1. Child benefit and guardian's allowance

When your child is away at school, your child benefit – and guardian's allowance if you get it – continues to be paid.[1]

2. Means-tested benefits

How your benefit is affected can depend on whether or not your child counts as 'looked after' by the local authority.[2] Ask the social work department of your local authority if you are not sure whether your child is looked after.

Universal credit

If your child is not looked after by the local authority

If your child does not count as 'looked after' by the local authority, s/he should still be included in your universal credit (UC) claim if her/his absence from home is temporary. However, s/he is no longer included in the claim if the stay away from home is expected to last for more than six months, or has lasted for more than six months.[3] There is no rule 'linking' two or more periods of absence from home and, therefore, arguably, even a brief stay at home followed by a return to residential school could start a new temporary period of absence. DWP guidance suggests that a child who is away at school during term-time, but who returns home during holidays, would still be included in your UC claim.[4] While the child is still included in your UC claim, you continue to get the child element and any disabled child element, even if disability living allowance (DLA) care component or personal independence payment (PIP) daily living component has stopped being paid (see p89).[5] Your work allowance (see p48) is calculated taking into account that you have a dependent child.[6] If your UC includes the carer element, it stops when you no longer have 'regular and substantial' caring responsibilities for your child (see p47), including if your child's DLA care component or PIP daily living component has stopped being paid.[7] If you receive help with childcare costs in your UC, this may change if you are no longer paying for childcare because your child is away at school.

Note: if the only reason you are exempt from the benefit cap (see p2) is because a child for whom you are responsible is entitled to DLA (or PIP), this exemption ends if the child no longer counts as part of the household.[8]

If your child is looked after by the local authority

If your child is away at school and counts as 'looked after' by the local authority, s/he is no longer included in your UC claim unless it is a 'planned short break' (respite).[9] This means that any child element you receive for her/him stops.[10] If you are in rented accommodation, the housing costs element is calculated as if the child is still living with you for the first six months of absence from home.[11] If your UC includes the carer element, it stops when you no longer have 'regular and substantial' caring responsibilities for your child (see p47), including if your child's DLA care component or PIP daily living component has stopped being paid.[12] If the child element has stopped and you have no other dependent children, you will not get a work allowance (see p48) unless you or your partner have limited capability for work.[13] Any help with childcare costs for the child in your UC stops.[14] The work-related requirements which apply to you may also change (see p49).

Note: if the only reason you are exempt from the benefit cap (see p2) is because a child for whom you are responsible is entitled to DLA (or PIP), this exemption ends if the child no longer counts as part of your household.[15]

Income support and income-based jobseeker's allowance

If your child is not looked after by the local authority

If your child is not looked after by the local authority and her/his absence is treated as temporary, s/he continues to be part of your household for income support (IS)/income-based jobseeker's allowance (JSA).[16] **'Temporary'** means that the absence is unlikely to exceed 52 weeks or, in exceptional circumstances, unlikely to substantially exceed 52 weeks. See below if the absence is not temporary.

However, even if the absence is temporary, the amount of IS/income-based JSA may change because of the impact on premiums (part of your 'applicable amount' – see p28).

If your IS/income-based JSA does not include amounts for children (ie, you get child tax credit (CTC) instead), the amount you get may be affected if you get a carer premium. If you are claiming IS as a carer, you are no longer able to do so from eight weeks after your carer's allowance (CA) stops (see p91).

If your IS/income-based JSA still includes amounts for children (ie, you have been getting IS/JSA since before April 2004 and have not claimed CTC), the amount may change because of the impact on premiums (carer premium, disabled child premium and enhanced disability premium).

The **carer premium** stops eight weeks after your CA stops (see p91).[17]

If you get CA again (see p90), the carer premium should start again and continue while you are getting CA and for eight weeks after it stops again.

If your child is away at school, the **disabled child premium** stops when the child's DLA care component or PIP daily living component stops (see p89), unless there is another basis for getting it – ie, if your child is still getting DLA or PIP mobility component or is severely sight impaired or blind.[18] The **enhanced disability premium** stops when the DLA care component or PIP daily living component stops.[19]

If your child's DLA/PIP starts being paid again (eg, when s/he comes home for a weekend or a holiday – see p89), the disability and enhanced disability premium should be paid for the days you are entitled to them.[20]

If the absence is not temporary

If the absence is not temporary, your child does not count as part of your household for IS/income-based JSA. If you still receive amounts for the child in your IS/income-based JSA, these stop.

If you are a lone parent and do not have another dependent child aged under five living with you, you can no longer claim IS as a lone parent.

If your child is looked after by the local authority

How your IS/income-based JSA is affected depends on whether or not you still get amounts in your IS/income-based JSA for your child. Normally, your IS/income-

based JSA does not include amounts for children – you get CTC instead. In this case, if your child goes to a residential school, your IS/JSA may be affected in two situations.
- If you get a carer premium, it stops eight weeks after your CA stops (see p90). If you are getting IS because you are a carer, from eight weeks after your CA stops you can no longer claim IS on that basis.
- If you are a lone parent and do not have another dependent child aged under five living with you, as soon as your child is away at school, you can no longer claim IS as a lone parent.

If your IS/income-based JSA does still include amounts for children (ie, you have been getting IS/JSA since before 6 April 2004 and have not claimed CTC – see p30), your entitlement to the personal allowance for the child and any disability or enhanced disability premium stops as soon as your child is away at school if s/he counts as 'looked-after'.[21] If you do not have another dependent child at home, your family premium also stops. Any carer premium, or your continued eligibility for IS as a carer or lone parent, is affected in the same way as described above (see p86).

Income-related employment and support allowance

There are no amounts in employment and support allowance (ESA) for dependent children and, therefore, your ESA is not normally affected if your child is away at school. The exception is if you are entitled to CA and this stops. The **carer premium** (part of your income-related ESA applicable amount) stops eight weeks after your entitlement to CA ends.[22]

If you get CA again (see p90), the carer premium should start again and continue while you are getting CA, and for eight weeks after it stops again.

Pension credit

If you are entitled to CA and this stops, the carer addition (part of your pension credit (PC)) stops eight weeks after your entitlement to CA stops (see p90).[23] Some PC claimants who are responsible for a child or qualifying young person get an additional amount for her/him in their PC (instead of getting CTC). If you get a PC additional amount for a child and s/he goes to residential school, and the child does not count as looked after by the local authority, the additional amount continues during a temporary period away at school which is unlikely to last for more than 52 weeks or, in exceptional circumstances, unlikely to last for substantially more than 52 weeks.[24] The higher amounts that may be paid because your child has a disability (see p35) continue even if DLA care component or PIP daily living component for your child has stopped being paid.[25] If your child is away at school and counts as looked after by the local authority you no longer get the PC additional amount unless it is a 'planned short break' (respite).[26]

Chapter 5: Disabled children at residential school
2. Means-tested benefits

Housing benefit and council tax reduction

If your child is not looked after by the local authority

If your child is not looked after by the local authority and the absence is temporary, s/he continues to be treated as part of your household for housing benefit (HB)/council tax reduction (CTR).[27] For HB, **'temporary'** means that the absence is unlikely to exceed 52 weeks or, in exceptional circumstances, unlikely to substantially exceed 52 weeks. For CTR, there is no '52 week' rule. This gives the local authority more flexibility with CTR than with HB. However, even if your child is still treated as part of your household, the amount of HB/CTR may change because of the impact on premiums (part of your 'applicable amount' – see p25) or, if you are getting UC and CTR, your applicable amount changes. See below if the absence is not temporary.

The **carer premium** stops eight weeks after your CA stops (see p90).[28]

If you get CA again (see p90), the carer premium should start again and continue while you are getting CA, and for eight weeks after it stops again.

If your child is away at school, the **disabled child premium** stops when the child's DLA care component or PIP daily living component stops (see p89), unless there is another basis for getting it – ie, your child is still getting DLA/PIP mobility component, or is severely sight impaired or blind.[29] The **enhanced disability premium** stops when the DLA care component or PIP daily living component stops.[30]

If you are on IS, income-based JSA, income-related ESA or the guarantee credit of PC, changes to the premiums in your applicable amount do not affect the amount of HB/CTR you get, as you are 'passported' to maximum HB/CTR.

If the absence is not temporary

If the absence is not temporary, the child does not count as part of your household for HB/CTR purposes and the personal allowance and premiums for her/him stop. If you do not have any other children still at home, the family premium, if you are receiving it, also stops.

If you are on IS, income-based JSA, income-related ESA or the guarantee credit of PC, changes to the personal allowance and premiums in your applicable amount do not affect the amount of HB/CTR you get, as you are 'passported' to maximum HB/CTR. However, your HB may still be reduced because of the impact on the number of bedrooms you are deemed to require (the 'size criteria'). This means that if your HB is calculated using the local housing allowance rules (see p24), it may be affected if the child no longer counts as occupying the home and as a result you need fewer bedrooms.[31]

If you are under pension age and living in the social rented sector and your child no longer counts as occupying the home, you may be deemed to need fewer bedrooms and be subject to the 'under-occupation penalty' (bedroom tax).[32]

If your child is looked after by the local authority

If your child is looked after by the local authority, the personal allowance and premiums for her/him stop as soon as s/he is away at school.[33] If you do not have any other children still at home the family premium, if you are receiving it, also stops.

If your child comes home for some of the time (eg, at weekends), the personal allowance and premiums (if appropriate) can be included again in your HB/CTR applicable amount for the whole of the benefit week if it is 'reasonable to do so', taking into account the nature and frequency of the child's visits.[34]

If you are on IS, income-based JSA, income-related ESA or the guarantee credit of PC, changes to the personal allowance and premiums in your applicable amount do not affect the amount of HB/CTR you get, as you are 'passported' to maximum HB/CTR. However, your HB may still be reduced because of the number of bedrooms you are deemed to require (the 'size criteria'). This means that if your HB is calculated using the local housing allowance rules (see p24), it may be affected if the child no longer counts as occupying the home and as a result you need fewer bedrooms.[35] If you are under pension age and living in the social rented sector and your child no longer counts as occupying the home, you may be deemed to need fewer bedrooms and be subject to the 'under-occupation penalty' (bedroom tax).[36] It may be possible to argue that, even though the child is not part of your 'household' for HB/CTR, s/he should still count as an 'occupier' and s/he should still be included in the size criteria – eg, if s/he is not likely to be away indefinitely.[37] Seek advice if you are in this situation.

Note: if the only reason you are exempt from the benefit cap (see p2) is because a child for whom you are responsible is entitled to DLA (or PIP), this exemption ends if the child no longer counts as part of your household (either because s/he counts as 'looked after' or because s/he has been absent for more than 52 weeks).[38]

3. Non-means-tested benefits

Disability living allowance and personal independence payment

If your child is away at school and the local authority is paying any of the costs of the accommodation, board or personal care, the disability living allowance (DLA) care component or personal independence payment (PIP) daily living component for the child stops after four weeks.[39] The mobility component of DLA/PIP is not affected and continues to be paid.

Two or more periods away at school separated by 28 days or less count as the same period.[40] This means that once the DLA care component/PIP daily living component has stopped, if your child comes home for a period of 28 days or less, the DLA care component/PIP daily living component is payable while s/he is at home (see below), but it stops again as soon as s/he goes back to school.

The day on which your child goes away to school and the day s/he comes home do not count as days away at school.[41]

If your child comes home temporarily

Once the DLA care component/PIP daily living component has stopped, it should be paid for any day your child spends at home, including the day s/he comes home and the day s/he leaves to go back to school. It is important to tell the Disability Service Centre (see Appendix 1) when your child goes away to school and about any days spent at home. The amount of DLA care component/PIP daily living component you get for days your child spends at home is worked out by using a daily rate of the care/daily living component (one-seventh of the weekly amount).[42]

Example
Sanjit is aged 10 and starts attending a residential school because of his disability. He is entitled to the DLA mobility component at the higher rate and the care component at the highest rate. His first day at his new school is 2 September 2019. Every few weeks he comes home for a long weekend. He comes home on Thursday afternoon and returns to school on Tuesday morning. The dates of his first weekend at home are Thursday 3 October 2019 to Tuesday 8 October 2019. Sanjit's DLA remains in payment for the first 28 days away at school. After that, the mobility component remains in payment, but the care component stops. This means that the last day for which the care component is payable is 30 September 2019. When Sanjit comes home for the weekend, the care component is payable for six days (Thursday 3 October to Tuesday 8 October).

Carer's allowance

If you are getting carer's allowance (CA) for caring for your child, there are two main reasons why your entitlement may be affected if s/he is away at school.
- You cannot get CA unless the person for whom you care is getting DLA care component at the middle or highest rate or PIP daily living component. If your child has been away at school for four weeks or more, the care component/daily living component stops. This means your CA entitlement stops.
- In order to qualify for CA, you have to be caring for the disabled person for at least 35 hours a week. If your child is away at school, you are unlikely to satisfy this rule. However, you can have some time off from caring and still be entitled to CA. See below for how this rule works.

Time off from caring

You can still be entitled to CA during temporary breaks from caring. You can have a break from caring of up to four weeks in any period of 26 weeks (or a break of up to 12 weeks if either you or the person for whom you care is having treatment in a hospital or 'similar institution' for at least eight of the 12 weeks).[43] If your child is away at school, you can probably make use of this rule to keep your CA for the first four weeks s/he is away (unless you have already had a break in caring within the last 26 weeks, or your child's care component stops before the end of the four-week period).

If your child comes home temporarily

DLA care component/PIP daily living component is payable for the days your child spends at home (see p89). You may also be able to get CA for periods your child spends at home, provided you can show that you spend at least 35 hours a week caring for her/him. A 'week' for CA runs from Sunday to Saturday.[44] The time you spend caring does not have to be spread across seven days, provided it amounts to 35 hours in the period from Sunday to the following Saturday.

Time spent preparing for your child's time at home and cleaning after s/he has gone can count as time spent caring for her/him – eg, any shopping or cooking that relates solely to the visit, and cleaning up afterwards, can count as caring.[45]

Example

Sanjit is aged 10 and is at a residential school because of his disability. He is entitled to DLA mobility component at the higher rate and care component at the highest rate. Every few weeks he comes home for a long weekend. He comes home on Thursday afternoon and returns to school on Tuesday morning. When Sanjit comes home for the weekend, the care component is payable for six days (Thursday to Tuesday – see the example on p89). Sanjit's mother claims CA for the time he is at home. She spends four hours preparing for his arrival on the Thursday and three hours cleaning up after he goes away on the Tuesday. While Sanjit is at home, the care his mother provides is very intensive and includes being up for long periods during the night.

Provided Sanjit's mother can show she spends at least 35 hours caring for him between Thursday afternoon and Saturday at midnight (including the four hours preparing for his arrival), and again between Saturday midnight and Tuesday (including the three hours cleaning up), she should get CA for two weeks.

Carer element, carer premium or carer addition

If you get universal credit (UC), the carer element stops when you no longer have 'regular and substantial' caring responsibilities for your child (see p47). If your entitlement to CA stops, the carer premium or carer addition in your income support, income-based jobseeker's allowance, income-related employment and support allowance, pension credit or housing benefit stops eight weeks after your entitlement to CA stops. This rule applies to council tax reduction unless you are also getting UC.[46]

Chapter 5: Disabled children at residential school
4. Tax credits

If you get CA again, the carer premium/addition/element should start again and continue while you are getting CA and for eight weeks after it stops again, unless you are on UC in which case you get the carer element while you have 'regular and substantial' caring reponsibilities for your child (see p47).

When your CA stops (and starts again), let the Department for Work and Pensions and/or local authority know immediately to avoid overpayments and underpayments.

If you have lost entitlement to a benefit because the carer premium or carer addition has stopped being included in your applicable amount, you will usually have to claim UC instead if you were previously on a different means-tested benefit.

See Chapter 1 for more information about the carer element/premium/addition.

4. Tax credits

Child tax credit (CTC) remains payable for a child, provided s/he is treated as 'normally living with' you.[47] HM Revenue and Customs (HMRC) guidance says this means that the child 'regularly, usually, typically' lives with you and that this allows for temporary or occasional absences.[48]

In addition, the tax credit rules allow your child to be treated as 'normally living with you' while s/he is in residential accommodation provided:[49]
- s/he is there solely because of her/his disability, or on the grounds that her/his health would be significantly impaired or further impaired were s/he not in that accommodation; *and*
- you were treated as responsible for her/him for tax credit purposes before s/he went into that accommodation.

This means you should keep receiving CTC for your child even though s/he is away at school. Your child also continues to count as a dependent child for working tax credit (WTC) purposes.

The amount of tax credits

If your child's disability living allowance (DLA) care component or personal independence payment (PIP) daily living component has stopped (see p89), this will affect the disability and severe disability elements as follows.[50]
- The disabled child element stops being included in your CTC calculation from the date the DLA care component/PIP daily living component stops (see p89), unless there is another basis for getting it – ie, your child is still getting DLA mobility component, PIP mobility component or is severely sight impaired or blind.

- The severely disabled child element stops being included in your CTC calculation from the date the DLA care component/PIP daily living component stops (see p89).

If your child's DLA care component/PIP daily living component starts being paid again (eg, because s/he comes home for a weekend or a holiday – see p89), the disabled child element/severely disabled child element should be included in your CTC for the days DLA is paid.

If you are getting help with childcare costs in your WTC, this may change when your child is away at school. If your childcare costs stop or reduce by £10 or more over a period of four weeks, you must let HMRC know.

Make sure you report changes to HMRC to avoid underpayments and overpayments.

5. Help visiting your child

If you are on a low income, you may be able to get help from the Scottish Welfare Fund (see p38) with the cost of visiting your child.[51]

If you are eligible, it may be possible to get a community care grant or crisis grant to help with travel expenses to visit your child at school. The amount awarded usually covers the cost of standard public transport. If public transport is not available or suitable, the cost of petrol or a taxi may be given. A travel voucher may be issued.

If you are on universal credit, income support, income-based jobseeker's allowance, income-related employment and support allowance or pension credit, it should be accepted that you are on a low income, but you do not need to be on one of these benefits to get help from the Scottish Welfare Fund.

Chapter 5: Disabled children at residential school
Notes

1. **Child benefit and guardian's allowance**
   1. ss77(5) and 143(3)(a) and (c) SSCBA 1992; regs 9 and 10 CB Regs. Any day your child is away from home solely for the purpose of receiving education is disregarded. Any time your child is away from home in residential accommodation solely because of her/his disability or to prevent deterioration in her/his health is disregarded for up to 84 days and beyond 84 days provided you regularly incur expenditure on the child.

2. **Means-tested benefits**
   2. As defined by s17(6) C(S)A 1995
   3. Reg 4(7) UC Regs
   4. para F1073 ADM
   5. Reg 24 UC Regs
   6. Reg 22 UC Regs
   7. Regs 29 and 30 UC Regs
   8. Regs 79 and 83 UC Regs
   9. Reg 4 and 4A UC Regs
   10. Reg 24 UC Regs
   11. Sch 4 part 3 para 11(2) UC Regs
   12. Regs 29 and 30 UC Regs
   13. Reg 22 UC Regs
   14. Reg 33 UC Regs
   15. Regs 79 and 83 UC Regs
   16. **IS** Reg 16(1) and (2) IS Regs
       JSA Reg 78(1) and (2) JSA Regs
   17. **IS** Sch 2 para 14ZA(2) and (4) IS Regs
       JSA Sch 1 para 17 (3) JSA Regs
   18. **IS** Sch 2 para 14, pre-amendment by SI 2003/455
       JSA sch 1para 16, pre-amendment by SI 2003/455
   19. **IS** Sch 2 para 13A, pre-amendment by SI 2003/455
       JSA Sch 1 para 15A, pre-amendment by SI 2003/455
   20. Sch 3A para 3 SS&CS(DA) Regs
   21. Reg 16(5)(c) IS Regs. Note that in Scotland, the regulations have to be read in their pre-SI 1992 No.468 amendment form.
   22. Sch 4 para 8(2) ESA Regs
   23. Sch 1 para 4(3) SPC Regs
   24. Sch 2A para 6 SPC Regs
   25. Sch 2A para 9 SPC Regs
   26. Sch 2A para 4 SPC Regs
   27. **HB** Reg 21(1) and (2) HB Regs; reg 21(1) and (2) HB(SPC) Regs
       CTR Reg 11(1) CTR(S) Regs; reg 11(1) CTR(SPC)(S) Regs
   28. **HB** Sch 3 para 17(2) HB Regs; Sch 3 para 9(2) HB(SPC) Regs
       CTR Sch 1 para 14(4) CTR(S) Regs; Sch 1 para 10(2) CTR(SPC)(S) Regs
   29. **HB** Sch 3 para 16 HB Regs; Sch 3 para 8 HB(SPC) Regs **CTR** Sch 1 para 13 CTR(S) Regs; Sch 1 para 9 CTR(SPC)(S) Regs
   30. **HB** Sch 3 para 15 HB Regs; Sch 3 para 7 HB (SPC) Regs
       CTR Sch 1 para 12 CTR(S) Regs; Sch 1 para 8 CTR(SPC)(S) Regs
   31. Reg 13D HB Regs
   32. Reg B13 HB Regs
   33. **HB** Reg 21(4)(a) HB Regs; reg 21(4)(a) HB(SPC) Regs
       CTR Reg 11(3)(a) CTR(S) Regs; reg 11(3)(a) CTR(SPC)(S) Regs
   34. **HB** Reg 21(5) HB Regs; reg 21(5) HB(SPC) Regs
       CTR Reg 11(4) CTR(S) Regs; reg 11(4) CTR(SPC)(S) Regs
   35. Reg 13D HB Regs; reg 13D HB(SPC) Regs
   36. Reg B13 HB Regs
   37. Regs B13(5) and 13D(12) HB Regs define 'occupier' as a person whom the relevant authority is satisfied occupies the claimant's dwelling as her/his home
   38. Regs 75A and 75F HB Regs

3. **Non-means-tested benefits**
   39. Regs 9 and 10 SS(DLA) Regs; regs 28 and 30 SS(PIP) Regs
   40. Reg 10(5) SS(DLA) Regs; reg 32(4) SS(PIP) Regs
   41. Reg 9(7) SS(DLA) Regs; reg 32(2) SS(PIP) Regs
   42. Reg 25 SS(C&P) Regs; reg 50(1) UC,PIP,JSA&ESA(C&P) Regs
   43. Reg 4(2) SS(ICA) Regs
   44. s122 SSCBA 1992
   45. CG/006/1990; para 60041 DMG

46 **IS** Sch 2 para 14ZA(3) IS Regs
JSA Sch 1 para 17(3) JSA Regs
ESA Sch 4 para 8(2) ESA Regs
PC Sch 1 Part II para 4(3) SPC Regs
HB Sch 3 para 17(2) HB Regs; Sch 3 para 9(2) HB(SPC) Regs
CTR Sch 1 para 14(2) CTR(S) Regs; Sch 1 para 10(2) CTR(SPC)(S) Regs

4. Tax credits
47 Reg 3 CTC Regs
48 para 02202 TCTM
49 Reg 3 r4.2 CTC Regs
50 Reg 8 CTC Regs

5. Help visiting your child
51 SWFG para 6.5

Chapter 6
Children who are 'looked after and accommodated'

This chapter covers:
1. Benefits and tax credits for children who are 'looked after and accommodated' (below)
2. When your child comes home (p102)

Your benefit and tax credit entitlement changes if your child is no longer living with you because s/he is 'looked after and accommodated' under the Children (Scotland) Act 1995 or the Children's Hearings (Scotland) Act 2011 – eg, s/he goes to stay in a residential unit or secure accommodation, or s/he has been placed with foster carers. You may have agreed to this or it may be because of a legal order. In this chapter, we use the term 'looked after and accommodated' to describe this situation. Sometimes this may be referred to as 'looked after away from home'.

The information in this chapter applies *unless* the residential accommodation has been provided solely:
- because of the child's disability; *or*
- because the child's health would be significantly impaired if the accommodation were not provided.

If this is the case, see Chapter 4 instead.

1. Benefits and tax credits for children who are 'looked after and accommodated'

Child benefit

Your entitlement to child benefit stops if your child has been looked after and accommodated for at least one day a week for eight consecutive weeks.[1] A 'day' for this purpose means midnight to midnight[2] and a 'week' means a period of seven days starting on a Monday.[3]

Chapter 6: Children who are 'looked after and accommodated'
1. Benefits and tax credits for children who are 'looked after and accommodated'

You have a duty to notify the Child Benefit Office of any changes in your circumstances, including if your child has been looked after and accommodated for eight weeks. Contact the Child Benefit Office (see Appendix 1) as soon as you know your child is likely to be looked after and accommodated for eight weeks or more. HM Revenue and Customs (HMRC) provides a form (CH193) for local authorities to use to notify the Child Benefit Office if a child has started to be looked after by them. This can be completed online at www.gov.uk/government/publications/child-benefit-local-authority-or-care-trust-notification-ch193.

However, you should not rely on the local authority advising the Child Benefit Office and, to avoid overpayment, make sure you also tell the Child Benefit Office about any change.

Do not assume that by telling one section of the Department for Work and Pensions (DWP) or HMRC that all the other sections will get the same information. You need to tell the Child Benefit Office even if you have already told the Tax Credit Office, DWP or local authority.

Means-tested benefits

Universal credit

If your child is looked after and accommodated, s/he is no longer included in your universal credit (UC) claim.[4] This means that any child element you receive stops.[5] If you are in rented accommodation, the housing costs element is calculated as if the child is still living with you for the first six months of absence from home.[6] If your child is looked after and accommodated, s/he does not count as a dependent child for the purpose of calculating your work allowance (see p48). If you have been getting help with childcare costs for the child, this stops. The changes to your UC take effect from the start of the assessment period in which they happen. The 'assessment period' is a period of one month.

Example
Jill is on UC. She claimed on 15 May 2019. This means that her first assessment period for UC is 15 May 2019 to 14 June 2019 and every assessment period after that follows the same dates (15th of the month to 14th of the following month). Her child becomes looked after and accommodated on 30 September 2019. All the changes that happen as a result of that take effect from the start of the assessment period in which that date falls – ie, 15 September 2019 to 14 October 2019. For example, the child element will stop being included in her UC from 15 September 2019.

Your 'claimant commitment' (see p49), which sets out what you have to do to keep receiving your full UC, might change.

Note: if the only reason you are exempt from the benefit cap (see p2) is because a child for whom you are responsible is entitled to disability living allowance

Chapter 6: Children who are 'looked after and accommodated'
1. Benefits and tax credits for children who are 'looked after and accommodated'

(DLA) (or personal independence payment – PIP), this exemption ends if the child no longer counts as part of your household.[7]

Income support and jobseeker's allowance

If you do not get amounts for your child

If your income support (IS) or income-based jobseeker's allowance (JSA) does not include amounts for your child, the amount of these benefits is not normally affected when your child becomes looked after and accommodated (but see below for other implications).

If, as a result of your child being looked after and accommodated, you are no longer caring for a child aged under five, you are not able to claim IS as a lone parent. This is because the child no longer counts as a member of your household.[8] This takes effect as soon as your child is looked after and accommodated.

If you are getting carer's allowance (CA) for your disabled child and the child is looked after and accommodated, any carer premium in your IS/income-based JSA may be affected or the basis for your IS claim might be affected (see p101).

Tell the DWP immediately if your child is looked after and accommodated.

If you still get amounts for your child

Your IS or income-based JSA might still include amounts for your child (personal allowances and premiums). This will only be the case if you have been getting IS/income-based JSA including amounts for a child since before 6 April 2004 and have not claimed child tax credit (CTC). Your entitlement to the personal allowance for that child and any disability or enhanced disability premium relating to that child stops as soon as your child is looked after and accommodated.[9] If you then have no children included in your IS/income-based JSA claim, the family premium also stops. The child benefit for that child, which you continue to get for eight weeks, does not count as income during that period.[10]

If you are getting CA for your disabled child and the child is looked after and accommodated, any carer premium in your IS/income-based JSA may be affected (see p101).

Tell the DWP immediately if your child is looked after and accommodated.

Income-related employment and support allowance

Income-related employment and support allowance (ESA) does not include any amounts for children and is not normally affected when your child is looked after and accommodated. If, however, you are getting CA for a disabled child and the child is looked after and accommodated, any carer premium in your income-related ESA may be affected (see p101).

Chapter 6: Children who are 'looked after and accommodated'
1. Benefits and tax credits for children who are 'looked after and accommodated'

Pension credit

If you are entitled to CA and this stops, the carer addition (part of pension credit – PC) may be affected (see p101). Some PC claimants who are responsible for a child/qualifying young person get an additonal amount for her/him in their PC (instead of CTC). If you get a PC additional amount for a child and s/he becomes looked after and accommodated, you will no longer get the PC additional amount unless it is a 'planned short break' (respite).[11]

Housing benefit and council tax reduction

If your child becomes looked after and accommodated, your applicable amount (the figure used to calculate how much housing benefit (HB)/council tax reduction (CTR) you get) no longer includes amounts (personal allowance and premiums) for the child.[12] See Chapter 1 for more about how HB/CTR is calculated. Your entitlement to the allowance and premiums stops as soon as your child is looked after and accommodated.

If you are on IS, income-based JSA, income-related ESA or the guarantee credit of PC, changes to the personal allowance and premiums in your applicable amount do not affect the amount of HB/CTR you get, as you are 'passported' to maximum HB/CTR. However, your HB may still be reduced because of the number of bedrooms you are deemed to require (the 'size criteria'). This means that if your HB is calculated using the local housing allowance rules (see p24), it may be affected if the child no longer counts as occupying the home and as a result you need fewer bedrooms.[13] If you are under pension age and living in the social rented sector and your child no longer counts as occupying the home, you may be deemed to need fewer bedrooms and be subject to the 'under-occupation penalty' (bedroom tax).[14] It may be possible to argue that, even though the child is not part of your 'household' for HB/CTR, s/he should still count as an 'occupier' and still be included in the size criteria – eg, if s/he is not likely to be away indefinitely.[15] Seek further advice if you are in this situation.

Your income may reduce (eg, because CTC has stopped) and this also affects the amount of HB/CTR to which you are entitled, unless you are already getting the maximum amount of HB/CTR.

If you are struggling to pay your rent because of changes to your HB entitlement, apply for a discretionary housing payment (see p26).

Tell the HB/CTR office immediately if your child is looked after and accommodated. Also inform the local authority when your CTC stops. This is because CTC counts as income for HB/CTR, so if you are no longer getting it, you may be entitled to more HB/CTR.

Note: if the only reason you are exempt from the benefit cap (see p2) is because a child for whom you are responsible is entitled to DLA (or PIP), this exemption ends if the child no longer counts as part of your household.[16]

Chapter 6: Children who are 'looked after and accommodated'
1. Benefits and tax credits for children who are 'looked after and accommodated'

Non-means-tested benefits

Disability living allowance and personal independence payment

If your child is entitled to DLA or PIP, it may be affected if s/he is looked after and accommodated. The rules are different depending on whether s/he is staying with foster carers or in residential accommodation – eg, a residential unit. If your child's DLA care component/PIP daily living component stops, and/or you are no longer caring for your child, any CA you get may be affected (see p101).

Foster care

DLA (both care and mobility components)/PIP (both daily living and mobility components) continues to be paid while your child is living with foster carers. However, the person to whom the benefit is paid may change. It is likely that you (or your partner) are the **'appointee'** for your child's DLA. This means that you are the person who receives payment. If your child is no longer living with you, this will probably change. Your child's foster carer or the local authority may become the appointee.[17]

Appointeeship for DLA should stop if your child is looked after and accommodated, unless the arrangement is expected to last for less than 12 weeks.[18] Tell the Disability Service Centre (see Appendix 1) immediately if your child goes to live with foster carers unless the arrangement is unlikely to last for more than 12 weeks. If there is disagreement about who should be a child's appointee, the DWP decides. There is no right of appeal against this decision.[19]

Residential accommodation

After 28 days in residential accommodation, the care component of DLA/daily living component of PIP stops.[20] The mobility component continues to be paid. Two or more periods in residential accommodation separated by 28 days or less are linked and count as the same period for this purpose.[21] See p104 if the child spends time away from residential accommodation – eg, at home with you.

Example

Seb is aged 12 and gets the DLA middle rate care component and lower rate mobility component. He becomes looked after and accommodated on 1 August and goes to stay in a residential unit on that date. On 21 August he goes to stay with his grandmother. At this point, he has been in the residential unit for 19 days (the day he went in and the day he left are not counted[22]). This arrangement lasts until 15 September, when he returns to the residential unit. He has been at his grandmother's for 26 days. The care component of DLA stops being payable on 25 September (assuming he remains in the residential unit until then) because he has been there for a total of 28 days. The two periods are linked because he was at his grandmother's for only 26 days. DLA mobility component continues to paid.

Chapter 6: Children who are 'looked after and accommodated'
1. Benefits and tax credits for children who are 'looked after and accommodated'

Tell the Disability Service Centre (see Appendix 1) immediately if your child is looked after and accommodated in residential accommodation. If your child is entitled to the mobility component of DLA or PIP (which continues to be paid), the person to whom this is paid may change because of the rules about appointees (these are the same as if your child goes to live with a foster carer – see p100).

Carer's allowance

Entitlement to CA stops if the care component of DLA/daily living component of PIP stops because your child has been in residential accommodation for more than four weeks (see p100).

In any event, and even if the care component/daily living component continues because your child is in foster care, you probably do not satisfy the rules for getting CA because you are not caring for the child for 35 hours or more a week. You can have a temporary break of up to four (or, in some circumstances, 12) weeks from caring and remain entitled to CA, provided the break is temporary (see p6).[23]

This may allow you to keep your CA for four weeks, although it may be difficult to argue that the break is temporary, depending on the circumstances of your case.

If you are getting UC, the carer element stops if you no longer have 'regular and substantial' caring responsibilities for your child (see p47).[24]

If you are getting IS, income-based JSA, income-related ESA, PC or HB/CTR, the carer premium/carer addition (see Chapter 1) stops eight weeks after your entitlement to CA stops.[25] If you were getting IS only because you were getting CA, eight weeks after CA stops your IS stops.

Tell the Carer's Allowance Unit (see Appendix 1) if your child is looked after and accommodated. Inform the office dealing with your UC, IS, JSA, ESA, PC or HB/CTR claim if your entitlement to CA stops.

Tax credits

Your tax credit entitlement for your child stops as soon as s/he becomes looked after and accommodated.[26] Your CTC may reduce or, if you no longer have any dependent children at home with you, stops altogether. If you are working and getting working tax credit, this might also be affected, either because having a dependent child is the basis of your entitlement or because you are getting help with childcare costs for the child.

Tell HMRC immediately, preferably in writing, if your child is looked after and accommodated to avoid being overpaid. Contact the Tax Credit Office to do this (see Appendix 1). If you do not tell HMRC within one month of the change, it can impose a penalty of up to £300 on you.[27]

Other benefits

Health benefits

If your child is looked after and accommodated, you may sometimes lose your entitlement to health benefits. This is because you may lose entitlement to a 'qualifying benefit' like IS or CTC, or because you are no longer treated as having a dependent child (for the Best Start food scheme). See p21 for who qualifies for health benefits. Check whether you still qualify even though your circumstances have changed – eg, you can get help with some costs on low-income grounds.

2. When your child comes home

If your child comes back to live with you full time, you can claim benefits and tax credits for her/him if you satisfy the normal rules (see Chapter 1). However, if you were previously getting extra amounts for your child in your income support (IS) or income-based jobseeker's allowance (JSA), you will not get these amounts again unless you have continued to get amounts for another child in the family. If tax credits or a means-tested benefit like IS has stopped, you will usually have to claim universal credit (UC) instead (see p46).

This section provides information about what happens when a child is staying with you some of the time – eg, if s/he is starting to come home for a couple of days a week on a trial basis.

Child benefit

If your child is looked after and accommodated, you can get child benefit for any week s/he comes home:[28]
- for seven nights in a row; *or*
- for any extra nights that follow immediately after the first seven; *or*
- on a regular basis for at least two consecutive nights every week.

> *Example*
> Jack has been looked after and accommodated for the past six months. He comes home on Thursday 19 September 2019 and stays with his mother until the following Thursday. His mother is entitled to child benefit for the week beginning Monday 16 September 2019. If he stays at least one extra night, following straight after this first period, his mother is also entitled to child benefit for the week beginning Monday 23 September 2019.

You have to make a new claim for child benefit for any periods your child spends at home. It is worth claiming not just for the income you get but also for the national insurance credits it gives you. This helps protect your state retirement pension by helping you satisfy the contribution conditions.

Chapter 6: Children who are 'looked after and accommodated'
2. When your child comes home

If, when your child comes back to live with you, you expect it to be on a permanent basis, child benefit should start being paid as normal again (provided you make a claim). If your child is then looked after and accommodated again, you should get child benefit paid for a further eight weeks (see p96).

Means-tested benefits

Universal credit

When your child comes home, your UC should be adjusted to include the child element. This should happen even if the child is still 'looked after' by the local authority.[29] However, if s/he is only coming home for short periods, your UC may not increase because of the way UC 'assessment periods' work – eg, if s/he both comes home and goes back to foster carers or residential accommodation within the same assessment period.

Income support and jobseeker's allowance

If you were getting IS or income-based JSA which included amounts (personal allowance and premiums) for your child before s/he was looked after and accommodated, you do not get these amounts again when your child comes back to live with you, unless you have continued to get amounts for another child in your IS/income-based JSA.

If you have continued to get a personal allowance for another child in the family while a child has been looked after and accommodated, your IS/income-based JSA can be increased when your child comes back to live with you. If s/he comes to stay part of the time, you can get the increase for the days s/he stays with you.[30] If this applies, make sure you tell the Department for Work and Pensions about any days your child spends at home and check that your IS/income-based JSA is adjusted correctly.

If you were not getting amounts for your child in your IS/income-based JSA before s/he became looked after and accommodated, your IS/income-based JSA is unlikely to be affected until your child comes home on a full-time basis, although you will usually have to claim UC instead (see p46).

Pension credit

If you are entitled to a pension credit (PC) additional amount for your child, your PC should be adjusted to include this again when your child comes home, even if your child is still 'looked after' by the local authority, provided you have parental responsibility for the child.[31]

Housing benefit and council tax reduction

When your child comes home, your housing benefit (HB) and council tax reduction (CTR) should be adjusted to include her/his personal allowance and any premiums. If you have not been getting maximum HB/CTR, this may mean you are entitled to more benefit. If your child comes home for part of a week, the

Chapter 6: Children who are 'looked after and accommodated'
2. When your child comes home

local authority can calculate your benefit as if s/he is at home for the whole week if it considers it is reasonable to do so, taking into account the nature and frequency of the child's visits.[32] The child should also be included in the 'size criteria'. Also tell the local authority if your income changes.

If your HB has stopped and you need to make a new claim, you may need to claim UC instead (see p46).

Non-means-tested benefits

Disability living allowance and personal independence payment

If the payment of disability living allowance (DLA) care component or personal independence payment (PIP) daily living component has stopped because your child is in residential accommodation (not foster care), it can be paid for days your child spends at home with you. The day s/he comes home and the day s/he goes back into local authority accommodation count as days at home. For example, if your child comes home on Friday evening and returns to local authority accommodation on Sunday evening, this counts as three days at home. The DLA care component/PIP daily living component is payable for these three days.

Tell the Disability Service Centre about any days your child spends at home.

If you are no longer your child's appointee for DLA, payments are not made to you. If your child starts to spend more time at home with you, it may be appropriate for you to become the appointee again. Apply by contacting the Disability Service Centre (see Appendix 1).

Carer's allowance

You receive carer's allowance (CA) if you are caring for a disabled person for at least 35 hours a week. The disabled person must be in receipt of DLA care component at the middle or highest rate or PIP daily living component (or attendance allowance). If your child is disabled and is entitled to the DLA care component at the middle or highest rate or PIP daily living component, you may be able to get CA if your child starts coming home for short spells (and DLA care component/PIP daily living component is payable). Provided you can show that you are caring for your child at least 35 hours a week (Sunday to Saturday) while s/he is at home, you should be able to get CA. The time does not have to be spread across the whole week. Time spent preparing for her/his visit and clearing up afterwards can count towards the 35 hours.[33] Even if you are not currently the appointee for the child's DLA, you can still claim CA, provided you satisfy the rules.

Example
Ahmed is aged seven and has been looked after and accommodated in a residential unit for the past nine months. He has a disability and is entitled to the DLA care component at the highest rate. He has recently started going home to his parents' house every weekend. He goes on Friday at 6pm and leaves on Monday at 8.30am. DLA care component is payable for Friday, Saturday, Sunday and Monday. His mother spends almost all of the time he is at home caring for him. She also spends at least two hours before he arrives preparing, and another three hours clearing up once he has left on Monday. Ahmed's mother claims CA. She must show that in the course of a week (Sunday to Saturday) she spends at least 35 hours caring for Ahmed. She should be entitled to CA.

If you become entitled to CA, any means-tested benefits (IS, income-based JSA, income-related ESA, PC, HB and CTR) you receive should include the carer premium or carer addition. If you get UC, it should include the carer element once you have 'regular and substantial' caring responsibilties for your child again (see p47).[34] If you have lost entitlement to a means-tested benefit such as IS, income-based JSA, income-related ESA or HB because of losing the carer premium, it is likely that you will have to claim UC instead.

If someone else is claiming carer's allowance

Only one person can get CA in respect of a particular disabled person.[35] If there is more than one person who could be entitled (eg, you and your child's foster carer), you can agree who will claim. If agreement is not possible, the DWP decides.[36] There is no right of appeal against this decision.

Tax credits

There is no provision in the tax credit rules to allow tax credits to be paid for days a child spends at home with you while s/he is still being looked after and accommodated. You can only get child tax credit (CTC) for a child when s/he is no longer looked after and accommodated and s/he is normally living with you. If you have not continued getting CTC for another child, you will usually have to claim UC instead.

Chapter 6: Children who are 'looked after and accommodated'
Notes

1. Benefits and tax credits for children who are 'looked after and accommodated'
1 s147(2) and Sch 9 para 1 SSCBA 1992; regs 16(1)(a) and 18 CB Regs
2 R(F) 3/85
3 s147(1) SSCBA 1992
4 Reg 4 UC Regs
5 Reg 24 UC Regs
6 Sch 4 para 11(2)(a) UC Regs. The rules say that the absence must be temporary, but it is unclear whether the DWP would question whether the child is temporarily or permanently absent.
7 Regs 79 and 83 UC Regs
8 Reg 16(5)(c) and Sch 1B para 1 IS Regs
9 **IS** Reg 16(5)(c) IS Regs
   JSA Reg 78(5)(f) JSA Regs
10 **IS** Sch 9 para 5B(2) IS Regs; reg 7(4) and (5)(c) SS(WTCCTC)(CA) Regs
   JSA Sch 7 para 6B(2) JSA Regs; regs 8(3) and 4(c) SS(WTCCTC)(CA) Regs
11 Sch 2A para 4 SPC Regs
12 **HB** Reg 21(4)(a) HB Regs; reg 21(4)(a) HB(SPC) Regs
   CTR Reg 11(3)(a) CTR(S) Regs; reg 11(3)(a) CTR(SPC)(S) Regs
13 Reg 13D HB Regs
14 Reg B13 HB Regs
15 Regs B13(5) and 13D(12) HB Regs define 'occupier' as a person whom the relevant authority is satisfied occupies the claimant's dwelling as her/his home.
16 Regs 75A and 75F HB Regs
17 Reg 43 SS(C&P) Regs
18 Reg 43(4) SS(C&P) Regs
19 Sch 2 para 5(y) SS&CS(DA) Regs; Sch 3 para 1(m) and (n) UC,PIP,JSA&ESA(DA) Regs
20 Regs 9 and 10 SS(DLA) Regs; regs 28 and 30 SS(PIP) Regs
21 Reg 10(5) SS(DLA) Regs; reg 32(4) SS(PIP) Regs
22 Reg 9(7) SS(DLA) Regs
23 Reg 4(2) SS(ICA) Regs
24 Regs 29 and 30 UC Regs
25 **IS** Sch 2 para 14ZA(3) IS Regs
   JSA Sch 1 para 17(3) JSA Regs
   ESA Sch 4 para 8(2) ESA Regs
   PC Sch 1 para 4(3) SPC Regs
   HB Sch 3 para 17(2) HB Regs; Sch 3 para 9(2) HB(SPC) Regs
   CTR Sch 1 para 14(2) CTR(S) Regs; Sch 1 para 10(2) CTR(SPC)(S) Regs
26 Reg 3 r4.1 Case A CTC Regs
27 s32 TCA 2002

2. When your child comes home
28 Reg 16(1)(b) CB Regs
29 Regs 4 and 4A UC Regs
30 **IS** Reg 16(6) IS Regs; Sch 3A para 3(b) SS&CS(DA) Regs
   JSA Reg 78(7) JSA Regs; Sch 3A para 8(b) SS&CS(DA) Regs
31 Sch 2A para 4(1) and (3)(b) SPC Regs
32 **HB** Reg 21(5) HB Regs; reg 21(5) HB(SPC) Regs
   CTR Reg 11(4) CTR(S) Regs; reg 11(4) CTR(SPC)(S) Regs
33 CG/006/1990
34 Regs 29 and 30 UC Regs
35 s70(7) SSCBA 1992
36 s70(7) SSCBA 1992; reg 7 SS(ICA) Regs

Chapter 7
Children living with kinship carers

This chapter covers:
1. What is kinship care (below)
2. Financial help from the local authority (p108)
3. Benefits and tax credits if a child is not looked after (p110)
4. Benefits and tax credits if a child is looked after (p119)

If a child is being cared for permanently, or for a considerable period, by extended family members or by friends, often called 'kinship care', issues about financial support can arise. Some kinship carers get financial support from the local authority, others do not. Kinship carers may be able to claim benefits and tax credits for the child for whom they care. Benefits and tax credits that a kinship carer claims for her/himself may also be affected by the care arrangements.

1. **What is kinship care**

In this chapter, **'kinship care'** means a full-time care arrangement provided by a child's extended family or wider network of friends.

The basis for kinship care arrangements varies and depends on the circumstances of the particular situation. In order to work out potential benefit and tax credit entitlement, it is crucial to know the basis of the care arrangements and whether the child counts as 'looked after' by the local authority. To use this chapter, first work out which of the following apply to you. A child can be living in a kinship care arrangement because:
- an informal arrangement has been made by the family – eg, not involving the children's hearing system or the courts. In this situation, the child is *not* 'looked after' (see p110);
- a residence order or kinship care order under section 11 of the Children (Scotland) Act 1995 has been granted in favour of the kinship carer. The child is *not* looked after as a result of this type of order (see p110);

Chapter 7: Children living with kinship carers
2. Financial help from the local authority

- the carer has been appointed as the child's guardian under section 7 of the Children (Scotland) Act 1995. The child is *not* looked after as a result of this appointment (see p110);
- s/he is subject to a compulsory supervision order or interim compulsory order under the Children's Hearings (Scotland) Act 2011, which requires her/him to live with the kinship carer. In this situation, the child is looked after (see p119);
- there is a permanence order in respect of her/him under Part II of the Adoption and Children (Scotland) Act 2007. In this situation, the child is looked after (see p119);
- s/he is accommodated with you under section 25 of the Children (Scotland) Act 1995. In this situation, the child is looked after (see p119).

2. Financial help from the local authority

Many, but not all, kinship carers get regular payments from the local authority. If a kinship carer receives payments from the local authority, these are likely to be made under either section 22 of the Children (Scotland) Act 1995 (Section 22 payments), section 50 of the Children Act 1975 (Section 50 payments) or regulation 33 of the Looked After Children (Scotland) Regulations 2009 (sometimes referred to as section 110 of the Adoption and Children (Scotland) Act 2007).

There is no national set minimum rate of kinship care payment and there is considerable variation in the level of payments made by local authorities to kinship carers.

Section 22 payments

Section 22 of the Children (Scotland) Act 1995 sets out the local authority's duty to safeguard and promote the welfare of children under 18 in its area who are 'in need'. Help can be given under this section either in cash or in kind. Section 22 powers are often used to make occasional or short-term payments, but are also used to make regular payments. Section 22 payments can be made to kinship carers of looked-after children and non-looked-after children and can be for a variety of purposes.

Section 50 payments

Section 50 of the Children Act 1975 allows the local authority to make payments towards the maintenance of a child who is under the age of 18 and living with a person other than her/his parent. Section 50 payments cannot be made to foster carers. Section 50 allows a local authority to make payments to kinship carers, but does not oblige it to do so. Section 50 payments can be made to kinship carers of looked-after children and non-looked-after children, and are for maintenance.

Regulation 33/Section 110 payments

Section 110 of the Adoption and Children (Scotland) Act 2007, together with regulation 33 of the Looked After Children (Scotland) Regulations 2009, allow the local authority to pay an allowance to kinship carers of looked-after children (called 'approved kinship carers'). The allowance can be for a variety of purposes.

Kinship care allowances guidance

In 2015, the Scottish government and the Convention of Scottish Local Authorities (COSLA) established an arrangement for payment of some kinship carers by local authorities.[1] The aim is that there should be parity between the amount the local authority pays for kinship care allowances and fostering allowances (not incuding fostering fees).

The arrangement covers:[2]
- kinship carers of looked-after children;
- kinship carers where the child is subject to a kinship care order under section 11 of the Children (Scotland) Act 1995 or the carer is the child's guardian under section 7 of the Children (Scotland) Act 1995; *and*
  - the child was previously looked after by the local authority;
  - the child is at risk of becoming looked after; *or*
  - was placed with the kinship carer by the local authority.

Scottish government guidance suggests that local authorities deduct any 'child-related benefits' to which the kinship carer is entitled, and that a foster carer would not get, from the amount of the allowance. Specifically, the guidance states that child benefit and child tax credit (CTC) (although not the disabled child or severely disabled child elements) should be deducted if the kinship carer is eligible for these benefits. Guardian's allowance, if payable, should **not** be deducted.[3]

Example

Betty cares for her eight-year-old grandson, Joe, and has been granted a kinship care order. Before she got the kinship care order, Joe was subject to a compulsory supervision order and was therefore 'looked after' by the local authority. Betty gets child benefit and CTC for Joe and this amounts to £84.33 a week. A foster carer would not get these benefits for a child in her/his care. The local authority's fostering allowance rate is £150 a week. The local authority deducts £84.33 from the fostering allowance rate and pays Betty £65.67 a week kinship care allowance.

Impact on benefits and tax credits

Local authority payments can sometimes affect your benefits or tax credits. This chapter explains the effect of local authority payments on each of the main benefits and tax credits. First check whether or not the child counts as looked

Chapter 7: Children living with kinship carers
3. Benefits and tax credits if a child is not looked after

after. If the child is not looked after, see below. If the child is looked after, see p119.

It can be important to know which type of payment you are receiving. Ask the social work department to confirm in writing the payment being made, which section of which Act it is using to make the payment, and what the payment is for. This will help you sort out your benefits and tax credits.

3. Benefits and tax credits if a child is not looked after

This section is for kinship carers of children who are not looked after by the local authority.

When you become a kinship carer, you may have to make new claims for benefits, or the amounts you get may change. This section provides information about which benefits you may be able to claim, and how your existing entitlement to benefits and tax credits might be affected. For more detailed information about the entitlement rules for benefits and tax credits, see Chapter 1.

Delays in getting a benefit claim sorted out can cause difficulties. See Chapter 2 for what you can do if your benefit payments are delayed, including information on short-term advances, interim payments, crisis grants and complaints.

Child benefit and guardian's allowance

Child benefit

When a child joins your household, someone else may already be claiming child benefit for her/him. There are rules that determine whose claim takes priority if there are competing claims.[4] The person with whom the child lives normally has priority, and this means you should get child benefit if you are the kinship carer for a non-looked-after child. However, if someone else is getting child benefit for the child when you make your claim, s/he will retain priority over you for three weeks after you make your claim.[5] This means that you will not normally become entitled to child benefit until three weeks after the week in which you claim (for child benefit purposes, a week starts on a Monday[6]). The only exception to this rule is if the other person gives up her/his entitlement at an earlier date.[7]

Example

Dot starts caring full time for her grandson, Adam, on 9 August 2019. Before this, Adam was living with his mum, Kate, but she is no longer able to look after him. Dot claims child benefit for Adam on 23 August 2019, but because Kate is still getting child benefit and does not give up her entitlement, Dot does not become entitled until Monday 16 September 2019.

Even if your claim has priority, you cannot receive child benefit for a period when it has already been paid to someone else for the same child, unless:[8]
- HM Revenue and Customs (HMRC) or, if the decision has been made following an appeal, the First-tier Tribunal or Upper Tribunal, has decided that the child benefit paid is recoverable because the person has failed to disclose or has misrepresented a 'material fact' and no appeal against that decision has been made within the time limit; *or*
- even though HMRC decided the benefit was not recoverable or has not made a decision on its recoverablity, the money has been repaid.

Once you are getting child benefit for a child, you can keep getting it during a period when the child is living temporarily away from you, provided that period is not for more than eight weeks out of the last 16.[9]

The effect of local authority payments

Child benefit is not affected by any payment you receive from the local authority.

Guardian's allowance

You can get guardian's allowance if you satisfy the rules on p20. Guardian's allowance is not affected by any payment you receive from the local authority.

Means-tested benefits

Universal credit

If you are getting universal credit (UC), a child element should be included in your UC award for a non-looked-after child you care for, as long as you are treated as being responsible for the child. You are responsible for the child if s/he normally lives with you.[10] You do not have to be getting child benefit for the child.

A 'two-child limit' was introduced on 6 April 2017 (see p47). Non-looked-after children in kinship care are exempt from the two-child limit if:[11]
- you have a kinship care order under section 11 of the Children (Scotland) Act 1995;
- you are appointed as guardian under section 7 of the Children (Scotland) Act 1995;
- you are entitled to guardian's allowance in respect of the child/children;
- one of the above bullet points applied prior to the child's 16th birthday and you have continued to be responsible for the child;
- you have undertaken care of the child/children where it is likely that otherwise s/he would have been looked after by the local authority.

This means that even if you already have two or more dependent children and you start caring for a child on or after 6 April 2017 in one of these circumstances, you can get the child element in your UC for the child who has come to live with you, providing you satisfy the normal conditions of entitlement. If you give birth to a child after taking on the care of a child or children in one of these circumstances, a child in kinship care is 'disregarded' when applying the two-child limit.[12]

Example
Sally and Bob have one child already when they take on the care of their niece and nephew for whom they have kinship care orders. They can get UC for all three children. Two years later, they have another baby and they are able to get UC for the baby as well because the two 'kinship' children are disregarded for the purposes of the 'two-child limit.' If they later have another baby, this child will be subject to the two-child limit.

The amount of the housing costs element for rent you get in your UC reflects the number of bedrooms you need, including for any 'kinship' child. Your work allowance should reflect the fact you have a dependent child (see p48). If you are working, you may be entitled to help with childcare costs (see p48). If you become a 'friend or family carer' (see below) of a child under 16 and you are the 'responsible carer' (see below), you are subject to the 'work-focused interview requirement' (see p49) only for the first 12 months (unless the child is under one, in which case the responsible carer has no work-related requirements).[13]

'**Friend or family carer**' means you are responsible for a child under 16 but are not her/his parent or step-parent. You must be taking care of the child because:[14]
- s/he has no parent, or has parents who are unable to care for her/him; or
- it is likely that s/he would otherwise be looked after by the local authority.

'**Responsible carer**' means you are a lone parent or, if you are in a couple, you and your partner have nominated you as responsible for the child. Only one of you can be nominated and the nomination applies to all your children.[15]

Local authority payments are disregarded as income for UC.[16]

Income support
Note: if you are not already getting income support (IS) you are very likely to have to claim UC instead.

Claiming income support as a lone parent
If you are a lone parent with at least one child aged under five you can get IS, provided you satisfy the other rules (see p27). The child must be a member of your household.[17] You are treated as responsible for a child if:[18]
- you get child benefit for her/him; or
- no one gets child benefit for her/him and s/he usually lives with you, or you are the only person who has claimed child benefit for her/him.

Note: you do not have to be the child's parent to count as a lone parent for IS.

If there is a delay in transferring child benefit to you so that you cannot count as a lone parent, you may still be eligible for IS in the meantime if the reason you are caring for the child is because her/his parent is temporarily ill or away from home.[19]

Claiming income support as a carer

If you care for a disabled person, you may be able to get IS, provided you satisfy the other rules (see Chapter 1). This applies if the child (or other person for whom you care) is getting disability living allowance (DLA) care component at the middle or highest rate or personal independence payment (PIP) daily living component (if s/he is aged 16 or over) and you are getting carer's allowance (CA), or you are 'regularly and substantially' engaged in caring for her/him. It can also apply after a claim for DLA/PIP has been made for a period of up to 26 weeks or until the decision is made, whichever is the earlier date. See p27 for how this rule works.

Claiming income support on other grounds

There are other groups who can get IS (see p27).

The effect of local authority payments

If you are not receiving amounts in your IS for a child, Section 50 payments are disregarded as income for IS.[20] If you are still receiving amounts in your IS for a child and you are not receiving CTC, Section 50 payments count as income up to the amount equal to the child's personal allowance and any disabled child premium for the child concerned. The amount of any payment above this level is ignored.[21] If you are in this situation, you may be better off claiming UC. Seek advice about this as soon as possible.

Section 22 payments are disregarded as income for IS.[22]

Income-related employment and support allowance

If you are already getting income-related employment and support allowance (ESA), it is not normally affected when you become a kinship carer. However, if you claim UC in order to get support for the child, your income-related ESA will stop.

The effect of local authority payments

Local authority payments are disregarded as income for income-related ESA.[23]

Contributory ESA is not affected by local authority payments as it is not a means-tested benefit.

Jobseeker's allowance

Note: if you are not already getting income-based jobseeker's allowance (JSA), you are very likely to have to claim UC instead.

When a child joins your household, your JSA is not normally affected. However, if you claim UC in order to get support for the child, your income-based JSA will stop.

The effect of local authority payments
If you are not receiving amounts in your income-based JSA for a child, Section 50 payments are disregarded as income.[24] If you are still receiving amounts in your income-based JSA for a child and you are not receiving CTC, Section 50 payments count as income up to the amount equal to the personal allowance and any disabled child premium for the child concerned. The amount of any payment above this level is ignored.[25] If you are in this situation, you are probably better off claiming UC instead. Seek advice as soon as possible.

Section 22 payments are disregarded as income.[26]

Contribution-based JSA is not means tested and is not affected by any payments you get from the local authority.

Pension credit
Some pension credit (PC) claimants who are responsible for a non-looked-after child or qualifying young person get an additional amount for the child/ren in their PC (instead of CTC).[27] You are responsible for the child if s/he normally lives with you. You do not have to be getting child benefit for the child. If you are getting child benefit for the child, it is not taken into account as income for PC.[28]

The effect of local authority payments
Local authority payments are disregarded as income for PC.[29]

Housing benefit and council tax reduction
Being a kinship carer can change the amount of housing benefit (HB) and council tax reduction (CTR) you get, or can mean you become entitled to HB/CTR, although you are very likely to have to claim UC instead of HB if you are under pension age and are not already getting HB. Your entitlement to HB/CTR might change for the following reasons.
- Being responsible for a non-looked-after child increases your applicable amount (see p25). This is the figure used to calculate how much HB/CTR you get. For a child to count as your dependant, s/he must be 'normally living' with you.[30] This means s/he spends more time with you than with anyone else.[31] If it is unclear in whose household the child normally lives, or if s/he spends equal time in more than one household, you are treated as having responsibility if:[32]
  – you get child benefit for the child; or
  – no one gets child benefit but you have claimed it; or
  – no one has claimed child benefit, or more than one person has claimed it but you appear to have most responsibility.

- If your HB is calculated on the basis of a 'local housing allowance' (this only affects tenants in the private rented sector – see p24), the local housing allowance that applies to you may change because you require more rooms. Your HB entitlement may increase as a result.
- If you are under pension age and living in the social rented sector, any deduction you have to your HB because you are considered to be under-occupying your accommodation might be affected by a non-looked-after child joining your household. If you have had an under-occupation deduction applied to your HB but you are no longer treated as under-occupying, this deduction should stop. See p24 for more details.

The effect of local authority payments
Section 22 payments and Section 50 payments are disregarded in full.[33]

Non-means-tested benefits

Disability living allowance, personal independence payment and attendance allowance

Disability living allowance and personal independence payment for children
When a child under 16 gets DLA, the DWP appoints an adult to act on the child's behalf. This adult receives DLA payments on behalf of the child. The appointee is normally the person with whom the child lives.[34]

If, when you start to look after a child as a kinship carer, s/he is already getting DLA, you can apply to become the appointee. Write to the Disability Service Centre (see Appendix 1), giving the child's name, date of birth and reference number if you have it (you will find it on any letters from the Disability Service Centre about the DLA). Also provide your details (name, address, date of birth and national insurance number) and explain the circumstances. For example, you may wish to explain that the arrangement is expected to be permanent, or long term, that you have claimed or are in receipt of child benefit for the child, and the circumstances which led to the child living with you.

If there is disagreement about who should be a child's appointee for DLA, the DWP decides. There is no right of appeal against this decision,[35] but you could complain if you are unhappy with the outcome (see p59).

If you are already looking after a child as a kinship carer, and you think s/he may be entitled to DLA, you can make the claim on her/his behalf. See Chapters 1 and 2 for more information on the conditions of entitlement and how to claim. If the child/young person you care for is aged 16 or over, s/he can make a claim for PIP.

Disability living allowance, personal independence payment and attendance allowance for adults
Being a kinship carer does not affect your own entitlement to DLA, PIP or attendance allowance (AA).

Chapter 7: Children living with kinship carers
3. Benefits and tax credits if a child is not looked after

The effect of local authority payments

DLA, PIP and AA are not means tested and, therefore, local authority payments do not affect the amount of benefit you receive, either for yourself or for the child.

Carer's allowance

If you are already entitled to CA (eg, because you are caring for an elderly relative), becoming a kinship carer does not affect your entitlement, unless you no longer satisfy the conditions of entitlement – eg, because you are no longer able to spend at least 35 hours a week caring for the disabled person.

If the child for whom you care gets the DLA care component at the middle or highest rate or PIP daily living component, you may be able to claim CA in respect of her/him if you satisfy the normal condtions of entitlement (see p5). Only one person can claim CA for a particular disabled person. If there is more than one person who could be entitled, you can agree who will claim. If agreement is not possible, the DWP decides. There is no right of appeal against this decision.[36]

The effect of local authority payments

CA is not means tested and, therefore, local authority payments do not affect the amount of CA you receive.

Tax credits

Child tax credit

Note: if you are not already getting tax credits you are very likely to have to claim UC instead.

You may already be getting CTC when you become a kinship carer – eg, if you already have a child. If you are already getting CTC, starting to care for a non-looked-after child may increase the amount of CTC to which you are entitled.

To get CTC, you must have at least one child for whom you are responsible.[37] You are treated as responsible for a child if:[38]

- s/he normally lives with you; *or*
- you have the main responsibility for her/him. This only applies if there are competing claims for CTC for the same child.

From 6 April 2017, a 'two-child limit' applies to child elements in CTC (see p43). Non-looked-after children in kinship care are exempt from the 'two-child limit' if:[39]

- you have a kinship care order under section 11 of the Children (Scotland) Act 1995;
- you are appointed as guardian under section 7 of the Children (Scotland) Act 1995;
- you are entitled to guardian's allowance in respect of the child/children;
- one of the above bullet points applied prior to the child's 16th birthday and you have continued to be responsible for the child;

Chapter 7: Children living with kinship carers
3. Benefits and tax credits if a child is not looked after

- you have undertaken care of the child/children where it is likely that otherwise s/he would have been looked after by the local authority.

This means that even if you already have two or more dependent children and you start caring for a child on or after 6 April 2017 in one of these circumstances, you can get the child element in your CTC for the child who has come to live with you, providing you satisfy the normal conditions of entitlement. If you give birth to a child after taking on the care of a child or children in one of these circumstances, a child in kinship care is 'disregarded' when applying the two-child limit.[40]

Only one person (or one couple making a joint claim) can get tax credits for a particular child.[41] You should get tax credits if the child 'normally lives with you'. HMRC says this means that the child 'regularly, usually, typically' lives with you.[42] You do not have to be getting child benefit for the child.

If a child is living with you full time and the arrangement is reasonably settled, it is very likely that HMRC will decide the child 'normally lives with you'. This means that if someone else has been getting tax credits for the child, her/his payments will stop. If s/he has continued to get tax credits during a period when, in fact, the child has been normally living with you, HMRC may decide s/he has been overpaid and could apply a penalty to her/him if s/he failed to report the change within one month.

If a child normally lives in more than one household (eg, s/he shares her/his time between two different households), there may be more than one potential tax credits claimant. You and any other potential claimant/s can decide between yourselves who should make the claim. If you cannot agree, HMRC decides whose claim should take priority by deciding who has the 'main responsibility' for the child.[43] HMRC is likely to take account of:[44]

- whether there is a court order which states where the child should live or who should care for her/him. This is not binding on HMRC: it should consider the factual care arrangements as well as the terms of any court order;[45]
- how many days a week the child lives in the different households;
- who pays for the child's food and clothes;
- where the child's belongings are kept;
- who is the main contact for nursery, school or childcare;
- who does the child's laundry;
- who looks after the child when s/he is ill and takes her/him to the doctor.

If you disagree with HMRC's decision (eg, it decides you cannot get CTC because another person has the main responsibility for the child), you can ask for a review and then appeal against it (see p58).

If a child stops living with you, tell HMRC as soon as possible to avoid being overpaid and within one month to avoid a possible penalty.

Chapter 7: Children living with kinship carers
3. Benefits and tax credits if a child is not looked after

Working tax credit

Note: if you are not already getting tax credits you are very likely to have to claim UC instead.

You may already be getting WTC when you become a kinship carer – eg, you or your partner are in low-paid work. To get WTC you, or your partner (if you have one), must be in full-time paid work.[46]

If you are single and responsible for at least one dependent child (see p41), full-time paid work means at least 16 hours a week. If you are a couple, see p44 for what full-time work means. If, as a result of becoming a kinship carer, you pay a childminder, nursery or other childcare provider, you may become entitled to an increased amount of WTC (see Chapter 1).

The effect of local authority payments

Any payments you get from the local authority do not affect your tax credit entitlement. They are disregarded as income.[47]

Other benefits

Scottish Welfare Fund payments

As a kinship carer, you may have expenses which could be met by a Scottish Welfare Fund payment – eg, to buy a new bed and bedding for the child. See p38 for who can qualify.

If you are not able to get a Scottish Welfare Fund payment, ask the local authority social work department if it can help you with the extra expenses you have.

Best Start grant

There are three payments which make up the Best Start grant: a pregnancy and baby payment, an early learning payment and a school-age payment. If you are a kinship carer you may be able to get one, two or all of these payments depending on the age of the child when s/he comes to live with you.

Pregnancy and baby payment

If you are a kinship carer of a child aged under one, you may be able to get a Best Start grant pregnancy and baby payment of £600 (or £300 if you have another child aged under 16 in your household). You must be responsible for the child (see p4) and usually you must be on a qualifying benefit (see p3). You have to claim before the child's first birthday. You may be able to get a pregnancy and baby payment even though someone else (eg, the baby's mother or father) has already received a payment for the child (eg, before the child came to live with you).

Early learning payment

If you are a kinship carer of a child aged between two and three and a half, you may be able to get a Best Start grant early learning payment of £250. You must be responsible for the child (see p4) and usually you must be on a qualifying benefit (see p3). You have to claim while the child is between two and three and a half.[48] You may be able to get an early learning payment even though someone else (eg, the child's mother or father) has already received a payment for the child (eg, before the child came to live with you).[49]

School-age payment

If you are a kinship carer of a child who is around the age to start school, you may be able to get a school-age payment of £250. You must be responsible for the child (see p4) and usually you must be on a qualifying benefit (see p3).

If the child's date of birth is between 1 March 2014 and 28 February 2015, you must claim between 3 June 2019 and 29 February 2020.

If the child's date of birth is between 1 March 2015 and 29 February 2016, you must claim between 1 June 2020 and 28 February 2021.[50]

You may be able to get a school-age payment even though someone else (eg, the child's mother or father) has already received a payment for the child (eg, before the child came to live with you).[51]

Health benefits

Becoming a kinship carer may mean that you become entitled to health benefits. For example, entitlement to CTC and having an income below a specified level means you are 'passported' to certain health benefits. If you are caring for a child aged under three, you may be entitled to help through the Best Start food payment card. For more information about health benefits, see p21.

Children are automatically entitled to free dental treatment and vouchers for glasses.

4. Benefits and tax credits if a child is looked after

This section applies if you are a kinship carer and you are caring for a child living with you because:
- of a supervision order or interim supervision order under the Children's Hearings (Scotland) Act 2011;
- the local authority has placed the child with you under section 25 of the Children (Scotland) Act 1995;
- there is a permanence order in respect of the child under Part II of the Adoption and Children (Scotland) Act 2007;

- the child is looked after for some other reason – eg, there is a child protection order in place.

It can be important to know what type of payment the local authority is making and what it is for (see p108). Ask your local authority to provide details in writing of the type of payment, in particular what legal power it is using to make the payment, and what it is for.

Child benefit and guardian's allowance

If you are caring for a looked-after child, you should be entitled to child benefit.[52] The exception to this is if the local authority is making payments to you under regulation 33 of the Looked After Children (Scotland) Regulations 2009 (this may be referred to as a payment under s110 of the Adoption and Children (Scotland) Act 2007) *and* this payment is for either accommodation or maintenance. In this situation, you are not entitled to child benefit.[53]

To be entitled to guardian's allowance, you must be entitled to, or treated as being entitled to, child benefit[54] and satisfy the other conditions of entitlement for guardian's allowance (see p20).

Means-tested benefits

Universal credit

If you are a kinship carer of a looked-after child or children, your universal credit (UC) does not include any child element for the child(ren) unless you have legal parental responsibilities for the child(ren). Most kinship carers of looked-after children do not have legal parental rights and, therefore, do not get a child element for the child or children they care for.

A 'two-child limit' was introduced on 6 April 2017 (see p47). There are some exemptions from this rule, including a child in kinship care where you have parental rights or responsibilities for her/him as a result of a permanence order. S/he continues to be exempt after her/his 16th birthday, providing you are still responsible for her/him.[55]

UC includes a housing costs element. If you live in rented accommodation the amount is based on how many rooms you need (the 'size criteria'). A looked-after child in kinship care is not allocated a room in the size criteria. However, kinship carers of looked-after children are allowed one extra bedroom in the size criteria.[56] A looked-after child in kinship care does not count as a dependent child for the purposes of the work allowance (see p48) or the childcare costs element (see p48).

If you are caring for a looked-after child aged under one and you are single, or you are in a couple and are nominated as the main carer, you are not subject to any work-related requirements (see p49).[57] If you are caring for a looked-after child aged between one and 16 and you are single, or you are in a couple and are nominated as the main carer, you are subject to the work-focused interview only requirement (see p49). This can extend beyond the child's 16th birthday if s/he has care needs which would make it unreasonable for you to meet the work search or work availability requirements, even if these were limited.[58]

If you are in a couple and your partner is the main nominated carer, you can be subject to the work-focused interview only requirement if you and your partner are caring for a child or qualifying young person (see p8) who has care needs which would make it unreasonable for either of you to meet the work search or work availability requirements, even if these were limited.[59]

Local authority payments are disregarded as income for UC.[60]

Income support

Note: if you are not already getting income support (IS), you are very likely to have to claim UC instead.

If you are a kinship carer, your IS may be affected in the following ways.
- If you are caring for a child aged under 16 and you do not have a partner you can claim IS on the basis of being an kinship carer of a looked-after child.[61]
- If you have been getting IS since before 6 April 2004 and you have a dependent child, you may still be getting amounts in your IS for her/him. This is only the case if you have not claimed child tax credit (CTC). See p30 for more information. If this applies to you because you get IS for other children in the family and you now want to include the child who has come to live with you, s/he must be considered to be part of your household (see below).

Part of your household

Sometimes, even though a child lives with someone, s/he is not treated as part of her/his household for IS purposes. It is possible that the Department for Work and Pensions (DWP) may not treat the child for whom you care as part of your household for IS purposes. This is because the rules that affect kinship carers are not clear.[62] If the DWP decides the child is not part of your household for IS purposes and you lose benefit as a result, seek advice.

The effect of local authority payments

The local authority may be paying you under section 22 of the Children (Scotland) Act 1995, section 50 of the Children Act 1975 or regulation 33 of the Looked After Children (Scotland) Regulations 2009.

Any payment the local authority makes should be disregarded in full,[63] except if you are still getting amounts in your IS for a child. In this case, Section 50 payments count as income up to the amount equal to the child's personal allowance and any disabled child premium for that child.[64]

Income-related employment and support allowance

You can get income-related employment and support allowance (ESA) if you satisfy the rules in Chapter 1. There are no additional amounts in ESA for dependent children.

Chapter 7: Children living with kinship carers
4. Benefits and tax credits if a child is looked after

The effect of local authority payments

The local authority may be paying you under section 22 of the Children (Scotland) Act 1995, section 50 of the Children Act 1975 or regulation 33 of the Looked After Children (Scotland) Regulations 2009.

Any payment the local authority makes should be disregarded in full.[65]

Jobseeker's allowance

Note: if you are not already getting income-based jobseeker's allowance (JSA), you are very likely to have to claim UC instead.

If you are a kinship carer, your JSA may be affected in one of two ways.

- If you have been getting JSA since before 6 April 2004 and you have a dependent child, you may still be getting amounts in your JSA for her/him. This is only the case if you have not claimed CTC. If this applies to you because you get JSA for other children in the family and you now want to include the child who has come to live with you, s/he must be considered to be a member of your household for JSA purposes (see below).
- Some couples have to make a joint claim for JSA, which means that you both need to claim, 'sign on' and look for work. This does not apply if you and your partner are caring for a child.

Part of your household

Sometimes, even though a child lives with someone, s/he is not treated as part of their household for JSA purposes. It is possible that the DWP may not treat the child for whom you care as part of your household for JSA. This is because the rules that affect kinship carers in this situation are not clear.[66] If the DWP decides that a child is not part of your household for JSA purposes, and you lose benefit as a result, seek advice.

The effect of local authority payments

The local authority may be paying you under section 22 of the Children (Scotland) Act 1995, section 50 of the Children Act 1975 or regulation 33 of the Looked After Children (Scotland) Regulations 2009.

Any payment the local authority makes should be disregarded in full,[67] except if you are still getting amounts in your JSA for a child. In this case, Section 50 payments count as income up to the amount equal to the child's personal allowance and any disabled child premium for that child.[68]

Pension credit

You can get pension credit (PC) if you satisfy the rules on p35. Some PC claimants who are responsible for a child or qualifying young person get an additional amount for the child/ren in their PC (instead of CTC). You will not get this additional amount for a looked-after child unless you have legal parental responsibilities for the child.[69] Most kinship carers of a looked-after child do not have parental rights: the exception is if you have a permanence order when you may also have parental responsibility.

Local authority payments are disregarded as income for PC.[70]

Housing benefit and council tax reduction

Note: if you are not already getting housing benefit (HB), you are very likely to have to claim UC instead, unless you are over pension age.

HB and council tax reduction (CTR) may be affected in several ways if you are a kinship carer of a looked-after child.

Housing benefit

The child you care for may not be treated as part of your household/occupying your home for HB purposes, even though s/he lives with you.[71] This can affect your HB in a number of ways.

- If the child is not part of your household, your applicable amount does not include amounts for the child. If you are on IS, income-based JSA, income-related ESA or the guarantee credit of PC you are passported to the maximum amount of HB (see p24). However, your HB may still be affected – see the next two bullet points.
- If you live in private rented accommodation and your HB is calculated using the 'local housing allowance' (see p24), the 'size criteria' used to work out your local housing allowance does not include the child(ren) you care for. However, you are allowed one extra room in the size criteria because you are a kinship carer of a looked-after child.[72]
- If you are under pension age and you live in the social rented sector, the child is not included in the 'size criteria' and you may be treated as under-occupying your home. This may result in your being subject to an under-occupation penalty ('bedroom tax'). However, you are allowed one extra room in the size criteria because you are a kinship carer of a looked-after child.[73]

If you are struggling to pay your rent because of the HB rules, you should claim a discretionary housing payment (see p26).

Council tax reduction

If you are on IS, income-based JSA, income-related ESA or the guarantee credit of PC, you are passported to maximum CTR. If you are not passported to maximum CTR, the amount you get depends on whether the child you care for counts as part of your household for CTR purposes and, therefore, whether s/he is included in your applicable amount (see p25). Sometimes, even though a child lives with you, s/he is treated as not part of your household, and it is possible that this may happen to you. This is because the rules that affect kinship carers in this situation are not clear.[74] If the local authority decides that the child is not part of your household for CTR purposes and you lose money as a result, seek advice.

Chapter 7: Children living with kinship carers
4. Benefits and tax credits if a child is looked after

The effect of local authority payments

The local authority may be paying you under section 22 of the Children (Scotland) Act 1995, section 50 of the Children Act 1975 or regulation 33 of the Looked After Children (Scotland) Regulations 2009. Any payment the local authority makes should be disregarded in full for HB and CTR.[75]

Non-means-tested benefits

Disability living allowance, personal independence payment and attendance allowance

The information on disability living allowance, personal independence payment and attendance allowance on p115 applies equally to any kinship care arrangement.

Carer's allowance

The information on carer's allowance (CA) on p116 applies equally to any kinship care arrangement.

Tax credits

Note: if you are not already getting tax credits, you are very likely to have to claim UC instead.

Child tax credit

Note: if the local authority payment (kinship care allowance) is not for accommodation or maintenance (usually a Section 22 payment – see p108), you should be entitled to CTC for the child providing you satisfy the normal conditions of entitlement.

The 'two-child limit' (see p43) generally means that you cannot get CTC for a child born on or after 6 April 2017 if you already have child elements included in your CTC for two or more children. If you are a kinship carer and have parental rights or responsibilities for a child as a result of a permanence order, that child is exempt from the 'two-child limit'. S/he continues to be exempt after her/his 16th birthday providing you are still responsible for her/him.[76] This is the only exception to the 'two-child limit' which affects kinship carers of looked-after children.

If the child is looked after by the local authority and the local authority is paying towards her/his accommodation and/or maintenance, you cannot get CTC in respect of the child for whom you care.[77] This is because the tax credit rules prevent you from being treated as responsible for a child if s/he is provided with or placed in accommodation under Part 2 of the Children (Scotland) Act 1995 or under the Children's Hearings (Scotland) Act 2011, and the cost of the child's accommodation or maintenance is borne wholly or partly out of public funds.

This rule only applies if the local authority payment is for accommodation or maintenance.

Working tax credit

If the child for whom you care is looked after by the local authority and the local authority is paying towards the child's accommodation and/or maintenance, s/he does not count as a dependent child for working tax credit (WTC) purposes.[78] However, being a kinship carer of a looked-after child may help you qualify for WTC.

In order to get WTC, you have to be in 'qualifying remunerative work'. This means that you are working (either employed or self-employed) for a certain number of hours a week and fall into at least one of five categories (see below). If the local authority makes a payment to you, being a kinship carer of a looked-after child can count as self-employed work for tax credit purposes, except if you have legal parental responsibilities for the child (eg, as a result of a permanence order).[79] HMRC guidance states that kinship carers should be treated as 'being in remunerative work'.[80] If you are a kinship carer of a looked-after child and you are refused WTC on the basis that you are not self-employed, seek further advice immediately.

You may be able to claim WTC if:[81]
- you are aged at least 25 and work for at least 30 hours a week; or
- you are aged at least 60 and work for at least 16 hours a week; or
- you are a single claimant, you have a dependent child, and you work for at least 16 hours a week. If the local authority is paying you in respect of the child's accommodation and/or maintenance, the child for whom you care as a kinship carer does *not* count as dependent for this purpose, but if you have a child of your own, s/he does count; or
- you are a couple, have a dependent child and your combined working hours are at least 24 a week. If the local authority is paying you for the child's accommodation and/or maintenance, the child for whom you care as a kinship carer does *not* count as dependent for this purpose, but if you have a child of your own, s/he does count. If you both work, one must work at least 16 hours a week. If only one of you works, you must work at least 24 hours. **Note:** if you are a couple with a dependent child and the non-working partner is incapacitated, a hospital inpatient, in prison or entitled to CA, you can qualify if you work at least 16 hours a week; or
- you have a disability which puts you at a disadvantage in getting a job, and you work for at least 16 hours a week.

The effect of local authority payments

Under the HMRC tax relief scheme, if you are claiming WTC as a self-employed carer under the rules described above, up to £10,000 a year, plus £200 a week for each child under 11 and £250 a week for each child aged 11 or over, is not liable for tax.

Local authority payments below these amounts are ignored as income for tax credit purposes.[82]

If you claim WTC as a kinship carer, your WTC counts as income for any means-tested benefits you get – eg, HB or CTR.

If you are not claiming tax credits as a self-employed earner, but are getting tax credits anyway (eg, because you are employed or you have other children for whom you can claim CTC), local authority payments are disregarded as income.[83]

National insurance credits

You are entitled to be credited with class 3 national insurance (NI) contributions for any week in which you are a kinship carer of a looked-after child.[84] These credits can help you qualify for retirement pension and some other benefits. You must apply to HMRC to be credited with NI contributions.[85] Complete Form CF411A (available from www.gov.uk) after the end of the tax year and send it to HMRC with a letter of confirmation from the local authority.

Notes

2. **Financial help from the local authority**
 1 www.gov.scot/Topics/People/Young-People/protecting/lac/kinship
 2 Arts 4 and 5 KCA(S)O; Part 2 CYP(S)A 2014: National Guidance on Part 13: Support for Kinship Care, www.gov.scot/Publications/2016/07/1045
 3 Appendix E paras 4, 6 and 7 CYP(S)A 2014: National Guidance on Part 13: Support for Kinship Care, www.gov.scot/Publications/2016/07/1045

3. **Benefits and tax credits if a child is not looked after**
 4 Sch 10 SSCBA 1992
 5 Sch 10(1) and (2) SSCBA 1992
 6 s147 SSCBA 1992
 7 Sch 10 SSCBA 1992; reg 15 CB Regs
 8 s13(2) SSAA 1992; reg 38 CB Regs
 9 s143(2) SSCBA 1992
 10 Reg 4(2) UC Regs
 11 Sch 12 para 4 UC Regs
 12 Reg 24A(1)(za) UC Regs
 13 Reg 91(2)(e) UC Regs
 14 Reg 919(31)(b) UC Regs
 15 s19(6) WRA 2012; reg 86 UC Regs
 16 Reg 66 UC Regs
 17 Sch 1B para 1 IS Regs
 18 Reg 15 IS Regs
 19 Sch 1B para 3 IS Regs; R(IS) 11/08
 20 Sch 9 para 25(1)(ba) IS Regs
 21 Sch 9 para 25 IS Regs, unamended by SI 2003 No.455 for claimants still receiving amounts for children in IS
 22 Sch 9 para 28(1)(c) IS Regs
 23 **s50** Sch 8 para 26(1)(b) ESA Regs
 s22 Sch 8 para 30(1)(c) ESA Regs
 24 Sch 7 para 26(1)(ba) JSA Regs
 25 Sch 7 para 26 JSA Regs, unamended by SI 2003 No.455 for claimants still receiving amounts for children in JSA
 26 Sch 7 para 29(1)(c) JSA Regs
 27 Sch 2IIA para 3 SPC Regs
 28 s15 SPCA 2002; reg 15(1)(j) SPC Regs

Chapter 7: Children living with kinship carers
Notes

29 s15 SPCA 2002; reg 15 SPC Regs
30 **HB** Reg 20(1) HB Regs; reg 20(1) HB(SPC) Regs
 CTR Reg 10(1) CTR(S) Regs; reg 10(1) CTR(SPC)(S) Regs
31 CFC/1537/1995
32 **HB** Reg 20(2) HB Regs; reg 20(2) HB(SPC) Regs
 CTR Reg 10(2) CTR(S) Regs; reg 10(2) CTR(SPC)(S) Regs
33 **HB** Sch 5 paras 25(1)(ba) and 28 HB Regs; reg 29(1) HB(SPC) Regs
 CTR Sch 4 paras 29(1)(b) and 32 CTR(S) Regs; reg 27(1) CTR(SPC)(S) Regs
34 Reg 43(2) SS(C&P) Regs
35 Sch 2 para 5(y) SS&CS(DA) Regs
36 s70(7) SSCBA 1992; reg 7 SS(ICA) Regs; Sch 2 para 3 SSA 1998
37 s8(2) TCA 2002
38 Reg 3(1) rr1 and 2 CTC Regs
39 Regs 7(2A), 9 and 12 CTC Regs
40 Reg 9 CTC Regs
41 Reg 3(1) r2.2 CTC Regs
42 para 02202 TCTM
43 Reg 3(1) r2.2 CTC Regs
44 para 02204 TCTM
45 *GJ v HMRC* (TC) [2013] UKUT 561 (AAC)
46 Reg 4 WTC(EMR) Regs
47 HMRC email to CPAG, 22 April 2009, and because they are not defined as income under reg 3 TC(DCI) Regs. If residence order in place, reg 19 Table 6 para 11(b) TC(DCI) Regs.
48 Sch 3 para 1(b) EYA(BSG)(S) Regs
49 Sch 3 para 2 EYA(BSG)(S) Regs
50 Sch 4 para 2 EYA(BSG)(S) Regs
51 Sch 4 para 32 EYA(BSG)(S) Regs

4. Benefits and tax credits if a child is looked after

52 Reg 16(1) CB Regs
53 Reg 16(3) CB Regs
54 ss77 and 122(5) SSCBA 1992
55 Reg 24B(2Ab) and Sch 12 para 4(f) UC Regs
56 Reg 2 and Sch 4 paras 9 and 12 UC Regs
57 Reg 89(1)(f) UC Regs
58 Reg 91(2)(a) and (b) UC Regs
59 Reg 91(2)(c) UC Regs
60 Reg 66 UC Regs
61 Sch 1B para 2 IS Regs
62 Reg 16 IS Regs sets out circumstances in which a person is to be treated as not being a member of the household. Arguably, your situation does not fall within this because the arrangement does not amount to the child being 'boarded out under a relevant enactment'.
63 Sch 9 paras 25(1)(ba), 26 and 28(1)(c) IS Regs; vol 5 chap 28 para 28378 DMG
64 Sch 9 para 25 IS Regs, unamended by SI 2003 No.455 for claimants still receiving amounts for children in IS
65 Sch 8 paras 26(1)(b), 28 and 30(1)(c) ESA Regs; para 51255 DMG vol 9 ch 51
66 Reg 78 JSA Regs sets out circumstances in which a person is to be treated as not being a member of the household. Arguably, your situation does not fall within this because the arrangement does not amount to the child being 'boarded out under a relevant Scottish enactment'.
67 Sch 7 paras 26(1)(ba), 27 and 29(1)(c) JSA regs; para 28378 DMG vol 5 ch28
68 Sch 7 para 26 JSA Regs, unamended by SI 2003 No.455 for claimants still receiving amounts for children in JSA
69 Sch 2IIA para 4(1) and (3)(b) SPC Regs
70 Reg 15 SPC Regs
71 Reg 21(3) HB Regs; reg 21(3)(a) HB(SPC) Regs. These regulations state that the child is treated as not being part of your household and not occupying your home where s/he is placed with you under a 'relevant enactment'. Relevant enactment includes the Children (Scotland) Act 1995, the Adoptions and Children (Scotland) Act 2007 and the Children's Hearings (Scotland) Act 2011.
72 Reg 13D(3A)(b) HB Regs; reg 13D(3A)(b) HB(SPC) Regs
73 Reg B13(6)(b) HB Regs
74 Reg 11(2)(a) CTR(S) Regs; regs 11(2)(a) CTR(SPC)(S) Regs. These rules state that a child is not part of your household if s/he is 'boarded out with you under a relevant enactment'. It is arguable that this should not apply to you.

Chapter 7: Children living with kinship carers
Notes

75 **HB** Sch 5 paras 25(1)(ba), 26(a)(ii) and (iii) and 28 HB Regs; reg 29(1) HB(SPC) Regs
   CTR Sch 4 paras 29(1)(b), 30(a) and 32 CTR(S) Regs; reg 27(1) CTR(SPC)(S) Regs
   If payment is made under s50 and the child is not treated as part of your household, the payment should be disregarded provided you spend the payment on the child: reg 46(6)(c) HB regs; reg 41(3)(c) CTR(S) Regs
76 Regs 7(2A), 9 and 12(f) and (g) CTC Regs
77 Reg 3(1) r4 Case A CTC Regs
78 Reg 2(2) WTC(EMR) Regs
79 ss803-65 and 806(3)(c) IT(TOI)A 2005; reg 4(1) WTC(EMR) Regs fourth condition; BIM 52755 and 52758
80 para 124100 TCM
81 Reg 4 WTC(EMR) Regs
82 Reg 19 Table 6 para 9 TC(DCI) Regs
83 Because they are not defined as income under reg 3 TC(DCI) Regs (confirmed for s50 and s22 payments in HMRC email to CPAG, 22 April 2009).
84 s23A(2) and (3)(b) SSCBA 1992; regs 4 and 9 SS(CCPC) Regs
85 Reg 9(a) SS(CCPC) Regs

Chapter 8
Children living with foster carers

This chapter covers:
1. What is foster care (below)
2. Benefits and tax credits for foster carers (p130)

When a child goes to live with foster carers, there can be benefit and tax credit issues for both the foster carer(s) and the child's birth parent(s). This chapter explains what happens to foster carers' benefits and tax credits. For information about what happens to the birth parents' benefits and tax credits when their child goes to live with foster carers, see Chapter 6.

1. What is foster care

'Fostering' is where a child or young person is being cared for in a family home with carers who do not have parental responsibility for her/him. There are two different types of fostering:
- public fostering; *and*
- private fostering.

The difference depends on who makes the arrangement for the child to live with foster carers.

Public fostering

Public fostering is where the local authority arranges for the child to live with a foster carer(s). This may be done through the local authority's own fostering service or through an arrangement with a voluntary organisation – eg, Barnardo's or Action for Children. This type of fostering is governed by the Children (Scotland) Act 1995 and the Looked After Children (Scotland) Regulations 2009. All public foster carers must be approved by the local authority.[1]

Chapter 8: Children living with foster carers
2. Benefits and tax credits for foster carers

A child who is in public foster care is 'looked after' by the local authority. The information in this chapter is aimed at public fostering arrangements and the term 'foster carers' is used to mean public foster carers.

Foster carers are usually paid a fostering allowance and also a 'fee'. There are no set rates for fostering allowances or fees and the amount paid may vary depending on the local authority or fostering agency.[2]

Private fostering

Private fostering is where a parent (or person with parental responsibility) arranges for the child to live with another person for 28 days or more, and the other person is not a relative. 'Relative' means mother, father, grandparent, brother, sister (or half-brother or half-sister), aunt or uncle (including by marriage). If the child's parents have never married, it also includes any person who would be defined as a relative had the parents been married.[3] This type of fostering is governed by the Foster Children (Scotland) Act 1984 and the Foster Children (Private Fostering) (Scotland) Regulations 1985.

The information in this chapter does *not* apply to private fostering arrangements. If you are a foster carer in a private fostering arrangement, or if your child lives with a private foster carer, there are no special benefit or tax credit rules. This means that if you satisfy the conditions of entitlement for a benefit or tax credit (see Chapter 1), you are able to claim. See p9, p41 and p47 for more information on the priority between potential claimants.

2. Benefits and tax credits for foster carers

Child benefit

If a child has been placed in foster care with you and the local authority or fostering agency is paying towards the child's maintenance and/or accommodation (eg, a fostering allowance), you cannot get child benefit (or guardian's allowance) for the child.[4]

Means-tested benefits

Universal credit

If you are on universal credit (UC), it does not include any child element for a child you are fostering.[5] You do not get any help with childcare costs in your UC for a child you are fostering. The housing costs element for rent is limited depending on how many bedrooms you are deemed to need (called the 'size criteria'). The size criteria does not include a child you are fostering. You are allowed one extra room in the size criteria, regardless of how many children you foster. This applies while you have a foster child or children living with you and also during a period of up to one year while you are an approved foster carer but do not have a child placed with you.[6] Any income from fostering that you receive does not count as income for UC.[7]

If you are the 'responsible foster parent' (see below) and you are caring for a child aged under one, you are not subject to any work-related requirements (see p49).[8] If you are the 'responsible foster parent' and you are caring for a child aged between one and 16, you are subject to the work-focused interview only requirement (see p49). This can extend beyond the child's 16th birthday if s/he has care needs which would make it unreasonable for you to meet the work search or work availability requirements, even if these were limited.[9]

If you are claiming UC as a couple and your partner is the 'responsible foster carer', you can be subject to the work-focused interview only requirement if you and your partner are caring for a child or qualifying young person (see p8) who has care needs which would make it unreasonable for either of you you to meet the work search or work availability requirements, even if these were limited.[10]

If you have a gap between placements where you do not have a child living with you, you can continue to be subject to the work-focused interview only requirement for up to eight weeks, providing this requirement applied to you before the break started.[11]

Responsible foster parent

'Responsible foster parent' means that either you are the child's only foster carer or, if you are a member of a couple who are foster carers, you and your partner have nominated you as the 'responsible foster parent'. Only one of you can be nominated. The nomination applies to all your children and can only be changed once in the 12 months after the nomination or if there has been a relevant change of circumstances.[12]

Income support

If you are on income support (IS) when you become a foster carer, your IS is not normally affected (but see p134 for information about claiming working tax credit (WTC) instead).

You cannot normally get IS if you are in 'remunerative work' of 16 hours or more a week. However, provided you are receiving a fostering allowance, fostering does not count as remunerative work for IS purposes.[13]

If you are a single person fostering a child under 16, you can claim IS on this basis.[14] You must actually have a child placed with you to be able to claim IS under this rule – ie, not be between placements.

Note: because of the introduction of UC, you cannot usually make a new claim for IS, but you can continue to get it at the moment if you are already entitled.

Any payment you receive for fostering is disregarded as income for IS.[15] However, if you are paid any type of payment (such as a retainer) while you do not have a child accommodated with you, this is treated as income.[16]

Chapter 8: Children living with foster carers
2. Benefits and tax credits for foster carers

Income-related employment and support allowance

If you are getting income-related employment and support allowance (ESA) when you become a foster carer, your income-related ESA is not normally affected (but see p134 for information about claiming WTC instead). You cannot get ESA if you are working. However, provided you are receiving a fostering allowance, fostering does not count as work for ESA purposes.[17] Any payment you receive for fostering is disregarded as income for income-related ESA.[18] However, if you are paid any type of payment (such as a retainer) while you do not have a child accommodated with you, this is treated as income.[19]

Jobseeker's allowance

If you are on jobseeker's allowance (JSA) when you become a foster carer, your JSA is not normally affected.

You cannot get JSA if you are in 'remunerative work'. However, provided you are receiving a fostering allowance, fostering does not count as remunerative work for JSA purposes.[20] Any payment you receive for fostering is disregarded as income for income-based JSA.[21] However, if you are paid any type of payment (such as a retainer) while you do not have a child accommodated with you, this is treated as income and may reduce the amount of your income-based JSA.[22]

Contribution-based JSA is not means tested and is not affected by any income you have from fostering.

Pension credit

Some pension credit (PC) claimants who are responsible for a child or qualifying young person get an additional amount for the child/ren in their PC (instead of child tax credit – CTC). You will *not* receive an additional amount in your PC for a child you are fostering.[23] Any payment you receive for fostering is disregarded for PC purposes. If you receive a payment while you do not have a child accommodated with you (eg, a retainer), this should not count as income unless it is treated as earnings.[24]

Housing benefit and council tax reduction

If you are on housing benefit (HB)/council tax reduction (CTR) when you become a foster carer, your HB/CTR is not normally affected. There are no amounts included in your 'applicable amount' (see p24) for foster children,[25] and any payment you receive for fostering is disregarded as income for HB/CTR.[26] However, if you are under pension age and you are paid any form of payment (such as a retainer) while you do not have a child accommodated with you, this is treated as income.[27] If you have reached pension age and you are paid a retainer, this should not count as income unless it is treated as earnings.[28]

If you are a tenant in the private rented sector (not local authority or housing association), your HB is probably calculated on the basis of a 'local housing allowance' (see p24). This means that the maximum HB you can get is an amount determined by where you live and how many rooms you and your family require (the 'size criteria'). The size criteria does not include room(s) for any child(ren) you are fostering, although you are allowed one extra room if you are a foster carer. This applies while you have a foster child or children living with you and also during a period of up to one year while you are approved as a foster carer but do not have a foster child living with you.[29]

If you are under pension age and living in the social rented sector, your HB may be reduced if you are under-occupying your home (see p24). When assessing whether you are under-occupying your home, you are not counted as needing rooms for any children you are fostering, although you are allowed one extra room because you are a foster carer. This applies while you have a foster child or children living with you and also during a period of up to one year while you are approved as a foster carer but do not have a foster child living with you.[30]

If you are struggling to pay your rent as a result of this or the local housing allowance rules, apply for a discretionary housing payment (see p26).

Non-means-tested benefits

Disability living allowance and personal independence payment

If the child you are fostering gets disability living allowance (DLA), s/he keeps getting it while in foster care as long as s/he continues to satisfy the usual conditions of entitlement.[31] Once the young person reaches age 16, if s/he is still on DLA, or if s/he gets personal independence payment (PIP), the mobility component continues. The care component (DLA) or daily living component (PIP) continues if either:[32]
- her/his health or development is likely to be significantly or further impaired without provision of services; *or*
- s/he is in need of care and attention because s/he is disabled.

If you think the child for whom you care is entitled to DLA, you can make a claim on her/his behalf. Once s/he is aged 16, the young person makes the claim for PIP (see p36) in her/his own right.

If the child has been in local authority accommodation (eg, a residential unit) before coming to live with you, her/his DLA care component may have stopped being paid. Let the Disability Service Centre know s/he is now living with you and the care component should be paid again.

If a child under 16 gets DLA, an adult is appointed to act on her/his behalf. This person receives payment of the child's DLA. The appointee is usually the child's parent. Appointeeship should stop if a child becomes 'looked after and accommodated', unless the arrangement is expected to last for less than 12 weeks.[33] When a child comes to live with you, you can apply to take over being the appointee by writing to the Disability Service Centre, giving the child's name, date of birth and reference number if you have it (you will find it on any letters from the Disability Service Centre about the DLA). You should also provide your details (name, address, date of birth and national insurance (NI) number) and explain the circumstances. Alternatively, the local authority can be appointed to deal with the child's DLA.[34]

If there is disagreement about who should be a child's appointee for DLA, the DWP decides. There is no right of appeal against this decision[35] but you could consider using the complaints procedures if you are unhappy with the decision (see Chapter 2).

Carer's allowance

You cannot get carer's allowance (CA) if you are 'gainfully employed', which means if you are earning more than £123 a week. Any payment you receive for fostering does not count as earnings for this purpose.[36]

If you are entitled to CA and you also get UC, IS, income-related ESA, income-based JSA, PC or HB/CTR, you should get a carer element, carer premium or carer addition in your applicable amount (see Chapter 1).

Tax credits

Child tax credit

You cannot get CTC for a child you are fostering if you are getting a fostering allowance.[37] You may still qualify for CTC for other dependent children who are not fostered.

Working tax credit

Note: because of the introduction of UC, you cannot usually make a new claim for tax credits but currently you can continue to get tax credits, and renew your claim at the end of tax year, if you are already entitled.

In order to get WTC, you have to be in 'qualifying remunerative work'. This means that you are working (either employed or self-employed) for a certain number of hours a week and fall into at least one of five categories (see below). Fostering should count as self-employed work for tax credit purposes, provided you are paid, and so you may be able to get WTC.[38] If you are a foster carer and you are refused WTC on the basis that you are not self-employed, seek advice immediately.

You may be able to get WTC if:
- you are aged at least 25 and you work at least 30 hours a week; *or*
- you are aged at least 60 and you work at least 16 hours a week; *or*
- you are a single claimant, have a dependent child, and you work for at least 16 hours a week. The child you are fostering does not count as dependent for this purpose, but if you have a child of your own s/he does count; *or*
- you are a couple, have a dependent child and your combined working hours are at least 24 a week. The child you are fostering does not count as dependent for this purpose, but if you have a child of your own, s/he does count. If you

both work, one must do at least 16 hours a week. If only one works, s/he must do at least 24 hours a week. **Note:** if you are a couple with a dependent child and the non-working partner is incapacitated, a hospital inpatient, in prison or entitled to CA, you can qualify if you work at least 16 hours a week; *or*
- you have a disability which puts you at a disadvantage in getting a job, and you work for at least 16 hours a week.

Fostering payments up to £10,000 a year, plus £200 a week for each child under 11 and £250 a week for each child aged 11 or over, are not liable for tax, according to the HMRC tax relief scheme. Fostering payments that come below this level are therefore ignored as income for tax credit purposes.[39] HMRC produces a helpsheet (HS236) on the tax relief scheme (available at www.gov.uk).

National insurance credits

You are entitled to be credited with class 3 NI contributions for any week in which you are an approved foster carer.[40] These credits can help towards your retirement pension and some other benefits. You must apply to HMRC to be credited with these contributions.[41] Apply online or print off Form CF411A at www.gov.uk after the end of the tax year and send it to HMRC with a letter of confirmation from your fostering agency or local authority.

Notes

1. **What is foster care**
   1 Reg 2 LAC(S) Regs
   2 Payment of fostering allowances is governed by reg 33 LAC(S) Regs
   3 s21 Foster Children (Scotland) Act 1984

2. **Benefits and tax credits for foster carers**
   4 Sch 9 SSCBA 1992; regs 16 and 18 CB Regs
   5 Reg 4 UC Regs
   6 Sch 4 paras 8, 9, 10 and 12 UC Regs
   7 Reg 66 UC Regs
   8 S19(2)(c) WRA 2012; regs 85 and 89(1)(f) UC Regs
   9 Reg 91 UC Regs
   10 Reg 91(2)(c) UC Regs
   11 Reg 91(2)(d) UC Regs
   12 Regs 85 and 86 UC Regs
   13 Reg 6(1)(k) IS Regs
   14 Sch 1B para 2 IS Regs
   15 Sch 9 para 26 IS Regs
   16 Sch 9 para 26 IS Regs
   17 Reg 40(2)(d) ESA Regs
   18 Sch 8 para 28 ESA Regs
   19 Sch 8 para 28 ESA Regs
   20 Reg 53(f) JSA Regs
   21 Sch 7 para 27 JSA Regs
   22 Sch 7 para 27 JSA Regs
   23 Sch 2IIA para 4 SPC Regs
   24 s15 SPCA 2002; reg 17B SPC Regs
   25 **HB** Reg 21(3) HB Regs; reg 21(3) HB(SPC) Regs
   CTR Reg 11(2) CTR(S) Regs; reg 11(2) CTR(SPC)(S) Regs

Chapter 8: Children living with foster carers
Notes

26 **HB** Sch 5 para 26 HB Regs; reg 38(2) HB(SPC) Regs
   CTR Sch 4 para 30(a) CTR(S) Regs; reg 27(1) CTR(SPC)(S) Regs
27 **HB** Sch 5 para 26 HB Regs
   CTR Sch 4 para 30 CTR(S) Regs
28 **HB** Reg 29 HB(SPC) Regs
   CTR Reg 27(1) CTR(SPC)(S) Regs
29 Regs 2 and 13D(3A)(b) HB Regs; regs 2 and 13D(3A)(b) HB(SPC) Regs
30 Regs 2 and B13(6)(b) HB Regs
31 Reg 9(4) and (5) SS(DLA) Regs
32 Reg 9(4)(b) SS(DLA) Regs; reg 28(3) SS(PIP) Regs; s93(4)(a)(ii) and (iii) C(S)A 1995
33 Reg 43(4) SS(C&P) Regs
34 Reg 43(5) SS(C&P) Regs
35 Sch 2 para 5(y) SS&CS(DA) Regs
36 Sch 1 para 6 SSB(CE) Regs
37 Reg 3(1) r4 CTC Regs
38 Reg 4 WTC(EMR) Regs
39 Reg 19 Table 6 para 9 TC(DCI) Regs
40 s23A(2) and (3)(b) SSCBA 1992; regs 4 and 9 SS(CCPC) Regs
41 Reg 9(a) SS(CCPC) Regs

Chapter 9
Adoption

This chapter covers:
1. Adoption allowances (below)
2. Benefits and tax credits when a child is placed with you for adoption (p139)
3. Benefits and tax credits once you have adopted a child (p146)

Benefit and tax credit issues can arise when a child goes to live with adoptive parents or prospective adoptive parents. The effect on benefits and tax credits depends on whether the child has been placed with you before being adopted by you (often referred to as being 'placed for adoption') or whether you have formally adopted the child (an adoption order has been granted in your favour by the court). This chapter explains both situations, and also explains how adoption allowances affect benefits and tax credits.

> **Definitions**
> **Agency adoptions** are where adoption agencies (local authorities and voluntary agencies) formally place children for adoption under adoption law. Most of the information in this chapter only applies to agency adoptions and adopters.
> Any other adoptions are **non-agency adoptions.** These may be adoptions by relatives, step-parents or other people, including inter-country adopters. Non-agency adoptions also include cases when former foster carers adopt, but have not been formally approved as agency adopters.
> An **adoption allowance** is a payment that may be made by the local authority or adoption agency to adoptive parents or to someone with whom a child has been placed for adoption. Adoption allowances are not paid to every adoptive parent.[1]

1. Adoption allowances

An adoption allowance can be paid by the local authority or adoption agency to adoptive parents or to someone with whom a child has been placed for adoption if:[2]
- it is needed to ensure that the adopter(s) can look after the child; *or*

Chapter 9: Adoption
1. Adoption allowances

- the child needs special care, involving extra expense, because of illness, disability, emotional or behavioural difficulties, or the continuing consequences of past abuse or neglect; *or*
- the adoption agency has to make special arrangements to aid the placement or adoption of the child because of her/his age or ethnic origin or the desirability of placing her/him with either a sibling or with a child with whom s/he has previously lived; *or*
- it is needed to meet recurring costs of travel to allow visits between the child and a relative; *or*
- the adoption agency considers it appropriate to make a contribution to meet:
  - the legal costs in relation to the adoption; *or*
  - expenses relating to introducing the child to the adopter; *or*
  - expenses needed for the accommodation and maintenance of the child, including the provision of furniture and domestic equipment, alterations and adaptations to the home, transport and clothing, toys and other items necessary to look after the child.

An adoption allowance can be paid from the date of the placement for adoption or from a later date.[3]

In deciding how much, if any, adoption allowance to pay, the local authority or adoption agency must take into account any other grant, benefit, allowance or resource which is available to you as a result of the adoption.

In addition, the local authority or adoption agency must normally take account of:[4]

- your financial resources, including any benefits or tax credits that would be available to you if the child lived with you; *and*
- your reasonable outgoings and commitments; *and*
- the financial needs of the child.

However, the local authority or adoption agency *must* disregard the factors listed in the three bullet points above if the allowance is for legal costs or to cover the costs involved in introducing you to the child. These factors *may* be disregarded if the allowance is for:

- the initial costs of accommodating the child; *or*
- recurring travel costs for the child to visit a relative; *or*
- a child who needs special care because of illness, disability, emotional or behavioural difficulties, or the continuing consequences of past abuse or neglect; *or*
- special arrangements that have to be made to aid the placement of a child because of her/his age, ethnic origin, disability or the desirability of placing her/him with either a sibling or a child with whom s/he has previously lived.

An adoption allowance stops if:[5]
- the adoptive child no longer lives with you (unless the local authority or adoption agency considers it necessary to continue to pay because of the needs of the child or other exceptional circumstances); or
- the child stops full-time education or training and starts work; or
- the child qualifies for universal credit, income support or jobseeker's allowance in her/his own right; or
- the child reaches 18, unless still in full-time education or training, in which case the allowance may continue to the end of the course/training; or
- the period agreed between you and the local authority or adoption agency for payment of the allowance has expired.

2. Benefits and tax credits when a child is placed with you for adoption

This section describes what happens to benefits and tax credits when a child you plan to adopt comes to live with you, but before you have an adoption order in place. See p146 for what happens to benefits and tax credits once you have an adoption order.

Child benefit

Provided you statisfy the normal rules (see p7), you are entitled to child benefit as soon as the child comes to live with you, unless the local authority is making payments to you under regulation 33 of the Looked After Children (Scotland) Regulations 2009.[6] **Note:** adoption allowances are *not* paid under this regulation.[7]

Child benefit is not means tested and, therefore, any adoption allowance paid does not affect it.

For information on what happens to benefits and tax credits once you have an adoption order for a child, see p146.

Statutory adoption pay, statutory paternity pay and statutory shared parental pay

You may be entitled to statutory adoption pay (SAP) if you are adopting or jointly adopting a child, or statutory paternity pay (SPP) if your partner is adopting a child or if you are jointly adopting a child with your partner. If you have a partner, you and/or your partner may be entitled to statutory shared parental pay (SSPP).

If you are jointly adopting a child with your partner, you can choose whether to request SAP or SPP. SAP is payable for 39 weeks, whereas SPP is only payable for two weeks. In this situation, your partner may be able to claim SAP while you claim SPP, or vice versa. However, you cannot both qualify for SAP for the same

Chapter 9: Adoption
2. Benefits and tax credits when a child is placed with you for adoption

adoption and you cannot receive SPP for any week in which you are entitled to SAP.[8] Both men and women can qualify for SAP and SPP (adoption).

SAP and SPP can be paid if a child has been newly placed for adoption by an adoption agency, but not if you adopt a child who is already living with you – eg, if you are a step-parent adopting your stepdaughter or stepson.[9]

If you are adopting more than one child, no additional SAP, SPP or SSPP is payable, unless this happens as part of a different adoption arrangement.[10]

Statutory adoption pay

SAP can be paid by an employer when an employee is adopting a child. If you qualify, SAP is the minimum to which you are entitled. You may be entitled to a higher amount under your contract and/or conditions of employment.

To get SAP you must:[11]

- be adopting a child under UK law. See CPAG's *Welfare Benefits and Tax Credits Handbook* if you are adopting a child from abroad; *and*
- have worked for the same employer for 26 weeks ending with the week in which you are told you have been matched with a child for adoption; *and*
- have average gross earnings of at least £118 (in tax year 2019/20) a week; *and*
- not be carrying out any work for the employer who is paying you SAP. It does not mean you have given up your job. You are allowed to work for up to 10 'keeping-in-touch' days within your SAP period (see below) without affecting your entitlement; *and*
- give your employer the correct notice. This means notice, usually at least 28 days in advance (in writing if required), of:
  – when you want the SAP to start; *and*
  – the date you expect the child to be placed with you.

In addition, you must provide:

- a written declaration that you want to claim SAP rather than SPP; *and*
- documents from the adoption agency giving details of the adoption (matching documents).

The earliest date SAP can start to be paid is normally 14 days before the day you expect the child to be placed with you. The latest is normally the day the placement starts.[12] Payment can then continue for a maximum of 39 weeks, unless the child:

- returns to the adoption agency after being placed with you; *or*
- dies after being placed with you for adoption; *or*
- is not actually placed with you, even though your adoption pay period has already started.

If one of the above situations occurs, the adoption pay period ends eight weeks after the end of the week the child returns or dies, or you are notified that the placement is not going to take place, if this is earlier than SAP would otherwise have ended.[13]

For the first six weeks, SAP is paid at a weekly rate of 90 per cent of your average earnings and after that at either £148.68 or 90 per cent of average weekly earnings, whichever is the lower amount.[14]

Statutory paternity pay

SPP can be paid by an employer when an employee and/or her/his partner is adopting a child. To get SPP you must:[15]

- be adopting a child jointly with your partner (or your partner is adopting a child) under UK law. See CPAG's *Welfare Benefits and Tax Credits Handbook* if you are adopting a child from abroad; *and*
- have, or expect to have (along with the adopter or joint adopter), the main responsibility for the upbringing of the child; *and*
- intend to care for the child or support the person adopting the child while receiving SPP; *and*
- not have elected to receive SAP; *and*
- have worked for the same employer for 26 weeks ending with the week in which you are told you have been matched with a child for adoption; *and*
- have average gross earnings of at least £118 (in tax year 2019/20) a week; *and*
- not be carrying out any work for the employer who is paying you SPP. It does not mean you have given up your job; *and*
- give your employer the correct notice (see below).

Within seven days of being notified of the adoption match or, if that is not practicable, as soon as is reasonably practicable after that date,[16] you must tell your employer:

- when you would like your SPP to start; *and*
- whether you want to get SPP for one week or two; *and*
- the date you expect the child to be placed for adoption (or the date s/he was placed, if the placement has already happened); *and*
- the date on which the adopter was notified that the child had been matched with her/him for adoption.

You must also give your employer a declaration, stating that:

- you and your spouse, civil partner or partner are jointly adopting a child, or your spouse, civil partner or partner is adopting a child; *and*
- you have, or expect to have, the main responsibility for the upbringing of the child (apart from the responsibility of the adopter or co-adopter); *and*
- while getting SPP, you intend to care for the child or support the child's adopter; *and*
- you elect to be paid SPP rather than SAP.

Chapter 9: Adoption
2. Benefits and tax credits when a child is placed with you for adoption

You can use Form SC4 for SPP to provide this information to your employer. The form is available at www.gov.uk.

If you give your employer less notice than this, or you do not provide the information within the time limit, your SPP can begin later, once the necessary time limit for providing the notice or information has passed, provided payment would still fall within the eight-week period in which SPP can be paid.

SPP can normally be paid for a maximum of two consecutive weeks. However, you can choose to receive it for just one week.[17] It is paid at either £148.68 or 90 per cent of your average weekly earnings, whichever is the lower amount. The earliest date it can be paid is the date of the child's placement for adoption.[18] The latest is eight weeks after that date.[19]

Statutory shared parental pay

If your partner chooses to end her/his SAP early, you may be able to get SSPP for the weeks your partner has 'given up' her/his SAP. For example, if your partner opts to get 19 weeks of SAP, you could potentially get 20 weeks of SSPP. You can also 'share' SSPP with your partner. So, if your partner opts to get 19 weeks SAP, you could share the remaining 20 weeks and both, for example, have 10 weeks SSPP each. SSPP can only be paid within one year of the child being placed for adoption.

You are eligible for SSPP if if you are eligible for SAP (see p140), or you are eligible for SPP (adoption) (see p141) and your partner is eligible for SAP. Your partner must have opted to stop receiving SAP. SSPP is paid at either £148.68 or 90 per cent of your average weekly earnings, whichever is the lower amount.

See CPAG's *Welfare Benefits and Tax Credits Handbook* for more information.

Means-tested benefits

Universal credit

If the child placed with you for adoption is 'looked after' by the local authority, your universal credit (UC) does not include any child element for the child.[20] You do not get any help with childcare costs in UC if the child is still 'looked after' by the local authority.[21] The housing costs element for rent is limited depending on how many bedrooms you are deemed to need (called the 'size criteria'). The size criteria will not include a child placed for adoption. You are allowed one extra room in the size criteria.[22] Any adoption allowance you receive does not count as income for UC.[23] If you are a single person, for the first 12 months after the child has been placed with you, you are not subject to any work-related requirements. If you are a couple, the person who is the main carer for the child is not subject to any work-related requirements. For what happens to UC once you have an adoption order, see p146.

Income support

If you are a single person or lone parent with whom a child aged under 16 has been placed for adoption, you may be able to claim income support (IS) on that basis (although if you are not already on IS you will usually have to claim UC instead).[24] If you are on IS when a child is placed with you for adoption, your IS is not normally affected. If you are paid an adoption allowance (before the adoption order is granted), any amount of this that you spend on the child is disregarded in full when working out your income. If you keep any for your own use, it is taken into account as income.[25]

For what happens to benefits and tax credits once you have an adoption order for a child, see p146.

Income-related employment and support allowance

If you are getting income-related employment and support allowance (ESA) when a child is placed with you for adoption and you are paid an adoption allowance (before the adoption order is granted), any amount of this that you spend on the child is disregarded in full. If you keep any for your own use, it is taken into account as income for income-related ESA.[26]

For information on what happens to benefits and tax credits once you have an adoption order for a child, see p146.

Jobseeker's allowance

If you are getting jobseeker's allowance (JSA) when a child is placed with you for adoption and you are paid an adoption allowance (before the adoption order is granted), any amount of this that you spend on the child is disregarded in full. If you keep any for your own use, it is taken into account as income for income-based JSA.[27]

For information on what happens to benefits and tax credits once you have an adoption order for a child, see p146.

Pension credit

If you are getting pension credit (PC) and are paid an adoption allowance, it is disregarded as income for PC purposes.[28] Some PC claimants who are responsible for a child or qualifying young person get an additional amount for her/him in their PC (instead of child tax credit – CTC). If the child placed with you for adoption is still 'looked after' by the local authority, your PC will not include the additional amount for the child.[29]

For information on what happens to benefits and tax credits once you have an adoption order for a child, see p146.

Housing benefit and council tax reduction

If you are getting housing benefit (HB)/council tax reduction (CTR) when a child is placed with you for adoption, your HB/CTR is not normally affected. There are

Chapter 9: Adoption
2. Benefits and tax credits when a child is placed with you for adoption

no amounts included in your 'applicable amount' (see p25) for children placed for adoption.[30]

If either you or your partner have reached pension age (see p35), any adoption allowance you are paid is disregarded in full for HB/CTR purposes.[31]

If you and your partner are under pension age and you are paid an adoption allowance (before the adoption order is granted), any amount of this that you spend on the child is disregarded in full. If you keep any for your own use, it is taken into account as income for HB/CTR.[32]

If you are a tenant in the private sector (not local authority or housing association), your HB is probably calculated on the basis of a 'local housing allowance' (see p24). This means that the maximum HB you can get is an amount determined by where you live and how many rooms you and your family require (the 'size criteria'). You are allowed one room in the size criteria if you have a child (or children, if part of the same adoption arrangement) placed with you for adoption.[33]

If you are under pension age and living in the social rented sector, your HB may be reduced if you are under-occupying your home (see p24). When assessing whether you are under-occupying your home, you are not counted as needing a room for a child placed with you for adoption. However, you are allowed one extra bedroom in the size criteria because a child (or children if part of the same adoption arrangement) has been placed with you for adoption.[34]

If you are struggling to pay your rent, claim a discretionary housing payment (see p26).

For information on what happens to benefits and tax credits once you have an adoption order for a child, see p146.

Non-means-tested benefits

Disability living allowance

If the child placed with you for adoption gets disability living allowance (DLA), s/he continues to receive it when s/he comes to live with you, provided s/he continues to satisfy the normal conditions of entitlement. If the child has been in local authority accommodation (eg, in a residential unit) before coming to live with you, the DLA care component may have stopped being paid. Inform the Disability Service Centre (see Appendix 1) that the child is now living with you and the care component should be paid again.

When a child under 16 gets DLA, an adult is appointed to act on her/his behalf. This person receives payment of the child's DLA. The appointee is usually the child's parent. When a child comes to live with you, you can apply to become the appointee by writing to the Disability Service Centre, giving the child's name, date of birth and reference number if you have it (you will find it on any letters from the Disability Service Centre). Also provide your details (name, address, date of birth and national insurance number) and explain the circumstances.

Carer's allowance

If the child placed with you for adoption is getting the middle or highest rate care component of DLA, you may be able to claim carer's allowance (CA), provided you satisfy the normal rules (see p5). You cannot get CA if you are 'gainfully employed' – ie, you earn more than £123 a week. Adoption allowance does not count as earnings for this purpose,[35] although SAP, SPP and SSPP do count as earnings.[36]

If you are entitled to CA and you also get UC, IS, income-related ESA, income-based JSA, PC or HB/CTR, you should get the carer element, carer premium or carer addition in your applicable amount.

Tax credits

Most people are not able to make a new claim for tax credits, but have to claim UC instead. See p46 for more details. The information in this section applies to you if you are already getting tax credits or you are in the group who is still able to claim tax credits.

Any adoption allowance you receive is disregarded for tax credits.[37] £100 a week of SAP/SPP/SSAP is disregarded for tax credits.[38]

For information on what happens to tax credits once you have an adoption order for the child, see p149.

Child tax credit

If you are able to claim tax credits or are already getting CTC (eg, for another child) and providing you satisfy the normal conditions of entitlement, you can get CTC for the child you are going to adopt as soon as the child comes to live with you, unless the local authority is making payments to you under regulation 33 of the Looked After Children (Scotland) Regulations 2009.[39] **Note:** adoption allowances are not paid under this regulation.[40] The 'two-child limit' (see p43) does not apply if a child is placed with you for adoption (agency adoption). This means that even if you already have two or more dependent children and a child is placed with you for adoption, you can get the child element in your CTC for the child who has come to live with you, providing you satisfy the normal conditions of entitlement.[41] If you subsequently give birth to a child, the child placed for adoption is 'disregarded' when applying the two-child limit.[42]

Working tax credit

In order to get working tax credit (WTC), you have to be in 'full-time paid work' (see p44).

Note: if you cannot get CTC for a child (see above), s/he does not count as a dependent child for WTC.

You are treated as being in full-time paid work during any period when you are being paid SAP, SPP or SSPP and during any period when you are absent from work during adoption or paternity leave or during statutory shared parental leave

Chapter 9: Adoption
3. Benefits and tax credits once you have adopted a child

during which you could have received SSPP, provided you were in qualifying remunerative work before you went on adoption/paternity/shared parental leave,[43] or would have counted as being in full-time paid work if you had been responsible for a child.[44]

Note: because of the introduction of UC, you cannot usually make a new claim for tax credits but currently you can continue to get them, and renew your claim at the end of tax year, if you are already entitled.

Other benefits

Best Start grant

You can qualify for a Best Start grant pregnancy and baby payment if a child aged under 12 months is placed with you for adoption, and you satisfy the other conditions of entitlement (see p3). You must claim before the child is one year old.[45] The payment is £600, or £300 if you have another child under 16 in your household.[46] If an older child is placed with you for adoption, you may be entitled to an early years payment or a school-age payment (see p4).

3. Benefits and tax credits once you have adopted a child

This section describes what happens to benefits and tax credits once an adoption order has been granted in your favour by the court.

Child benefit

Once you have adopted a child, you can claim, or continue to claim, child benefit, provided you satisfy the normal rules set out on p7.

Any adoption allowance you receive does not affect child benefit.

Statutory adoption pay, statutory paternity pay and statutory shared parental pay

See p139 for when you can claim statutory adoption pay (SAP), statutory paternity pay (SPP) and statutory shared parental pay (SSPP).

Means-tested benefits

Universal credit

Once you have adopted a child and s/he is no longer 'looked after' by the local authority, your universal credit (UC) includes the child element for her/him, providing you are 'responsible' for her/him. The 'two-child limit' (see p47) does not apply if you adopt a child (agency adoption). This means that even if you

Chapter 9: Adoption
3. Benefits and tax credits once you have adopted a child

already have two or more dependent children and you adopt a child born on or after 6 April 2017, you can get the child element in your UC for the child who has come to live with you, providing you satisfy the normal conditions of entitlement.[47] You count as responsible for her/him if s/he normally lives with you.[48] If you subsequently give birth to a child, the child placed for adoption is 'disregarded' when applying the two-child limit.[49] The amount of housing costs element you get in your UC reflects the number of bedrooms you need, including for the child you have adopted. Your work allowance should reflect the fact you have a dependent child (see p48). If you are working, you may be entitled to help with childcare costs (see p48). If you are a single person, for the first 12 months after the child has been placed with you, you are not subject to any work-related requirements. If you are a couple, the person who is the main carer for the child is not subject to any work-related requirements.[50] Any adoption allowance you receive does not count as income for UC.[51]

Income support

Note: if you are not already getting income support (IS) you will usually have to claim UC instead.

Once you have adopted a child, s/he counts as part of your household for IS purposes, provided you are treated as responsible for her/him. You are responsible for the child if:[52]
- you get child benefit for her/him; *or*
- no one gets child benefit for her/him and s/he usually lives with you, or you are the only person who has claimed child benefit for her/him.

If you have adopted a child aged under five and you do not have a partner, you count as a lone parent for IS purposes. This means you may be able to get IS, provided you satisfy the other rules (see p27).

If you are not getting any amount in your IS for a child and you are claiming child tax credit (CTC), any adoption allowance paid for a child you have adopted is disregarded for IS.[53]

If you are still claiming amounts for a child in your IS (see p30) and you are receiving an adoption allowance, you may be better off claiming UC.[54] Seek advice if you are in this situation.

Income-related employment and support allowance

If you are getting income-related employment and support allowance (ESA) when you adopt a child, your income-related ESA may not be affected, although if you claim UC your income-related ESA will stop.

Any adoption allowance paid for a child you have adopted is disregarded for income-related ESA.[55]

Chapter 9: Adoption
3. Benefits and tax credits once you have adopted a child

Jobseeker's allowance

Note: if you are not already getting income-based jobseeker's allowance (JSA) you are likely to have to claim UC instead.

Once you have adopted a child, the child counts as part of your household for JSA purposes, provided you are treated as responsible for her/him. You are responsible for the child if:[56]
- you get child benefit for her/him; *or*
- no one gets child benefit for her/him and s/he usually lives with you, or you are the only person who has claimed child benefit for her/him.

If you are not getting any amount in your income-based JSA for a child and you are claiming CTC, any adoption allowance paid for a child you have adopted is disregarded for JSA.[57]

If you are still claiming amounts for a child in your income-based JSA (see p30) and you are receiving an adoption allowance, you may be better off claiming UC instead.[58] If you are in this situation, seek advice.

Contribution-based JSA is not means tested and, therefore, is not affected by any adoption allowance you receive.

Pension credit

You can get pension credit (PC) if you satisfy the rules set out on p34. Some PC claimants who are responsible for a child or qualifying young person get an additional amount for her/him in their PC (instead of CTC). Once you have adopted a child and s/he is no longer 'looked after' by the local authority, you can get the additional amount (see p35) providing the child is normally living with you and you are not getting CTC for her/him.[59] If you are paid an adoption allowance, it is disregarded as income for PC purposes.[60]

Housing benefit and council tax reduction

Note: if you are not already on housing benefit (HB) you are likely to have to claim UC instead.

Once you have adopted a child, s/he counts as part of your household for HB/council tax reduction (CTR) purposes, provided you are treated as responsible for her/him. You are responsible for the child if s/he normally lives with you. If there is any doubt, s/he is treated as living with you if:[61]
- you get child benefit for her/him; *or*
- no one gets child benefit but you have claimed it; *or*
- no one has claimed child benefit, or more than one person has claimed it, but you appear to have most responsibility.

Adopting a child can change the amount of HB/CTR you get. The reasons why HB/CTR entitlement might change include the following.

- Being responsible for a child increases your applicable amount (see p24). This is the figure used to calculate how much HB/CTR you get.
- If your HB is calculated on the basis of a 'local housing allowance' (this only affects tenants in the private rented sector), the local housing allowance that applies to you might change. See p24 for more information.
- You may have childcare costs, which can be allowed for in the HB/CTR calculation.
- If you are under pension age and live in the social rented sector, your HB may be reduced because you are considered to be under-occupying your accommodation (see p24). This may change when you adopt a child.

Any adoption allowance you are paid is disregarded in full for HB and CTR.[62]

Non-means-tested benefits

Disability living allowance

If the child you have adopted gets disability living allowance (DLA), s/he keeps getting it. If a child under 16 gets DLA, an adult is appointed to act on her/his behalf. That person receives payment of the child's DLA. The appointee is usually the child's parent. When a child comes to live with you, you can apply to become the appointee by writing to the Disability Service Centre (see Appendix 1), giving the child's name, date of birth and reference number if you have it (you will find it on any letters from the Disability Service Centre about the DLA). Also provide your details (name, address, date of birth and national insurance number) and explain the circumstances.

Carer's allowance

If the child you adopt is getting the middle or highest rate care component of DLA, you may be able to claim carer's allowance (CA), provided you satisfy the normal rules (see p5). You cannot get CA if you are 'gainfully employed' – ie, if you are earning more than £123 a week. Adoption allowance does not count as earnings for this purpose,[63] although SAP, SPP and SSPP do count as earnings.[64]

If you are entitled to CA and you also get UC, IS, income-based JSA, income-related ESA, UC, PC or HB/CTR, you should get the carer element, carer premium or carer addition in your applicable amount.

Tax credits

Most people are not able to make a new claim for tax credits, but have to claim UC instead. See p46 for more details. The information in this section applies to you if you are already getting tax credits or you are in the group who is still able to claim tax credits (see p41 and p44).

Once you have adopted a child, you can count as responsible for her/him for tax credits purposes – ie, you can claim tax credits in respect of her/him.

Chapter 9: Adoption
3. Benefits and tax credits once you have adopted a child

Child tax credit

You can claim CTC for the child you have adopted, provided you satisfy the normal rules explained on p41. The 'two-child limit' (see p43) does not apply if you adopt a child (agency adoption). This means that even if you already have two or more dependent children and you adopt a child born on or after 6 April 2017, you can get the child element in your CTC for the child you have adopted, providing you satisfy the normal conditions of entitlement.[65] If you subsequently give birth to a child, the child placed for adoption is 'disregarded' when applying the two-child limit.[66]

Working tax credit

To get WTC you, or your partner, must be in full-time paid work. If you are responsible for at least one dependent child (see p44), full-time paid work means at least 16 hours a week if you are a single claimant and usually means 24 hours a week if you are a couple (see p44).

If, as a result of adopting a child, you pay a childminder, nursery or other childcare provider, you may become entitled to an increased amount of WTC (see p44).

You are treated as being in full-time paid work during any period when you are being paid SAP, SPP or SSPP and during any period when you are absent from work during adoption or paternity leave or during statutory shared parental leave during which you could have received SSPP, provided you were in qualifying remunerative work before you went on adoption/paternity/shared parental leave,[67] or would have counted as being in qualifying remunerative work if you had been responsible for a child.[68]

Any adoption allowance you are paid is disregarded for tax credits.[69] £100 a week of SAP/SPP/SSPP is disregarded for tax credits.[70]

Other benefits

Best Start grant

You can qualify for a Best Start grant pregnancy and baby payment if you adopt a child aged under 12 months. You must claim before the child is one year old.[71] You cannot claim a pregnancy and baby payment if you already received the payment when the child was placed for adoption (see p146).[72] The payment is £600, or £300 if you have another child under 16 in your household.[73]

If you adopt an older child, you may be entitled to an early years payment or a school-age payment (see p4 and p4).

Health benefits

Adopting a child may mean you become entitled to health benefits. If you have adopted a child aged under three, you may be entitled to help under the Best Start food scheme payment card for fruit, vegetables and milk (see p22).

Children are automatically entitled to free dental treatment and vouchers for glasses.

Chapter 9: Adoption Notes

Notes

1 Regs 10-17 ASSA(S) Regs

1. Adoption allowances
2 Reg 10 ASSA(S) Regs
3 Reg 10(1) ASSA(S) Regs
4 Reg 13 ASSA(S) Regs
5 Reg 14 ASSA(S) Regs

2. Benefits and tax credits when a child is placed with you for adoption
6 Sch 9 para 1 SSCBA 1992; reg 16(4) CB Regs; CBTM 08065. This could be a fostering allowance, for example.
7 Paid under s71 AC(S)A 2007
8 ss171ZB(4) and 171ZL(4) SSCBA 1992
9 ss171ZB(2)(a) and 171ZL(2)(a) SSCBA 1992; reg 2(2) SPPSAP(G) Regs
10 ss171ZB(6), 171ZL(5) and 171ZV SSCBA 1992
11 s171ZL(2)-(4) and (7) SSCBA 1992; regs 3(2), 23 and 24 SPPSAP(G) Regs
12 Reg 21 SPPSAP(G) Regs
13 Reg 22 SPPSAP(G) Regs
14 s171ZN(2E) SSCBA 1992
15 ss171ZB(2) and (3), 171ZC and 171ZE(4)-(7) SSCBA 1992; reg 11 SPPSAP(G) Regs
16 s171ZC(1) and (2) SSCBA 1992; regs 9 and 15 SPPSAP(G) Regs
17 s171ZE(2) SSCBA 1992; reg 12(3) SPPSAP(G) Regs
18 Reg 12(1)(a) SPPSAP(G) Regs
19 Reg 14 SPPSAP(G) Regs
20 Reg 4 UC Regs
21 Reg 33 UC Regs
22 Sch 4 para 12((1)(b) and (4)(b) paras 8, 9 10 and 12(1) UC Regs
23 Reg 66 UC Regs
24 Sch 1B para 2A IS Regs
25 Reg 42(4)(b) IS Regs; para 28174 DMG
26 Reg 107(4) ESA Regs; para 51215 DMG
27 Reg 105(10)(b) JSA Regs; para 28174 DMG
28 s15 SPCA 2002
29 Sch II2A2A para 4 SPC Regs
30 **HB** Reg 21(3) HB Regs; reg 21(3) HB(SPC) Regs
   CTR Reg 11(2) CTR(S) Regs; reg 11(2) CTR(SPC)(S) Regs
31 **HB** Reg 29 HB(SPC) Regs
   CTR Reg 27(1) CTR(SPC)(S) Regs
32 **HB** Reg 42(6)(c) HB Regs
   CTR Reg 41(3)(c) CTR(S) Regs
33 Regs 2, 13D(3A) and (12) and 21(3) HB Regs; regs 2, 13D(3A) and (12) and 21(3) HB(SPC) Regs
34 Regs 2, B13 and 21(3) HB Regs
35 Regs 9 and 12 SSB(CE) Regs
36 Reg 9(1)(j) SSB(CE) Regs
37 Reg 19 Table 6 para 11(a) TC(DCI) Regs
38 Reg 4(1)(h) TC(DCI) Regs
39 Reg 3(1) r4 Case B CTC Regs. This could be a fostering allowance, for example.
40 Paid under s71 AC(S)A 2007
41 Reg 11 CTC Regs
42 Reg 9 CTC Regs
43 Reg 5 WTC(EMR) Regs
44 Reg 5A WTC(EMR) Regs
45 Sch 2 EYA(BSG)(S) Regs
46 Sch 2 EYA(BSG)(S) Regs

3. Benefits and tax credits once you have adopted a child
47 Sch 12 para 3 UC Regs
48 Reg 4(2) UC Regs
49 Reg 24A(1)(za) UC Regs
50 Reg 89(1)(d) and (3) UC Regs and s19(6) WRA 2012
51 Reg 66 UC Regs
52 Reg 15 IS Regs
53 Sch 9 para 25(1)(a) IS Regs
54 If you still receive IS amounts for children, adoption allowance counts as income up to the amount of the child's personal allowance. Sch 9 para 25 IS Regs, as saved by SI 2003 No.455
55 Sch 8 para 26(1)(a) ESA Regs
56 Reg 77 JSA Regs
57 Sch 7 para 26(1)(a) JSA Regs
58 An adoption allowance is taken into account in full as income up to the level of the child's personal allowance. Sch 7 para 26 JSA Regs, as saved by SI 2003 No.455
59 Sch II2A para 3 SPC Regs
60 s15 SPCA 2002

Chapter 9: Adoption
Notes

61 **HB** Reg 20 HB Regs; reg 20 HB(SPC) Regs
   CTR Reg 10 CTR(S) Regs; reg 10 CTR(SPC)(S) Regs
62 **HB** Sch 5 para 25(1)(a) HB Regs; reg 29 HB(SPC) Regs
   CTR Sch 4 para 29(1)(a) CTR(S) Regs; reg 27(1) CTR(SPC)(S) Regs
63 Regs 9 and 12 SSB(CE) Regs
64 Reg 9(1)(j) SSB(CE) Regs
65 Reg 11 CTC Regs
66 Reg 9 CTC Regs
67 Reg 5 WTC(EMR) Regs
68 Reg 5A WTC (EMR) Regs
69 Reg 19 Table 6 para 11(a) TC(DCI) Regs
70 Reg 4(1)(h) TC(DCI) Regs
71 Sch 2 EYA (BSG)(S) Regs
72 Sch 2 para 1 EYA (BSG)(S) Regs
73 Sch 2 EYA(BSG)(S) Regs

Chapter 10

Young people leaving care

This chapter covers:
1. Universal credit (p154)
2. Income support, income-based jobseeker's allowance and housing benefit (p155)
3. Other benefits (p156)
4. Financial support from the local authority for 16/17-year-old care leavers (p157)
5. Other help from the local authority (p159)
6. Other help (p160)
7. Challenging local authority decisions (p160)

Many 16/17-year-olds who have been 'looked after and accommodated' by the local authority (sometimes called 'looked after away from home') cannot get universal credit (UC), income support (IS), income-based jobseeker's allowance (JSA) or housing benefit (HB). Instead, the local authority is responsible for providing support under section 29 of the Children (Scotland) Act 1995. Local authorities often refer to this help as 'after care', 'after-care services' or 'leaving care services'. Young people in this situation are often referred to as 'care leavers' or 'care-experienced young people'. When someone turns 18, there are no special rules about benefits for care leavers, although they may still be eligible for support from the local authority that looked after them.

Some 16- and 17-year-olds are still 'looked after and accommodated' by the local authority. The information in this chapter on IS, income-based JSA and HB does not apply to young people who are still looked after. See p154 for UC.

Note: benefits other than UC, IS, income-based JSA and HB are not affected.

Continuing care

Since April 2015, some young people who are looked after by the local authority have been able to ask to remain in their placement after they stop being officially 'looked after'.[1] This is called 'continuing care'. Continuing care means the same accommodation and other assistance as was being provided for the young person before s/he stopped being looked after by the local authority.[2]

Chapter 10: Young people leaving care
1. Universal credit

Most care leavers aged 16 and 17 are not able to claim universal credit (UC). For UC, you are a care leaver if:[3]
- you are 16 or over; and
- you were looked after (see below) by the local authority for at least three months since the age of 14 (the three-month period does not have to be continuous). Any period during which you were placed with a member of your family is disregarded when calculating the three months; and
- you were looked after by the local authority at your 16th birthday or after that date; and
- you are no longer looked after by the local authority.

If this applies to you, you cannot normally get UC (see below for exceptions).

If you are aged 16 or 17 and you are in a continuing care arrangement and were looked after for at least three months since age 14, you cannot normally get UC (see below for exceptions). Again, in counting the three months, any period during which you were placed with a member of your family is disregarded.

If you are aged 16 or 17 and you are still looked after by the local authority, you cannot normally get UC (see below for exceptions).

'**Looked after**' means:[4]
- the local authority provides you with accommodation under section 25 of the Children (Scotland) Act 1995; or
- you are subject to a compulsory supervision order or interim supervison order under the Children's Hearing (Scotland) Act 2011; or
- you are subject to a permanence order under section 80 of the Adoption and Children (Scotland) Act 2007 (or you were subject to a parental responsibilities order under section 86 of the Children (Scotland) Act 1995);[5] or
- you have been moved to Scotland from another part of the UK, and are subject to an order made under section 33 of the Children (Scotland) Act 1995.

Exceptions

There are some exceptions to this rule. You are not excluded from UC but you still cannot get the housing element of UC if you:[6]
- are responsible for a child;
- are a member of a couple and your partner is responsible for a child;
- have limited capability for work or are waiting for an assessment to establish whether you have limited capability for work.

These exceptions also apply to 16/17 year olds who are still looked after by the local authority or who are in continuing care.

2. Income support, income-based jobseeker's allowance and housing benefit

Note: most people who need to claim a means-tested benefit now have to claim universal credit (UC). This means the rules about income support (IS), income-based jobseeker's allowance (JSA) and housing benefit (HB) are no longer relevant for many young people.

Most care leavers aged 16 or 17 cannot get HB and cannot get IS or income-based JSA. However, see below for exceptions.

You are a care leaver for these purposes if:[7]
- you are 16 or over; *and*
- you were looked after and accommodated by the local authority for at least 13 weeks since the age of 14; *and*
- you were looked after by the local authority at your 16th birthday or after that date; *and*
- you are no longer looked after by the local authority; *and*
- you are not living with your family (see below), or you are living with your family and are receiving regular financial support from the local authority under section 29(1) of the Children (Scotland) Act 1995.

Note: if you are in 'continuing care', these rules apply to you if all the bullet points above apply.[8]

'**Accommodated**' means provided with accommodation by the local authority, requiring you to live in a specified place, unless that specified place is with your own family.[9]

The **13-week period** does not have to be a continuous period. When calculating the 13-week period, do not include any pre-planned short-term placements (such as respite) of four weeks or less if you returned to your family at the end of the placement.[10]

'**Family**' includes anyone who has parental responsibility for you (except the local authority) and anyone with whom you were living before being looked after by the local authority.[11] You are still defined as a care leaver (and, therefore, cannot claim IS, income-based JSA or HB) if you live with your family and the local authority provides regular financial support under section 29(1) of the Children (Scotland) Act 1995 (see p157).

Exceptions

Even if you fall within the definition of care leaver (including if you are in continuing care), if you are a lone parent or if you are entitled to statutory sick pay, you are not excluded from IS or income-based JSA.[12] You are still excluded from HB. This also applies to you if you are in 'continuing care' and you fall within the definition of care leaver. **Note:** even if you are not excluded from IS/income-based JSA, you will probably have to claim UC instead.

3. Other benefits

Employment and support allowance and statutory sick pay

If you are a care leaver who is too unwell to work, you may be able to claim employment and support allowance (ESA). There are no special rules preventing you claiming ESA, provided you satisfy the normal entitlement rules. If you are in employment but off sick, you may get statutory sick pay.

Health benefits

There are fixed charges for some NHS items and services. Care leavers who are receiving financial support from the local authority under section 29 of the Children (Scotland) Act 1995 (see p157) are exempt from these charges.[13]
Charges covered are for:
- dental treatment;
- glasses/contact lenses (a voucher is issued to cover the cost of the glasses/lenses you require – this may not cover the cost of those you choose to buy);
- travel to hospital for treatment.

Complete Form HC1(SC) to apply, available from the local authority, Jobcentre Plus offices or NHS hospitals. You should then get an HC2 certificate showing you are exempt from charges. This lasts up to your 18th birthday or for one year, whichever is longest. If you are still entitled when the certificate runs out (ie, because you are still under 18 and still being supported by the local authority), make a new claim.

If you are a care leaver who does not receive regular financial support from the local authority, you may also be entitled to help with NHS fixed charges if you are on a qualifying benefit, such as universal credit (UC) (with earnings below a specified level), income support (IS) or income-based jobseeker's allowance (JSA), or on the grounds of low income (see Chapter 1).

Best Start grant

If you are pregnant or have a baby, you may be able to get a Best Start grant pregnancy and baby payment (see p3). If you are under 18, you do not have to be receiving a 'qualifying benefit' to be entitled to a pregnancy and baby payment.

Scottish Welfare Fund payments

Care leavers who are on a low income may be able to get a community care grant or crisis grant from the Scottish Welfare Fund. A community care grant may be particularly important to help with the costs of setting up home (see p39).

Other benefits and tax credits

There are no special rules for care leavers for benefits or tax credits, other than UC, IS, income-based JSA, HB and health benefits. If you are entitled to another benefit, such as personal independence payment, you can claim in the usual way (see Chapter 1).

4. Financial support from the local authority for 16/17-year-old care leavers

Local authorities are responsible for providing financial support and accommodation to 16/17-year-old care leavers who are excluded from universal credit (UC), income support (IS), income-based jobseeker's allowance (JSA) and housing benefit (HB).[14] The local authority that last looked after you is responsible for supporting you. This remains the case even if you subsequently move to an area covered by a different local authority,[15] although in this situation, the local authority to which you have moved might take on the responsibility for supporting you.[16]

Note: this section does not describe 'continuing care' assistance. See the Scottish government's guidance on continuing care.[17]

Who can get financial support

Care leavers excluded from UC, IS, income-based JSA and HB should get financial assistance from the local authority. Care leavers aged 16 and 17 who are not excluded from UC, IS or income-based JSA (eg, lone parents) do not normally get regular financial assistance from the local authority.[18] Where they are excluded from claiming the housing costs element of UC (and HB) the local authority must, where necessary, provide suitable accommodation (see p159).[19]

If you are living with your family

If you fall within the definition of care leaver, but have gone back to live with your family (see p155), you are not excluded from IS, income-based JSA and HB unless you are getting regular financial help from the local authority under section 29(1) of the Children (Scotland) Act 1995. You only get regular financial help from the local authority if it considers that you would otherwise experience severe hardship. This rule is now of limited relevance as most people cannot make a new claim for IS, income-based JSA or HB and have to claim UC instead.

If you have returned to live with your family, the local authority decides you should not be given any regular financial assistance and you are still a qualifying young person (see p8), your parent may be able to get benefits/tax credits for you. This may apply if, for example, you are still at school, or at college on a non-advanced course.

Note: for UC, there are no special rules about care leavers who have returned to live with their family. This means that, unless you come within one of the exceptions set out on p154, you are still excluded from UC if you have returned to live with your family even if you do not get any support from the local authority.

The amount of help

The amount you are paid by the local authority should be at least equal to the amount you would be paid if you were able to claim IS or income-based JSA, which is £57.90 a week.[20]

This is the minimum you should be paid. The local authority should carry out an assessment of your needs, and the guidance suggests that support should include amounts for utility bills, food/household goods, laundry, insurance, clothing, travel and leisure.[21] The local authority has the discretion to reduce the payments to take into account earnings and savings. The guidance suggests it should do so in the same way as the DWP. The guidance specifically states that criminal injuries compensation payments should be ignored and, therefore, should not affect the amount you get.[22]

The guidance suggests that local authorities may use incentives, including additional payments, to encourage you to take part in employment, training and education.[23] If you are in higher education, the local authority support should be sufficient for you not to need to take out a full student loan.[24]

The local authority should not take into account as income anything which would be ignored if you were claiming means-tested benefits – eg, personal independence payment or disability living allowance.[25]

How you are paid

Payments are usually paid directly into your bank account, although local authorities can use another method of payment if it is appropriate.[26] It is also possible for the local authority to provide assistance in kind. The guidance suggests that this might be appropriate if there is reason to believe that cash payments are likely to be spent on drugs.[27]

Treatment of local authority payments for benefits

It is unlikely that you will be receiving regular payments from the local authority while also receiving a means-tested benefit because of the rules described above, but if you are, payments made under section 29 of the Children (Scotland) Act 1995 (payments to care leavers) and payments made under section 26A of the Children (Scotland) Act 1995 (continuing care) are disregarded for UC, IS, income-based JSA, income-related ESA and HB.[28] Section 29 payments are disregarded for council tax reduction.[29]

5. Other help from the local authority

Financial support is only one form of help available to young care leavers from the local authority. This section provides a short description of the help and support you should expect. For more information, see the government's guidance, *Supporting Young People Leaving Care in Scotland*.[30]

Help with accommodation

The local authority must provide, where necessary, suitable accommodation.[31] When considering what is suitable, the local authority should, as far as it is reasonably practicable, take into account your views, your health, any needs you have arising from disability, and your education, training and employment needs.[32] Guidance suggests that you should not be placed in unsuitable bed and breakfast or hostel accommodation, and that factors such as being close to support networks should be taken into account.[33]

Support once you are 18

The local authority's responsibility to support you does not end when you are 18. Unless the local authority is satisfied that your welfare does not require it, it is obliged to advise, guide and assist you if you:[34]
- were looked after by the local authority at your 16th birthday; *and*
- are no longer looked after; *and*
- are not yet 19.

This assistance can include financial help.

If you are aged over 18 and under 26 and you were looked after at your 16th birthday, you can request advice, guidance and assistance from the local authority. The local authority *may* help you, unless it is satisfied that your welfare does not require it.[35] The local authority can continue to provide advice, guidance and assistance beyond your 26th birthday but is not required to do so.[36]

Using local authority payments to pay your carer

If you get payments from the local authority and give some or all of the money to a person who is caring for you, there are special rules about how that money is treated. These rules affect your carer's benefits.

If you give some or all of the payment to another person, the payment is ignored when that person's income support, income-based jobseeker's allowance, income-related employment and support allowance, housing benefit and council tax reduction are calculated, provided:[37]
- you live with that person; *and*
- that person previously looked after you; *and*
- you are aged 18 or over.

If you are in continuing care (see p153) and you are 16 or over, this rule also applies to your carer.

If your carer is on universal credit, payment made by the local authority which you pass on to her/him is ignored.[38]

6. Other help

Students who have previously been looked after by a local authority in the UK and who are under 26 at the start of the course may be eligible for a care-experienced bursary. This is £8,100 a year (for 2019/20) in advanced education (eg, HNC/HND or degree course) and £202.50 (for 2019/20) a week in non-advanced education (eg, National Qualifications 1–5, Scottish Vocational Qualifications 1–3).

For students in advanced education, there is also a 'care-experienced accommodation grant' available from SAAS to help with accommodation costs during the summer vacation. The amount of this grant is up to £105 a week and, if you are eligible, it is paid direct to the person or organisation to whom you pay rent. For how to apply, see www.saas.gov.uk/_forms/ab06.pdf.

Care leavers who are aged 18 or over and are under 26 are exempt from council tax liablity. You are exempt if you were looked after on or after your 16th birthday and you are no longer looked after.[39] This means, for example, that if you live alone there is no council tax charge.

7. Challenging local authority decisions

Decisions you can challenge

You can challenge the level and nature of the support the local authority gives you. This includes the level of financial help you get. You can also challenge the local authority's decision if you are a care leaver aged 19 or over and the local authority decides not to provide you with with advice, guidance and assistance.[40] This challenge is called an 'appeal'.

How to appeal

You can either appeal in writing or tell the local authority (eg, by phone or in person) that you want to appeal. It is usually a good idea to put your appeal in writing to make sure all the issues you want to raise are included. In any case, if you make your appeal orally, the local authority must immediately make a written record of the details of your appeal and send it to you, giving you the opportunity to comment on it. This is your chance to add any further details that you think are relevant. The written record must be amended to reflect your comments.[41] You may want to get help with your appeal. The organisation Who Cares? Scotland may be able to help you (see Appendix 1).

The appeal process

The local authority should inform a nominated officer of the details of your appeal.[42] The nominated officer is a person appointed by the local authority to assist with the appeals process. The local authority must try to resolve the appeal informally. This means it should look again at your case and at the issues you have raised in your appeal. The time limit for this reconsideration is five working days from the date the appeal is received. This can be extended by agreement between you and the local authority.[43] If, after this reconsideration, the appeal remains unresolved, the local authority must notify the nominated officer.[44] The appeal will then be considered formally.

The appeal is heard by:[45]
- a senior officer of the local authority who has not been involved in your case and who is more senior than the officer who made the decision; *and*
- an 'independent person' appointed by the local authority.

The independent person takes part in the discussion, but the decision is made by the senior officer alone.

The appeal is heard at a meeting, to which you should be invited. You can take another person to the meeting for support or to speak on your behalf.

The decision

The decision must be made within 10 working days of the date the nominated officer is told it has not been informally resolved.[46] The local authority has a further two working days to notify you of the decision.[47]

Withdrawing your appeal

You can withdraw your appeal at any time during the process. You must do this by writing to the local authority.

Further appeals

There is no further right of appeal after this process, although you can use the local authority's complaints process if you are still unhappy with the outcome.

Chapter 10: Young people leaving care
Notes

You can also consider making a complaint to your MSP or MP, and/or to the Scottish Public Services Ombudsman (see Appendix 1). Who Cares? Scotland may be able to help you with this kind of complaint (see Appendix 1).

Scotland's Commissioner for Children and Young People (see www.cypcs.org.uk) has a particular interest in young people leaving care and, although not able to take on individual cases, may be able to provide helpful information.

It is also possible to challenge a local authority decision by judicial review. This is a legal remedy, generally only available after you have exhausted all other appeal routes (see Chapter 2).

Notes

1. s26A C(S)A 1995
2. s26A(4) C(S)A 1995

1. Universal credit
3. Reg 8(1), (2) and (4) UC Regs
4. s17(6) C(S)A 1995
5. Art 13 Adoption and Children (Scotland) Act 2007 (Commencement No.4, Transitional and Savings Provisions) Order 2009 No. 267
6. Reg 8(1) and (2); Sch 4 para 4 UC Regs

2. Income support, income-based jobseeker's allowance and housing benefit
7. Reg 2(2) C(LC)SSB(S) Regs
8. Reg 2(2)(b) C(LC)SSB(S) Regs
9. Reg 2(4)(b) C(LC)SSB(S) Regs
10. Reg 2(4)(a) C(LC)SSB(S) Regs
11. Reg 2(4)(c) C(LC)SSB(S) Regs
12. Reg 2(3) C(LC)SSB Regs

3. Other benefits
13. Regs 3-5 NHS(TERC)(S) Regs

4. Financial support from the local authority for 16/17-year-old care leavers
14. Regs 13 and 14 SAYPLC(S) Regs
15. Reg 2 SAYPLC(S) Regs
16. Scottish government guidance, *Supporting Young People Leaving Care in Scotland*, para 5.2
17. Scottish government, *Children and Young People (Scotland) Act 2014: Guidance on Part 11: continuing care*, 2016
18. Scottish government guidance, *Supporting Young People Leaving Care in Scotland*, para 8.10
19. Reg 14 SAYPLC(S) Regs
20. Reg 13(3) SAYPLC(S) Regs
21. Scottish government guidance, *Supporting Young People Leaving Care in Scotland*, para 8.2
22. Scottish government guidance, *Supporting Young People Leaving Care in Scotland*, para 8.6
23. Scottish government guidance, *Supporting Young People Leaving Care in Scotland*, para 8.3
24. Scottish government guidance, *Supporting Young People Leaving Care in Scotland*, para 8.4
25. Reg 13(3) SAYPLC(S) Regs
26. Scottish government guidance, *Supporting Young People Leaving Care in Scotland*, para 8.1
27. Scottish government guidance, *Supporting Young People Leaving Care in Scotland*, para 8.9

Chapter 10: Young people leaving care
Notes

28 **UC** Reg 66 UC Regs
IS Sch 9 para 28(1)(c) IS Regs
JSA Sch 7 para 29(1)(c) JSA Regs
ESA Sch 8 para 30(1)(c) ESA Regs
HB Sch 5 para 28 HB Regs
29 Sch 4 para 32 CTR Regs

5. Other help from the local authority
30 Scottish government guidance, *Supporting Young People Leaving Care in Scotland*, available at www.gov.scot/publications/supporting-young-people-leaving-care-scotland-regulations-guidance-services-young/
31 Reg 14 SAYPLC(S) Regs
32 Reg 14 SAYPLC(S) Regs
33 Scottish government guidance, *Supporting Young People Leaving Care in Scotland*, para 9.3
34 s29(1) C(S)A 1995
35 s29(2) C(S)A 1995
36 s29(5B) C(S)A 1995
37 **IS** Sch 9 para 28(2) IS Regs
JSA Sch 7 para 29(2) JSA Regs
ESA Sch 8 para 30 ESA Regs
HB Sch 5 para 28A(1) HB Regs; reg 29 HB(SPC) Regs
CTR Sch 4 para 33 CTR(S) Regs; reg 27(1) CTR(SPC)(S) Regs
38 Reg 66 UC Regs

6. Other help
39 Sch 1 para 6 CT(D)(S) Regs

7. Challenging local authority decisions
40 Reg 16(1) SAYPLC(S) Regs
41 Reg 17(2)-(5) SAYPLC(S) Regs
42 Reg 18(1)(a) SAYPLC(S) Regs
43 Reg 18(1)(b) and (2) SAYPLC(S) Regs
44 Reg 18(1)(c) SAYPLC(S) Regs
45 Reg 19(2) SAYPLC(S) Regs
46 Reg 19(8) SAYPLC(S) Regs
47 Reg 20 SAYPLC(S) Regs

Appendices

Appendix 1
Useful addresses

Government departments

Carer's Allowance Unit
Mail Handling Site A
Wolverhampton WV98 2AB
Tel: 0800 731 0297
Textphone: 0800 731 0317

Disability Service Centre
Disability living allowance
(claimants aged under 16)
Disability Benefit Centre 4
Post Handling Site B
Wolverhampton WV99 1BY
Tel: 0800 121 4600
Textphone: 0800 121 4523

Personal independence payment
Post Handling Site B
Wolverhampton WV99 1AH
Tel: 0800 121 4433
Textphone: 0800 121 4493

Child Benefit Office, Guardian's Allowance Unit
PO Box 1
Newcastle Upon Tyne NE88 1AA
Tel: 0300 200 3100
Textphone: 0300 200 3103
www.gov.uk/child-benefit

Tax Credit Office
Tax Credit Helpline
Tel: 0345 300 3900
Textphone: 0345 300 3909

Pension Credit
Tel: 0800 991 234
Textphone: 0800 169 0133
www.gov.uk/pension-credit

Complaints

The Adjudicator
Adjudicator's Office
PO Box 10280
Nottingham NG2 9PF
Tel: 0300 057 1111
www.adjudicatorsoffice.gov.uk

Scottish Public Services Ombudsman
Bridgeside House
99 McDonald Road
Edinburgh EH7 4NS
Tel: 0800 377 7330
www.spso.org.uk

Parliamentary and Health Service Ombudsman
Tel: 0345 015 4033
www.ombudsman.org.uk

Other organisations

Capability Scotland
Osborne House
1 Osborne Terrace
Edinburgh EH12 5HG
Tel: 0131 337 9876
Textphone: 0131 346 2529
www.capability-scotland.org.uk

Appendix 1: Useful addresses

Carers Scotland
Tel: 0808 808 7777
www.carersuk.org/scotland

Child Poverty Action Group in Scotland
Unit 9, Ladywell
94 Duke Street
Glasgow G4 0UW
Tel: 0141 552 3303
Advice line for advisers and support workers: 0141 552 0552 (Mon–Thurs 10am–4pm, Fri 10am–12noon)
advice@cpagscotland.org.uk
www.cpag.org.uk/scotland

Children 1st
83 Whitehouse Loan
Edinburgh EH9 1AT
Tel: 0131 446 2300
cfs@children1st.org.uk
www.children1st.org.uk

Contact Scotland
The Melting Pot
5 Rose Street
Edinburgh EH2 2PR
Helpline: 0808 808 3555

ENABLE Scotland
INSPIRE House
3 Renshaw Place
Eurocentral
Lanarkshire ML1 4UF
Tel: 01698 737 000
enabledirect@enable.org.uk
www.enable.org.uk

The Fostering Network
Ingram House
227 Ingram Street
Glasgow G1 1DA
Tel: 0141 204 1400

Scotland's Commissioner for Children and Young People
Bridgeside House
99 McDonald Road
Edinburgh EH17 4NS
Tel: 0131 346 5350
Young person's freephone: 0800 019 1179
www.cypcs.org.uk

The Scottish Child Law Centre
54 East Crosscauseway
Edinburgh EH8 9HD
Tel: 0131 667 6333
Under 21s freephone: 0800 328 8970
Under 21s freephone for mobiles: 0300 330 1421
enquiries@sclc.org.uk
www.sclc.org.uk

STAF (formerly the Scottish Throughcare and Aftercare Forum)
Edward House
199 Sauchiehall Street
Glasgow G2 3EX
Tel: 0141 465 7511
www.staf.scot

Who Cares? Scotland
5 Oswald Street
Glasgow G1 4QR
Tel: 0141 226 4441
hello@whocaresscotland.org
www.whocaresscotland.org

Appendix 2
Abbreviations used in the notes

Art(s)	Article(s)
EWCA	England and Wales Court of Appeal
HLR	Housing Law Reports
para(s)	paragraph(s)
QBD	Queen's Bench Division
r(r)	rule(s)
reg(s)	regulation(s)
s(s)	section(s)
Sch(s)	Schedule(s)
vol	volume

Acts of Parliament

Most Acts are available at www.legislation.gov.uk.

AC(S)A 2007	Adoption and Children (Scotland) Act 2007
CFA 2014	Children and Families Act 2014
C(S)A 1995	Children (Scotland) Act 1995
CSPSSA 2000	Child Support, Pensions and Social Security Act 2000
CYP(S)A 2014	Children and Young People (Scotland) Act 2014
E(S)A 1980	Education (Scotland) Act 1980
IAA 1999	Immigration and Asylum Act 1999
IT(TOI)A 2005	Income Tax (Trading and Other Income) Act 2005
JSA 1995	Jobseekers Act 1995
NHSCCA 1990	National Health Service and Community Care Act 1990
NHS(S)A 1978	National Health Service (Scotland) Act 1978
PA 2014	Pensions Act 2014
SPCA 2002	State Pension Credit Act 2002
SSA 1998	Social Security Act 1998

Appendix 2: Abbreviations used in the notes

SSAA 1992	Social Security Administration Act 1992
SSCBA 1992	Social Security Contributions and Benefits Act 1992
SW(S)A 1968	Social Work (Scotland) Act 1968
TCA 2002	Tax Credits Act 2002
WRA 2007	Welfare Reform Act 2007
WRA 2012	Welfare Reform Act 2012

Regulations

Most regulations are available at www.legislation.gov.uk. Each set of regulations has a statutory instrument (SI) number and a date.

ASPP(G)Regs	The Additional Statutory Paternity Pay (General) Regulations 2010 No.1056
ASSA(S)Regs	The Adoption Support Services and Allowances (Scotland) Regulations 2009 No.152
CB Regs	The Child Benefit (General) Regulations 2006 No.223
CB&GA(DA) Regs	The Child Benefit and Guardian's Allowance (Decisions and Appeals) Regulations 2003 No.916
C(LC)SSB Regs	The Children (Leaving Care) Social Security Benefits Regulations 2001 No.3074
C(LC)SSB(S) Regs	The Children (Leaving Care) Social Security Benefits (Scotland) Regulations 2004 No.747
CTC Regs	The Child Tax Credit Regulations 2002 No.2007
CT(D)(S) Regs	The Council Tax (Discounts) (Scotland) Regulations 1992 No.1409
CTR(S) Regs	The Council Tax Reduction (Scotland) Regulations 2012 No.303
CTR(SPC)(S) Regs	The Council Tax Reduction (State Pension Credit) (Scotland) Regulations 2012 No.319
DFA Regs	The Discretionary Financial Assistance Regulations 2001 No.1167
ESA Regs	The Employment and Support Allowance Regulations 2008 No.794
EYA(BSG)(S) Regs	The Early Years Assistance (Scotland) Regulations 2018 No.370
FEA(S)Regs	The Funeral Expense Assistance (Scotland) Regulations 2019 (draft)

Appendix 2: Abbreviations used in the notes

GA(Gen) Regs	The Guardian's Allowance (General) Regulations 2003 No.495
HB Regs	The Housing Benefit Regulations 2006 No.213
HB(SPC) Regs	The Housing Benefit (Persons who have Attained the Qualifying Age for State Pension Credit) Regulations 2006 No.214
HB&CTB(DA) Regs	The Housing Benefit and Council Tax Benefit (Decisions and Appeals) Regulations 2001 No.1002
HSS&WF(A) Regs	The Healthy Start Scheme and Welfare Food (Amendment) Regulations 2005 No.3262
IS Regs	The Income Support (General) Regulations 1987 No.1967
JSA Regs	The Jobseeker's Allowance Regulations 1996 No.207
KCA(S)O	The Kinship Care Assistance (Scotland) Order 2016 No.153
LAC(S) Regs	The Looked After Children (Scotland) Regulations 2009 No.210
NHS(CDA)(S) Regs	The National Health Service (Charges for Drugs and Appliances) (Scotland) Amendment Regulations 2009 No.37
NHS(TERC)(S) Regs	The National Health Service (Travelling Expenses and Remission of Charges) (Scotland) (No.2) Regulations 2003 No.460
PIP(TP) Regs	The Personal Independence Payment (Tranisitional Provisions) Regulations 2013 No.387
SAYPLC(S) Regs	The Support and Assistance of Young People Leaving Care (Scotland) Regulations 2003 No.608
SFM&FE Regs	The Social Fund Maternity and Funeral Expenses (General) Regulations 2005 No.3061
SPC Regs	The State Pension Credit Regulations 2002 No.1792
SPPSAP(G) Regs	The Statutory Paternity and Statutory Adoption Pay (General) Regulations 2002 No.2822
SS(AA) Regs	The Social Security (Attendance Allowance) Regulations 1991 No.2740
SS(C&P) Regs	The Social Security (Claims and Payments) Regulations 1987 No.1968
SS(CCPC) Regs	The Social Security (Contributions Credits for Parents and Carers) Regulations 2010 No.19

Appendix 2: Abbreviations used in the notes

SS&CS(DA) Regs	The Social Security and Child Support (Decisions and Appeals) Regulations 1999 No.991
SS(DLA) Regs	The Social Security (Disability Living Allowance) Regulations 1991 No.2890
SS(HIP) Regs	The Social Security (Hospital In-Patients) Regulations 2005 No.3360
SS(ICA) Regs	The Social Security (Invalid Care Allowance) Regulations 1976 No.409
SS(IFW) Regs	The Social Security (Incapacity for Work) (General) Regulations 1995 No.311
SS(PAOR) Regs	The Social Security (Payments on Account, Overpayments and Recovery) Regulations 1988 No.664
SS(PIP) Regs	The Social Security (Personal Independence Payment) Regulations 2013 No.377
SS(WTCCTC)(CA) Regs	The Social Security (Working Tax Credit and Child Tax Credit) (Consequential Amendments) Regulations 2003 No.455
SSB(CE) Regs	The Social Security Benefit (Computation of Earnings) Regulations 1996 No.2745
TC(A)(No.2) Regs	The Tax Credits (Appeals) (No.2) Regulations 2002 No.3196
TCA(No.3)O	The Tax Credits Act 2002 (Commencement No.3 and Transitional Provisions and Savings) Order 2003 No.938
TC(DCI) Regs	The Tax Credits (Definition and Calculation of Income) Regulations 2002 No.2006
TC(Imm) Regs	The Tax Credits (Immigration) Regulations 2003 No.653
TC(ITDR) Regs	The Tax Credits (Income Thresholds and Determination of Rates) Regulations 2002 No.2008
TC(R) Regs	The Tax Credits (Residence) Regulations 2003 No.654
TP(FT) Rules	The Tribunal Procedure (First-tier Tribunal) (Social Entitlement Chamber) Rules 2008 No.2685
UC Regs	The Universal Credit Regulations 2013 No.376
UC,PIP,JSA&ESA (C&P)Regs	The Universal Credit, Personal Independence Payment, Jobseeker's Allowance and Employment and Support Allowance (Claims and Payments) Regulations 2013 No.380

Appendix 2: Abbreviations used in the notes

UC,PIP,JSA&ESA(DA) Regs	The Universal Credit, Personal Independence Payment, Jobseeker's Allowance and Employment and Support Allowance (Decisions and Appeals) Regulations 2013 No.381
WF(BSF)(S) Regs	The Welfare Foods (Best Start Foods) (Scotland) Regulations 2019 No.193
WTC(EMR) Regs	The Working Tax Credit (Entitlement and Maximum Rate) Regulations 2002 No.2005

Other abbreviations

ADM	Advice for Decision Making
BIM	Business Income Manual
CBTM	Child Benefit Technical Manual
DMG	Decision Makers' Guide
GM	The Housing Benefit and Council Tax Benefit Guidance Manual
SWFG	The Scottish Welfare Fund Guidance
TCM	Tax Credit Manual
TCTM	Tax Credits Technical Manual

References like [2010] UKUT 208 (AAC) are references to decisions of the Upper Tribunal.
References like CIS/142/1990 and R(IS) 1/07 are references to commissioners' decisions.

Index

How to use this Index

Entries against the bold headings direct you to the general information on the subject, or where the subject is covered most fully. Sub-entries are listed alphabetically and direct you to specific aspects of the subject. The following abbreviations are used in the index:

AA	Attendance allowance		IS	Income support
CA	Carer's allowance		JSA	Jobseeker's allowance
CTC	Child tax credit		PC	Pension credit
CTR	Council tax reduction		PIP	Personal independence payment
DLA	Disability living allowance		SAP	Statutory adoption pay
ESA	Employment and support allowance		UC	Universal credit
HB	Housing benefit		WTC	Working tax credit

16/17-year-olds
   IS/JSA/HB 155
   leaving care 153
   local authority financial support 157
      amount 158
   local authority help 159
   returning to live with family 157
   UC 154

A
Adjudicator
   complaints 60
adoption 137
   Best Start grants 150
   child adopted
      benefits and tax credits 146
   child placed for adoption
      benefits and tax credits 139
   guardian's allowance 20
   health benefits 150
   SAP 40
adoption allowance 137
amount of benefit
   AA 3
   benefit cap 2
   Best Start grants
      early learning payment 4
      pregnancy and baby payment 3
      school-age payment 4

   CA 6
   child benefit 10
   CTC 42
   CTR 10
   DLA 14
   ESA
      contributory 18
      income-related 15
   guardian's allowance 21
   HB 24
   IS 28
   JSA
      contribution-based 34
      income-based 33
   PC 35
   PIP 38
   SAP 40
   UC 47
   WTC 44
appeals
   benefits and tax credits 58
   care leavers challenging local authority
      decisions 161
applicable amount
   ESA 16
   HB 25
   IS 28
   JSA 33

Index
approved training – carer's allowance

approved training 8
attendance allowance 2
   amount 3
   backdating 55
   claiming 52
   kinship carers
      child not looked after 115
      looked after child 124
   who can claim 2

B
backdating 54
bedroom tax 24, 75
   adoption 144, 149
   disabled child at residential school 88, 89
   disabled child in care home 75
   foster care 133
   kinship carers 115, 123
   looked after and accommodated child 99
benefit cap 2
benefits 1
Best Start foods 22
   adoption 150
   claiming 52
Best Start grants 3
   care leavers 156
   child adopted 150
   child placed for adoption 146
   claiming 52
   early learning payment 4
   kinship carers
      child not looked after 118
   pregnancy and baby payment 3
   qualifying benefits 3
   responsible for child 4
   school-age payment 4

C
care homes
   child comes home 80
   disabled child in care home 71
   linking rules 79
   visiting costs 79
care leavers
   16/17-year-olds 153
   aged 18 and over 159
   benefits and tax credits 157
   care-experienced accommodation grant 160
   care-experienced students' bursary 160
   challenging local authority decisions 160
   continuing care 153
   council tax 160
   definition 155
   ESA 156
   health benefits 156
   housing 159
   IS/JSA/HB 155
   local authority financial support 157
      amount 158
      treatment for benefits 158
   local authority help 159
   lone parent 155
   returning to live with family 157
   Scottish Welfare Fund payments 157
   UC 154
care-experienced accommodation grant 160
care-experienced students' bursary 160
carer addition 6, 36
   disabled child at residential school 91
   disabled child in care home 78
carer element 6, 48
   child in hospital 65
   disabled child at residential school 91
   disabled child in care home 78
carer premium 6
   child in hospital
      ESA 66
      HB/CTR 67
      IS/JSA 66
   disabled child at residential school 91
   disabled child in care home 78
   ESA 17
   IS 29
carer's allowance 5
   amount 6
   backdating 55
   care home stay ends 81
   carer's allowance supplement 6
   child adopted 149
   child in hospital 68
   child placed for adoption 145
   claiming 53
   disabled child at residential school 90
   disabled child in care home 77
   disabled person's benefit 5
   foster carers 134

Index
carer's allowance – council tax reduction

kinship carers
    child not looked after 116
    looked after child 124
looked after and accommodated child 101
looked after and accommodated child
    comes home 104
overlapping benefits 6
who can claim 5
carer's allowance supplement 6
carers
breaks in caring 6, 77, 90
CA 5
IS 27
kinship carers
    IS 113
local authority payments 159
young carer grant 7
challenging decisions
benefits and tax credits 58
local authority decisions on care leavers 160
change of circumstances
tax credits 45
child addition
PC 36
child benefit 7
amount 10
backdating 55
care home stay ends 80
child adopted 146
child in hospital 64
child placed for adoption 139
claiming 53
disabled child at residential school 84
disabled child in care home 71
extension period 8
foster carers 130
interim payments 57
kinship carers
    child not looked after 110
    looked after child 120
looked after and accommodated child 96
looked after and accommodated child
    comes home 102
priority of claimants 9
terminal date 9
who can claim 7

child element
CTC 42
UC 47
child tax credit 41
amount 42
backdating 56
care home stay ends 81
child adopted 150
child in hospital 68
child placed for adoption 145
claiming 54
disabled child at residential school 92
disabled child in care home 78
foster carers 134
kinship carers
    child not looked after 116
    looked after child 124
looked after and accommodated child 101
looked after and accommodated child
    comes home 105
who can claim 41
childcare element
UC 48
WTC 45
children
definition of child
    child benefit 8
    CTC 41
hospital inpatients 64
responsible for child
    Best Start grants 4
    child benefit 9
    CTC 41
claims
benefits and tax credits 52
community care grants 39
care leavers 157
hospital visiting 69
kinship carers 118
compensation payments 62
complaints
benefits and tax credits 59
components
ESA 17
HB 25
continuing care 153
council tax reduction 10
amount 10
backdating 55

177

Index
council tax reduction – employment and support allowance

calculating 10
care home stay ends 80
child adopted 148
child in hospital 67
child placed for adoption 143
claiming 53
disabled child at residential school 88
    child not looked after 88
    looked after child 89
disabled child in care home 74
foster carers 132
kinship carers
    child not looked after 114
    looked after child 123
looked after and accommodated child 99
looked after and accommodated child comes home 103
who can claim 10
crisis grants 39
  care leavers 157
  hospital visiting 69
  kinship carers 118

D
decisions
  benefits and tax credits 56
delays
  benefits and tax credits 56
  crisis grants 58
dental treatment
  charges 21
  free 21
disability
  AA 2
  DLA 11
  ESA 14
  PIP 36
disability living allowance 11
  amount 14
  backdating 55
  care component 12
  care home stay ends 81
  child adopted 149
  child in hospital 68
  child placed for adoption 144
  claiming 53
  disabled child at residential school 89
  disabled child in care home 77
  foster carers 133

future changes 14, 36
kinship carers
    child not looked after 115
    looked after child 124
looked after and accommodated child 100
looked after and accommodated child comes home 104
mobility component 13
who can claim 12
disability premium
  IS 29
disabled child element
  CTC 43
disabled child premium
  child in hospital
    HB/CTR 67
    IS/JSA 66
  HB 25
  IS 31
disabled children
  care homes 71
  DLA 12
  residential schools 84
disabled worker element
  WTC 45
discretionary housing payments 26
DWP
  complaints 59

E
early learning payment 4
employment and support allowance 14
  amount
    contributory ESA 18
    income-related ESA 15
  backdating 55
  calculating income-related ESA 15
  care leavers 156
  child adopted 147
  child in hospital 66
  child placed for adoption 143
  claiming 53
  contributory ESA 18
  disabled child at residential school 87
  disabled child in care home 74
  foster carers 132
  income-related ESA 15

kinship carers
　child not looked after 113
　looked after child 122
　looked after and accommodated child 98
　who can claim
　　contributory ESA 18
　　income-related ESA 15
enhanced disability premium
　child in hospital
　　HB/CTR 67
　　IS/JSA 66
　ESA 17
　for a child
　　HB 25
　　IS 31
　IS 30
evidence
　to support a claim 54

F
family element
　CTC 42
family premium
　HB 25
　IS 31
financial need 56
foster care 129
　benefits and tax credits 130
　definition 129
　looked after and accommodated child 96
　　DLA 100
　　PIP 100
　national insurance credits 135
　private fostering 130
　public fostering 129
full-time work
　WTC 44
funeral support payment 19
　claiming 53
　who can claim 19

G
glasses and contact lenses
　charges 21
　vouchers 22
guardian's allowance 20
　adoption 20
　amount 21

backdating 55
child in hospital 64
claiming 53
disabled child at residential school 84
disabled child in care home 71
eligible child 20
foster carers 130
interim payments 57
kinship carers
　child not looked after 111
　looked after child 120
　who can claim 20

H
health benefits 21
　adoption 150
　backdating 55
　care leavers 156
　claiming 53
　exemption from charges 21
　kinship carers
　　child not looked after 119
　looked after and accommodated child 102
　low income scheme 22
　qualifying benefits 21
HM Revenue and Customs
　complaints 60
hospital
　CA 68
　child benefit 64
　child in hospital 64
　CTC 68
　CTR 67
　DLA 68
　ESA 66
　fares to hospital 21, 22
　guardian's allowance 64
　HB 67
　IS 65
　JSA 65
　PC 66
　PIP 68
　UC 65
　visiting costs 69
　WTC 68
housing benefit 23
　16/17-year-olds 155
　amount 24
　backdating 55

179

benefit cap 2
calculating 24
care home stay ends 80
care leavers 155
child adopted 148
child in hospital 67
child placed for adoption 143
claiming 53
disabled child at residential school 88
    child not looked after 88
    looked after child 89
disabled child in care home 74
discretionary housing payments 26
foster carers 132
interim payments 57
kinship carers
    child not looked after 114
    looked after child 123
looked after and accommodated child 99
looked after and accommodated child comes home 103
social sector tenants under-occupying home 24
who can claim 23
who cannot claim 23
housing costs
care leavers 159
ESA 17
HB 23
IS 30
JSA 33
UC 48

I
illness
ESA 14
income support 26
16/17-year-olds 155
amount 28
backdating 55
calculating 28
care home stay ends 80
care leavers 155
child adopted 147
child in hospital 65
child placed for adoption 143
claiming 53
claiming for children 30
disabled child at residential school 86
    child not looked after 86
    looked after child 86
disabled child in care home 72
foster carers 131
kinship carers
    child not looked after 112
    looked after child 121
looked after and accommodated child 98
looked after and accommodated child comes home 103
who can claim 27
Independent Case Examiner
complaints 59
interim payments
benefits 56
HB 57

J
jobseeker's allowance 31
16/17-year-olds 155
amount
    contribution-based JSA 34
    income-based JSA 33
backdating 56
calculating income-based JSA 33
care home stay ends 80
care leavers 155
child adopted 148
child in hospital 65
child placed for adoption 143
claiming 54
contribution-based JSA 33
disabled child at residential school 86
    child not looked after 86
    looked after child 86
disabled child in care home 72
foster carers 132
income-based JSA 32
kinship carers
    child not looked after 113
    looked after child 122
looked after and accommodated child 98
looked after and accommodated child comes home 103
who can claim
    contribution-based JSA 33
    income-based JSA 32
judicial review
benefits and tax credits 63

K
kinship care 107
  allowance from local authority
    looked after child 109
  benefits and tax credits
    child not looked after 110
    looked after child 119
  definition 107
  financial help from local authority 108
  national insurance credits 126
  Regulation 33/Section 110 payments 109
  Section 22 payments 108
  Section 50 payments 108
  Social Welfare Fund payments 118

L
limited capability for work
  ESA 15
  UC 48
linking rules
  disabled child in care home 79
local authorities
  care leavers
    financial support 157
    other help 159
  complaints 61
  kinship care payments 108
  looked after and accommodated children 96
local housing allowance 24
lone parents
  care leavers 155
  IS 27
  kinship carers
    IS 112
looked after and accommodated children 96
  16/17-year-olds leaving care 153
  child comes home 102
looked after children
  continuing care 153
  definition 154
  disabled child in care home 75
  foster care 130
  kinship care 107
    allowance from local authority 109
  residential school
    HB/CTR 89
    IS/JSA 86

M
maternity
  Best Start foods 22
  Best Start grants 3
  pregnancy and baby payment 3
MPs
  complaints 60

N
national insurance contributions
  ESA 18
  foster carers 135
  JSA 34
  kinship carers 126

O
Ombudsman
  complaints 61

P
parents
  guardian's allowance 20
Parliamentary and Health Service Ombudsman
  complaints 62
pension credit 34
  amount 35
  backdating 56
  calculating 35
  child adopted 148
  child in hospital 66
  child placed for adoption 143
  claiming 54
  disabled child at residential school 87
  disabled child in care home 74
  foster carers 132
  guarantee credit 35
  kinship carers
    child not looked after 114
    looked after child 123
  looked after and accommodated child 99
  looked after and accommodated child comes home 103
  qualifying age 35
  savings credit 36
  who can claim 35

Index
pensioner premium – Section 22 payments

pensioner premium
   ESA 17
   IS 30
personal allowance
   ESA 16
   HB 25
   IS 28
   JSA 33
personal independence payment 36
   amount 38
   backdating 56
   care home stay ends 81
   child in hospital 68
   claiming 54
   daily living activities 37
   disability conditions 37
   disabled child at residential school 89
   disabled child in care home 77
   foster carers 133
   kinship carers
      child not looked after 115
      looked after child 124
   looked after and accommodated child 100
   looked after and accommodated child comes home 104
   mobility activities 38
   who can claim 37
pregnancy
   Best Start grants 3
   Healthy Start 22
   IS 28
   pregnancy and baby payment 3
pregnancy and baby payment 3
premiums
   ESA 17
   HB 25
   IS 29
   JSA 33
prescriptions 21

Q
qualifying young person
   child benefit 8
   CTC 41

R
Regulation 33 payments 109
   looked after child
      CB 120
      ESA 122
      HB/CTR 124
      IS 121
      JSA 122
      PC 123
      tax credits 126
      UC 121
relevant education 8
rent
   HB 23
residential accommodation 96
   CA 101
   DLA 100
   PIP 100
residential schools
   disabled children 84
   visiting costs 93
respite care 77

S
school-age payment 4
schools
   see: residential schools
Scottish Public Services Ombudsman
   complaints 62
Scottish Welfare Fund 38
   care leavers 157
   claiming 54
   community care grants 39
   crisis grants 39
   kinship carers 118
Section 22 payments 108
   child not looked after
      ESA 113
      HB/CTR 115
      IS 113
      JSA 114
      PC 114
      tax credits 118
      UC 112
   looked after child
      ESA 122
      HB/CTR 124
      IS 121
      JSA 122

Index
Section 22 payments – universal credit

PC 123
tax credits 126
UC 121
Section 50 payments 108
  child not looked after
    ESA 113
    HB/CTR 115
    IS 113
    JSA 114
    PC 114
    tax credits 118
    UC 112
  looked after child
    ESA 122
    HB/CTR 124
    IS 121
    JSA 122
    PC 123
    tax credits 126
    UC 121
Section 110 payments 109
severe disability addition
  PC 35
severe disability element
  WTC 45
severe disability premium
  ESA 17
  IS 30
severe hardship 158
severely disabled child element
  CTC 43
short-term advances
  benefits 56
Social Security Scotland
  complaints 61
statutory adoption pay 40
  adopting a child 140
  amount 40
  backdating 56
  choosing adoption pay or paternity pay 139
  claiming 54
  who can claim 40
statutory paternity pay
  adopting a child 141
  backdating 56
  choosing adoption pay or paternity pay 139
  claiming 54

statutory shared parental pay
  adopting a child 142
  backdating 56
  claiming 54
statutory sick pay
  care leavers 156

T
tax credits 1, 40
  benefit cap 2
  see also: child tax credit, working tax credit
travel expenses
  child at residential school 93
  child in hospital 69
  disabled child in care home 79
two-child limit
  CTC 43
  UC 47

U
universal credit 46
  16/17-year-olds 154
  amount 47
  backdating 56
  benefit cap 2
  calculating 47
  care home stay ends 80
  care leavers 154
  child adopted 146
  child in hospital 65
  child placed for adoption 142
  claimant commitment 49
  claiming 54
  disabled child at residential school 85
  disabled child in care home 71
  foster carers 130
  kinship carers
    child not looked after 111
    looked after child 120
  looked after and accommodated child 97
  looked after and accommodated child comes home 103
  severe disability premium gateway 46
  who can claim 46

Index
universal credit – young people

W
work allowance
  UC 48
working tax credit 44
  amount 44
  backdating 56
  care home stay ends 81
  child adopted 150
  child in hospital 68
  child placed for adoption 145
  claiming 54
  disabled child at residential school 92
  disabled child in care home 78
  foster carers 134
  kinship carers
    child not looked after 118
    looked after child 125
  looked after and accommodated child 101
  looked after and accommodated child
    comes home 105
  who can claim 44

Y
young carer grant 7
young people
  leaving care 153
  young carer grant 7